Placing Papers

A VOLUME IN THE SERIES
Studies in Print Culture and the History of the Book

EDITED BY
Greg Barnhisel
Robert A. Gross
Joan Shelley Rubin
Michael Winship

Placing Papers

The American Literary Archives Market

Amy Hildreth Chen

UNIVERSITY OF MASSACHUSETTS PRESS
Amherst & Boston

Copyright © 2020 by University of Massachusetts Press
All rights reserved
Printed in the United States of America

ISBN 978-1-62534-485-4 (paper); 484-7 (hardcover)

Designed by Jen Jackowitz
Set in Adobe Caslon

Cover design by Thomas Eykemans
Cover photo by Tommy Gildseth

Library of Congress Cataloging-in-Publication Data
Names: Chen, Amy, 1984– author.
Title: Placing papers : the American literary archives market / Amy Hildreth Chen.
Description: Amherst : University of Massachusetts Press, 2020. | Series: Studies in print culture and the history of the book | Includes bibliographical references and index.
Identifiers: LCCN 2019042714 | ISBN 9781625344847 (hardcover) | ISBN 9781625344854 (paperback) | ISBN 9781613767306 (ebook) | ISBN 9781613767313 (ebook)
Subjects: LCSH: Libraries—Special collections—American literature. | Archives—Administration—United States—History. | Archives—Acquisitions—United States—History. | Authors, American—Archives.
Classification: LCC Z692.A7 C44 2020 | DDC 025.17/140973—dc23
LC record available at https://lccn.loc.gov/2019042714

British Library Cataloguing-in-Publication Data
A catalog record for this book is available from the British Library.

A portion of Jeredith Merrin's "Hummingbird—for Patricia C. Willis" is reprinted here with permission of the Jeredith Merrin.

All tables created by the author.

For William Ju Chen

CONTENTS

ACKNOWLEDGMENTS IX

INTRODUCTION
Outside the Literary Archives Market   1

CHAPTER 1
Inside the Literary Archives Market   11

CHAPTER 2
Brand   24
Authors and Families

CHAPTER 3
Profit   43
Agents and Dealers

CHAPTER 4
Competition   55
Directors and Curators

CHAPTER 5
Provenance   80
Archivists and Digital Archivists

CHAPTER 6
Access   106
Scholars and the Public

CONCLUSION
The Matthew Effect   122

NOTES   135
INDEX   169

The author's full dataset is available at doi:10.25820/data.003114.

ACKNOWLEDGMENTS

This book would not be what it is without the many people whose time and talents informed and improved my work. My first acknowledgment must be to my editor, Brian Halley, and the staff at the University of Massachusetts Press. Thank you for believing in this project. My copyeditor Nancy J. Raynor's meticulous attention fixed my errors. I am grateful to those who took their time to improve this book. W. Bartley Hildreth interrogated my use of economic terms and history. Loren Glass deepened my bibliography. Jodi Reeves Eyre and Robin Israel, of Eyre & Israel, evaluated my figures. Robyn Fivush and Rodger Hildreth discussed my data analysis. Willow Fuchs improved my sentences. Claire Clark modeled how to write an interdisciplinary topic with an approachable, narrative-driven style. Jen Buckley reminded me that my title should appear more frequently as a theme in the manuscript. Joel Minor provided background information not only about the literary collections at Washington University in St. Louis but also about trade overall. David Faulds and Athena Jackson reassured me that my approach to the market was correct.

Creating that first full draft took years and the support of many people. Carmelita Pickett, Greg Prickman, Kathy Magarrell, and Ericka Raber approved my five weeks of research leave over the summer of 2017 while I worked at the University of Iowa as Special Collections Instruction Librarian and then English and American Literature Librarian; these weeks gave me the time I needed to finish the manuscript. Kevin Young inspired my topic by granting me the opportunity to work with him at Emory University's Stuart A. Rose Manuscript, Archives, and Rare Book Library during my doctoral studies. W. Bartley Hildreth developed my interest in how business and cultural heritage intersect. Carrie Smith and Lisa Stead paved with the way for this text with their excellent edited volume, *The Boundaries of the Literary Archive* (2013). Geraldine Higgins taught me the importance of anthologies. Erika Farr explained born-digital preservation practices. Stephen Enniss piqued my interest with his keynote at the 2014 meeting of Rare Book and Manuscript Section (RBMS) of the Association of College and Research Libraries (ACRL) in Las Vegas. Claire Clark, Jody DeRidder, and Erik Peterson guided me through the book proposal process. Christopher Prom helped me define what my book was and what it wasn't. Lise Jaillant gave me a venue to present my initial findings. Glenn Horowitz and Ken Lopez provided their client lists. Amy Koopmann explained how law libraries worked. Tina Colvin kept my prose proofread. Laura Hampton listened when stress became overwhelming. Attendees at the Modern Language Association (MLA) and Society of American Archivists (SAA) gatherings in 2016 workshopped my ideas.

In the process of creating my data set and manuscript, I contacted professionals across the country for help. The following administrators, archivists, curators, and librarians graciously answered my questions: Christina E. Barber, Melissa Barton, Alice Birney, Amy Braitsch, Jolie L. Braun, Nancy Brown-Martinez, Itza Carbajal, Lisa Carter, Courtney Chartier, Lynda Claassen, Heather Cole, Tara Craig, Stephen Davis, Erika Dowell, Amanda Faehnel, Kathleen Feeney, Moira Fitzgerald, Anna Franz, Julia Gardner, Edward Gaynor, Isaac Gewirtz, Ashley Gosselar, Julie Grob, Susan Halpert, Sue Hamburger, Matthew Harris, Megan E. Hixon, Jennifer Holland, Kathryn Hujda, Stephen James, Rebecca Jewett, A. J. Johnson, Eric Johnson, Tim Johnson, Christian Kelleher, Mary Catherine Kinniburgh, Nancy Kuhl, Jennifer B. Lee, Merrilee Lee, Linda Long, Cecily Marcus, Maureen Maryanski, Cristina Meisner, Stephen C. Mielke, Daryl Morrison, Jennifer Motszko, Megan Mummey, Timothy D. Murray, Karla Nielsen, Ronald D. Patkus, Heather Pisani, Katherine Reagan, Dean Rogers, Laura Russo, Katherine A. Salzmann, Edward Sevcik, Kathy Shoemaker, Samuel Sisneros, Don Skemer, Curtis Small, Dean Smith, Holly A. Smith, Duane Swanson,

Kassandra Ware, Diane Warner, Melissa Watterworth, Dorothy Waugh, Penny White, Cherry Williams, Rebecca Wingfield, Hilary Dorsch Wong, Mylinda Woodward, and Stephen Young.

Twitter also gave me an interdisciplinary cohort to discuss concepts and problems as they arose. I particularly am grateful to the following people: Hannah Alpert-Abrams, Sarah Burke Calahan, Jennifer Douglas, Melissa Hubbard, Maarja Krusten, Erin Lawrimore, Erin O'Meara, Sara Powell, Kathleen Roe, John Russell, Shannon Supple, Mattie Taormina, Sarah Werner, Eric Willey, Tom Wilson, and Lorraine York. You are my community, my life of the mind.

I reserve my deepest gratitude for my husband, Muzel Chen, who knew this baby needed to come first. I couldn't have done it without you.

Placing Papers

INTRODUCTION

Outside the Literary Archives Market

The history of the market is the central, if submerged, element in the story of every great library and collection.

—William R. Reese

In the literary archives market, those who create the commodity—authors—have only one opportunity to make a deal. Their papers, which document their life and work, typically are sold together as a single collection. Consumers, researchers and the public prefer to work with and visit complete holdings. Researchers find the expense and time required to review multiple collections at geographically dispersed repositories too costly, while the public is less motivated to see a small set of materials. Likewise, repositories also prefer to purchase complete collections as institutions gain more prestige from major acquisitions. As a result, stakes are high.

Many writers decide to use executors, such as literary agents or manuscript dealers, to help them obtain the best price. After all, their families often depend on the financial support such sales provide. But the pressure is not just on authors and their representatives. Buyers also have only one chance to obtain their preferred collection. Library directors are keen to make newsworthy acquisitions that will enhance their institution's reputation. Subject curators know it is rare to gain the opportunity to add to their holdings significantly with a single purchase. And while archivists and digital archivists work for repositories to organize and provide access to collections once they are successfully obtained, they know that notable holdings can bolster their career, especially if incoming materials present cultural or technological challenges that will allow them to learn and advance professionally.

These stakeholders' concerns represent only their immediate motivations. Market participants are driven by history too. Authors may know others who sold their papers for top dollar to prestigious places and hope to equal, or best, their literary peers. Agents and dealers need to keep their businesses viable, which depends not only on continuing to represent the most important writers but also on maintaining positive and mutually beneficial relationships with repositories. Directors and curators must watch their budgets to ensure that they can make as many significant acquisitions as is financially possible. Their job is to identify their repository's preexisting strengths and build holdings over the course of their career that develop and expand those fields. Trained to imagine themselves as supporting the work of researchers and the interest of the public, archivists increasingly recognize that their interventions shape what documents are preserved and thus what narratives can be written. And researchers and the public come to collections and repositories with preconceived notions as to how these collections can be interpreted.

These stakeholders' current motivations and previous experiences generate a dynamic trade in literary papers. Within the United States, this market for collections of contemporary authors began in 1955 and continues today. While each collection is as unique as the writer who created it, the market's overall shape and direction can be tracked to show how it evolved from a trade that cheaply met the needs of a new, larger generation of researchers following World War II into the multimillion dollar market seen today. *Placing Papers: The American Literary Archives Market* documents this history by identifying the present and preceding needs of its stakeholders to argue that in the future the market will consolidate around the most privileged members of each group of stakeholders, a phenomenon widely known as the "Matthew Effect."

Although market histories, including this one, largely focus on successful trades, a market's power is shown by what it prevents from changing hands. Garbage may not seem to be a desirable commodity within a trade that mostly caters to academic and private research libraries. However, when that trash belonged to a two-time Pulitzer Prize winner, scholars would prefer to debate these materials' value rather than having repositories, even one as illustrious as Harvard's, foreclose their conversation.[1] As the collections that institutions choose not to acquire are rarely documented and discussed, scholars believe their work shapes the direction of literary history rather than realizing that the individuals and institutions that comprise the literary archives market decide what will be written long before they enter the reading room.

JOHN UPDIKE'S LITERARY COLLECTION

In February 2016, John Updike's trash came to auction for $20,000. It failed to sell.[2] But who put Updike's garbage up for sale? What was in it? Why was it supposed to be worth so much? And why did no one buy it?

This story begins in May 2006 when a man named Paul Moran was biking along a suburban road in Massachusetts. Moran saw Updike walk out of his house and place several bags on the curb. Among the contents were his honorary degrees. Moran paused as he realized the degrees were valuable. He immediately returned to Updike's house with his car and collected the garbage. Later, Moran recounted "with latex gloves and hand sanitizer, I retrieved the contents like a kid with a black plastic Christmas stocking. My hands were shaking from excitement and withdrawal. I was now in possession of John Updike's life in Kodachrome."[3]

At first, he sold his finds piecemeal at a local bookstore. Then he decided these items should not be used for immediate monetary gain. Instead, he decided to build a collection over time, to be sold later. He stopped by Updike's house frequently over the next several years, always picking up Updike's garbage. As a result, Moran gathered letters, photographs, clothing, and many other items related to Updike's life and literary career. He only ceased his errand when Updike died in January 2009. While Updike knew what Moran did, he never gave him explicit permission.[4]

Moran's eventual goal was to sell Updike's papers to the Harry Ransom Center at the University of Texas at Austin. To do this, he moved the collection from Massachusetts to a storage unit in Austin and created a website called the Other John Updike Archive (johnupdikearchive.com) to allow him to blog about his finds. Not content to promote his collection only on his own platform, he wrote an article, "Finding John Updike: And Taking His Trash" (2014) for the *Texas Monthly* to showcase the collection's value.[5] But the Ransom Center declined to purchase the collection. When Moran put it up for auction through R&R Auction in 2016, the papers failed to meet their reserve of $20,000.

Although Updike is a major twentieth-century American writer, it would be reasonable to assume that Moran got too greedy when he went to sell Updike's belongings. After all, asking $20,000 for trash seems like a bit much. Maybe the Ransom Center's problem with the collection was its price. But Updike's official literary collection, also comprised of letters, photographs, drafts, and other "personal miscellany," sold to Harvard University's Houghton Library for $3 million.[6] In comparison, Moran's collection was a steal.

The problem was many people thought Moran did steal. He was entitled to whatever he found on the curb legally owing to the Fourth Amendment, but Updike's family, literary agent, repository, the archivists employed at the repository, and biographer each agreed independently that what Moran did was unethical.[7] Was that enough to keep anyone from buying it, even if the garbage did have research value? Apparently so, given that no one purchased the collection, even though its holdings were intellectually valuable and reasonably priced and its contents did mirror many of the types of materials available in Updike's authorized collection.

The literary archives market controls who has access to the primary documents that shape the composition of literary history. Scholars write literary history by consulting primary sources found in literary archives, but they rarely consider how these papers became accessible because what matters to them is their ability to use them to learn about a writer's life and creative process.

Updike's trash reveals that the market is as defined by what it keeps out as by what it permits. As papers are curated before they ever come into the hands of scholars, scholarship is not an objective representation of its sources. Rather, authorities' preferences determine which sources remain available to generate an understanding of the past. In the case of literary history, stakeholders within the literary archives market determine what sources future scholars may access according to the stakeholder's rational best interests.

Moran saved Updike's trash because he saw financial, scholarly, and public value in the items. He realized they were worth something; researchers and fans would want to see them; some might even be willing to pay. Plus, he could not walk away—he had what Walter Benjamin would call a collecting instinct.[8] But what Moran did not count on was that the most important characteristic of a collection is the identity of its owner, not its research value.

Moran failed to sell his collection not because it was worthless but because he was not Updike or Updike's authorized heir or agent. Moran's failure proved how the literary archives market adjudicates who can own, sell, manage, and interpret writers' papers.

What Moran lacked was cultural capital, a form of knowledge transferred through socioeconomic privilege that equips a person to appreciate and decipher cultural relations and artifacts. Often those who possess a high cultural capital are said to understand the unspoken code governing social relations. Pierre Bourdieu described this code as not just a "*belief* concerning what constitutes a cultural (e.g., literary, artistic) work and its aesthetic and social value" but also a perception of which networks of people and organizations have the right to adjudicate value.[9] Moran did not realize initially that because he did not possess the correct cultural capital, his collection would fail to incite interest.

Moran's collection also challenged the monetary value of the original Updike collection. Author's papers are purported to be the final, authorized, but still enticingly backstage pass to a writer's life and work. To the institutions that purchase literary archives, this access is worth thousands or millions of dollars. But Moran offered an even more illicit carrot: the ability to see Updike as he did not wish to be seen, a tease to tempt even the most ethical researcher. If Moran's collection was bought by any university other than Harvard, where Updike sent his papers for decades, the institution that collected Updike's first set of papers would have its claim to exclusivity undercut.[10] Once Moran's holdings went unsold, Harvard remained secure that its collection is the primary set of papers related to Updike available to scholars.

When Adam Begley, Updike's official biographer, described the collection of Updike's trash as "completely worthless," he unwittingly designated that this collection was *supposed* to be worthless, for it fell outside the parameters of what he intended to provide.[11] After all, Begley's writing needed to be based on the authorized papers; his definitive account is less definitive when new sources become available. Begley acted in his rational best interest to validate only the sources he used. Similarly, when Leslie A. Morris, Updike's curator from Houghton Library, and Andrew Wylie, Updike's literary agent, condemned the collection, they asserted *their* best interests: their financial as well as intellectual monopoly on the author.[12] Morris defended her decision to decline Moran's papers by arguing "an archival collection derives meaning in part from what a person chooses to cull from it."[13] In effect, she reiterated that the only collection that was supposed to exist was the official one, properly prepared by Updike, managed by Wylie, bought by Harvard, curated by Morris, and researched by Begley. Moran's goal to sell Updike's trash challenged the existing institutional structure of the literary archives market. These stakeholders' combined authority prevented the Moran collection from achieving its reserve price.[14]

Furthermore, Moran's collection challenged the identity of these individuals and institutions. Professions are defined by their work as well as how access to that work operates. These features can be divided into four distinct requirements: knowledge, monopoly, autonomy, and service. Knowledge is obtained by completing specialized education. Monopolies are enforced by ensuring that such knowledge remains limited to those who can access this education. Autonomy requires controlling how this knowledge can be applied once it is obtained through an officially sanctioned program, and service justifies the entire system by appealing to a greater ideal, such as the public good. Professions follow these practices to guard their value, also known as "occupational privilege."[15] As literary agents, library administrators, curators, and scholars are all professionals, these individuals were primed to react protectively against the threat of an outsider engaging in their work. Disparaging the research value and provenance of Moran's collection is a rhetorical action intended to reify the speaker's own occupational privilege, the source of their cultural capital. Unfortunately for Moran, their ability to enforce their professional autonomy—their right to determine who can identify, sell, and purchase literary archives—held stable in the face of his test.

Once Moran realized he lacked cultural capital as a collector entering the literary archives market, he attempted to change his identity from collector to artist. He rechristened Updike's trash as postmodern assemblage and began a publicity campaign through his blog. Eleven links formed the blog's header, taking readers to longer explanations of Moran's approach, while the blog entries featured portions of the collection.[16] By doing so, Moran bracketed the collection within his chosen critical context. Seen in figure 1, three of these links are particularly insightful: "Culture Vulture," "Proust's Overcoat," and "Talking Heads '77."

Clicking "Culture Vulture" originally took readers to a *New York Times* article about an upcoming Swann Auction in New York. The auction followed a trend spearheaded by Christie's South Kensington to combine traditional auction items with more unusual offerings like preserved wedding

FIGURE 1. Screen capture of Paul Moran's website, The Other John Updike Archive.

cakes and used paint brushes to "give the sale a story."[17] Moran used this piece to suggest that prized materials like Updike's original literary collection can benefit from association with less collectible items, like his trash.

Choosing "Proust's Overcoat" allowed viewers to see a page that combined images of the collection with quotes from Lorenza Foschini's *Proust's Overcoat: The True Story of One Man's Passion for All Things Proust* (2010). Foschini documented Jacque Guérin's obsessive hunt for Marcel Proust's belongings.[18] By affiliating himself with Guérin, Moran highlighted how the ends justify the means when it comes to preserving literary papers.

Opting for "Talking Heads '77" provided visitors an opportunity to read a piece written by Moran himself arguing that Updike's trash was a postmodern assemblage. Moran found his tradition in the work of Joseph Beuys's *Felt Suit* (1970), René Magritte's *La Trahison des images* (1928–29), Joseph Cornell's *Manual of Marvels* (circa 1930), and Marcel Duchamp's *Fountain* (1917).[19] Beuys emphasized that art is a representation of the everyday; Magritte highlighted that images are simulations of the real artifacts; Cornell thought scavenged materials could be as evocative as traditional media; and Duchamp suggested art is determined by the context into which an item is placed.

As Moran repurposed common found objects into art by presenting these materials online, Moran felt that he continued the work of Dadaists and Surrealists. Moran saw how his finds were not legible to the literary archives market, but he thought these materials could be appreciated if he presented the items within an accepted critical framework. If Moran could have his collection accepted as his own art, comprised of belongings previously owned by Updike, rather than as Updike's literary collection, he thought he would have a better shot at selling the materials. In effect, he tried to rebrand himself to make his holdings more attractive. But Moran's recontextualization failed. What he described as an assemblage, others perceived as ephemera. What he said was art, others saw as garbage.

This example demonstrates that rather than reacting to the demands of researchers, the literary collection market's stakeholders shape their appetites. What is left by history gains value from what is discarded. But Morris admitted that what gets thrown away can later prove fascinating—and one prominent scholar agreed. Matthew G. Kirschenbaum included an image of one of the computer diskettes supposedly lost by Updike but found by a "private collector" in *Track Changes* (2016). He even discussed the Moran case in his chapter "What Remains," in which he stated, "It is fair to say that key members of the Updike establishment have taken a dim view of Moran's activities." Revealingly, Kirschenbaum then argued that these diskettes raise questions central to Updike scholarship.[20]

Yet even Kirschenbaum's support would not have helped Moran. After all, Pierre Bourdieu predicted that literature, like art, cannot exist outside the network that legitimates its value. As repositories are in the business of propagating cultural capital, those representing these institutions are unlikely to cede their authoritative role.[21] No matter how elevated Moran made his discourse, it was in the market's best interest to keep Moran out. Cultural authority becomes more important to maintain than research value.

Stakeholders in the literary archives market demonstrated their values through their treatment of Moran's collection. The presence of Moran's collection challenged the executors, institutions, and archivists who engaged in the sale, acquisition, and organization of Updike's papers. Researchers should remember that when these stakeholders decided to oppose an acquisition, they determined the direction of future scholarship.[22] The literary archives market does not support scholars, it feeds them. The distinction seems minute, but the difference is critical. Scholars are dependent on the market, not the market on scholars.

The literary archives market commodifies the personal papers of writers like John Updike.[23] After all, not all authors' papers have the potential to become commodities destined to live within a "conventional archive."[24] Think of a publisher's slush pile of rejected poems or a failed novelist's notebooks. While poem drafts and journals are types of items found in a literary collection, they do not have financial value unless they come from a successful author.[25] But once a writer becomes successful, institutions want to acquire his or her papers to satisfy scholarly interest and public curiosity. As a result, the author and her family, often with the help of a literary agent or manuscript dealer, donates or sells her papers to an institution. That institution can be represented during the acquisitions process by either a library director or a curator who advocates for the significance of the author and her work. Once a director or curator convinces the writer to place her material in their repository, staff archivists arrange and describe these papers before they become accessible.[26] The literary archives market transforms an author's personal papers into a commodity.

Updike's trash had to move through the authorized channels of the market's stakeholders to become a legible commodity. As Moran was not Updike's authorized heir or representative, Moran could not participate in the market even when he had a set of papers with research value. But the rules that worked to exclude Moran took time to develop. This book examines how the motivations of the literary archives market's American stakeholders generated the history and behavioral norms of the trade.

Quantitative data describe the stakeholder's historical behavior by illustrating correlations rather than proving causation owing to changing sample sizes for each variable and the relatively small size of the overall data set. All quantitative data in this book are based on the 102 writers listed in the seventh edition of *The Norton Anthology of American Literature* (*NAAL*). Since then, ten years have elapsed and two more editions have been published, offering scholars of the future literary archives market an opportunity to see how definitions of the canon shift over time.[27] While writers who appear in multiple editions of *NAAL* could be said to be more canonical than those who are included only once, for example, such analysis and its implications on how the literary archives market is depicted will be left to a future researcher.[28] Furthermore, data collection concluded in January 2016, indicating that information includes only authors who placed their collections prior to December 2015.

The names found in the anthology became constants, while the information sought in finding aids formed variables. ArchiveGrid, Google, and university library catalogs located these guides. As authors often have several institutions collecting their papers, the data set included only the largest collections.²⁹ Size served as a proxy for the likelihood that the collection represented an author's primary deposit of papers rather than a synthetic collection;³⁰ for this reason, only collections larger than 0.5 linear feet were included. When an author had multiple collections, the larger set of papers was selected.³¹

Once a *NAAL* writer's primary collection was identified, I populated the study's data set with information found in the collection's finding aid. In the case that the finding aid did not provide the necessary information, the repository was contacted via email. Footnotes record and explain any inconsistencies or omissions in the resulting data set. Furthermore, the data set employs both interval and nominal data. Interval data signals a value difference, whereas nominal data involves numbers that do not have a set order. Nominal data in this study is coded as either a 0 or a 1. For example, an author is either alive (0) or dead (1) when institutions acquire their literary collection. One cannot be simultaneously alive and dead, and while being alive might seem superior to being deceased, neither state is quantitatively set as better than the other.³²

Case studies of individual acquisitions from the stakeholders portrayed in each chapter complement the quantitative data. Whenever possible, this book uses the stakeholders' own published words. Generally, these stakeholders commented on their activities in nonscholarly locations such as popular newspapers and magazines, trade publications, finding aids, professional white papers, publicity statements, commercial websites, and personal blogs. The paratextual and often ephemeral location of these texts highlights how the literary archives market came to be overlooked in scholarship discussing twentieth- and twenty-first-century American literature.

Understanding how the market commodified creativity requires appreciating why authors create brands, executors turn a profit, institutions want to reduce competition, archivists influence research outcomes, and scholars and the public seek access. Synthesizing these perspectives demonstrates how these stakeholders together shaped not only the trade in writers' papers but also the direction and the future of academic inquiry in the humanities.

To begin, let's follow the money.³³

CHAPTER 1

Inside the Literary Archives Market

―――

The number of dissertations being written on Joyce, Faulkner, and Hemingway had, in a few short years after World War II, surpassed the number written on Shakespeare, Milton, and Johnson.

–Thomas F. Staley

In 2014, Gwendolyn Brooks, Billy Collins, Toni Morrison, and Flannery O'Connor, four of the most significant American writers of the twentieth century, placed their papers in academic libraries. Two of these authors, Billy Collins and Toni Morrison, selected their own repositories. Collins chose the University of Texas at Austin, home to the Harry Ransom Center, which he described as "the best orphanage in the world."[1] Morrison picked the Department of Rare Books and Special Collections at Princeton University. The University of Illinois acquired the literary collection of Gwendolyn Brooks, who died in 2000, while Emory University obtained the archives of Flannery O'Connor, who died in 1964.

The national news media enthusiastically recounted these acquisitions. National Public Radio reported that the Ransom Center now included Collins's "jottings on cocktail napkins, envelopes and other scraps." Christopher L. Eisgruber, Princeton University president, recounted in *Time* that "this extraordinary resource [of Morrison's papers] will provide scholars and students with unprecedented insights." The *Chicago Tribune* delighted readers with the fact that "the venerated poet" Gwendolyn Brooks "recorded everything she ate in spiral-bound notebooks," while the *New York Times* explained O'Connor's boxes included "charming juvenilia, including a hand-lettered children's book about a goose."[2] Each of these articles focused on how ephemera related to an author's private life highlight the relationships, habits, and intellectual environment authors bring to bear on their work. Such documents provide powerful contextual clues about the milieu in which a writer produced his or her texts. While the public is fascinated by the unique and surprising contents of writers' papers, scholars are preoccupied by the ability of these documents to capture the personal beside the professional. But this charm does not come cheap.

FINANCIAL VALUE

Writers' cultural capital, generated by public and scholarly interest, allows them to sell as well as donate their papers. When sold, prices may range from tens of thousands to millions of dollars. The cost of these papers defines which institutions choose to compete on the literary archives marketplace, favoring American universities with high endowments. The relative monopoly certain universities enjoy does not mean that they, or their competitors, feel satisfied with the market's current dynamics. Many repositories in the United States are frustrated with how the market's prices inflated over time.

Bookseller Glenn Horowitz, who often represents writers' collections, noted that his first literary collection sale of poet W. S. Merwin's papers sold for "$185,000 in 1983"—a small sum compared with novelist Vladimir Nabokov's papers, which are "widely believed to have been the first archive sale to top $1 million" in 1992. Novelist Norman Mailer obtained $2.5 million. Poet Allen Ginsberg's papers sold for $980,000. Prices for "typical" literary archives are between "$50,000 and $250,000," although writers associated with more modest prices are less likely to share their earnings.[3] Native American poet N. Scott Momaday received $500,000, a slightly above-average price but below the payments accorded to others. Nevertheless, Momaday felt satisfied by the exchange. He told the *Wall Street Journal* what he was paid even though Yale attempted to protect his privacy by refusing to comment.[4]

Institutions outside the United States are alarmed by the cost of writers' papers as they lose the opportunity to keep their cultural heritage at home when authors sell their collections to more moneyed American repositories. British academics lament that "the struggle to preserve valuable papers within the United Kingdom is always challenged by the deeper coffers and wealthier benefactors of American . . . libraries and private collections."[5] The primary American offender is the Harry Ransom Center at the University of Texas at Austin. For example, the *Guardian* reported that Jim Crace sold his papers to the Ransom Center for "a six-figure sum (in pounds, not dollars)," a price an unnamed university in England could not match. In frustration at their inability to compete, British archivists updated the proverb that "two things are inevitable: death and taxes." Now, they say, "two things are inevitable: death and Texas."[6]

Even literature documents the Ransom Center's reach: Brian Friel dramatized the problem in *Give Me Your Answer, Do!* (1997). In the play, Friel depicts the anxiety Tom Connolly, an Irish writer, feels when a university representative comes to evaluate his papers. After a scene in which Connolly debates what David Knight, "the agent from that University in Texas," meant when Knight said Connolly's papers were "substantial," Connolly begins to show how much stress he is under. Daisy, his wife, calms him: "My hope would be that he makes you a worthy offer . . . Because that acknowledgement, that affirmation might give you—whatever it is—the courage?—the equilibrium?—the necessary self-esteem?—just to hold on. Isn't that what everyone needs? So for that reason alone I really hope he does buy the stuff."[7] If Knight acquires Tom Connolly's papers at a good price, Tom's literary collection will give the family financial security. But Daisy concludes that Tom's creativity would be stymied if he sold his papers because Tom would become too confident. The play ends before the audience learns what Knight will offer for the collection and if Tom accepts his price or follows Daisy's advice, but the turn between the Connolly family's desperation to sell in the first act and Daisy's reticence in the second illustrates the potential conflict between an author's financial and emotional needs.

Give Me Your Answer, Do! downplays the problems American institutions incite when they seek the papers of international authors. Friel shows only Texas's wealth and ambition, not its competition with other repositories. In real life, however, many of these institutions fight back to keep the papers of their nation's writers at home. For example, to keep national manuscripts in British hands, the John Rylands Library of the University of Manchester founded the Group for Literary Archives and Manuscripts (GLAM) in 2005, the same year the United Kingdom Literary Heritage Working Group began to create a strategy to "raise awareness of the value of archives, offer guidance to writers over committing their papers and urge the government to offer tax incentives to living writers rather than to estates of the deceased."[8] Its outreach helped British writers become more aware of the importance of their archives to their home country.

Such outreach was essential as more American universities entered the field. Emory University's Stuart A. Rose Manuscript, Archives, and Rare Book Library also is interested in British literary archives. The university paid $600,000 for Poet Laureate Ted Hughes's papers and an "undisclosed sum" for those of Best of the Booker award winner Salman Rushdie. However, Emory does not focus only on British papers. In 2007, the university purchased American novelist Alice Walker's papers for around $1 million. But Emory's collecting policy favors writers from a third country—Ireland.[9] Emory decided to focus on the country as it had a rich literary heritage that had yet to be systematically collected. Now Emory holds most manuscripts related to the Belfast Group, a set of writers who dramatically reshaped the landscape of Anglophone poetry and whose most notable member, Seamus Heaney, would go on to win the Nobel Prize.

Whether British or American, many archivists and librarians believe that literary archives should not be sold. As costs rise, archivists and librarians note how their institutions struggle to provide the funding needed to continue supporting new acquisitions. Isaac Gewirtz, curator of the Henry W. and Albert A. Berg Collection of English and American Literature at the New York Public Library, commented that donations are decreasing while individual items can cost "hundreds of thousands of dollars."[10] Public institutions can accept donations of literary archives but cannot always pay for them due to lower funding levels. Even when they can pay, representatives from such schools often are not able to match the offers of their more-moneyed peers.[11]

Complaints about the high price for literary archives do not come solely from universities struggling to build their profile in contemporary literature. Major players, like the Ransom Center, also feel the strain of high prices. Stephen Enniss, the center's director, revealed how much his repository spent on Gabriel García Márquez's papers—$2.2 million—only after the Associated

Press and the *Austin American-Statesman* filed a Freedom of Information Act request. Enniss protested that "our competitive position is eroded" now that the cost of García Márquez's collection became public, for "we can't negotiate without showing the larger market our vulnerability."[12] Enniss did not want the price the Ransom Center paid for García Márquez's papers to be known because he believes that other authors will then expect higher amounts for their materials. Enniss's words demonstrate that although foreign and domestic repositories are frustrated that they cannot compete against their well-funded competitors for literary archives, the Ransom Center itself is beginning to complain about the costs associated with the trade.

Yet the market persists. Despite growing institutional objections to high costs, libraries need to continue acquiring research collections, and most writers prefer to sell their papers as Billy Collins and Toni Morrison did. Dan Piepenbring, reporting for the *Paris Review*, noted how ubiquitous the idea was: "One good thing about getting older, though, is that you can sell your papers—you know, all that junk that records your 'process.'" While Piepenbring jokes that literary archives are junk and dismisses scholarship based on them as creating an artificial understanding of how composition occurs, the market remains attractive to authors. Those who participate in the trade can profit; this prospect is too enticing to ignore. Even deceased authors get in on the game. When authors die before they can choose a repository for their papers, the executors employed to maximize estate assets also prefer to sell their literary archives. As the *Wall Street Journal* wryly commented, whether an author is living is beside the point: "Being dead helps but isn't required."[13]

Authors nevertheless find the process of transferring their archives from their homes to a repository emotionally fraught. Phillip Lopate noted that "the most gratifying event to have occurred this past year—my ambivalence about surrendering them aside—was selling my papers to Yale University's Beinecke Library." Lopate did not enjoy the undertaking, which required approaching several repositories, enduring appraisers who determined his papers' value, and waiting for universities to decide whether they were interested in his work. Lopate particularly resented the appraisal process, which required setting a financial value for a lifetime of work based on external market considerations. Lopate remarked that the men and women who came to survey his collection took only two hours to determine his papers' worth and maintained clinically detached expressions as they examined the intimate details of his life.[14] The process of transforming personal papers into a literary archive may be lucrative, but it requires writers to see their work as a commodity.

Appraisal can provoke an author's sense of competitiveness. Creating a literary archive out of an author's personal papers does not just commodify the work but also commodifies the life. Papers document a writer's experiences in addition to his or her creativity. If another author obtains a certain sum for his or her collection, why is it that the amount is higher or lower? Is it because that writer had a more interesting life? Or is it because the person's work obtained higher critical recognition? Or is it that one's peer found more popular success?

Once authors know what other authors can earn by selling their papers to repositories, they see that price as an anchor and are more likely to argue that their value is equal—or higher. As a result, library directors and curators try to conceal the amounts they pay partially to keep writers from negotiating their rate. Enniss's desire to suppress the amount paid by the Ransom Center for García Márquez's papers is a result of this concern. Other repositories manage authors' egos differently. Emory University either agrees to pay or not to pay the amount a third-party appraiser quotes for a collection; it does not negotiate with an author to find a lower price. This strategy keeps financial evaluations outside the university's control, simultaneously eliminating the need to negotiate with authors while maintaining their goodwill. In contrast, Washington University in St. Louis does not rule out negotiating acquisition prices with its authors, although it avoids comparing and contrasting prices among its writers.[15] While some institutions do not negotiate whereas others are open to debate, most institutions avoid public disclosure of prices.

Despite these emotions, authors are the winners in the literary archives marketplace. That is, writers who command enough scholarly and public interest to generate high prices for their papers are the trade's beneficiaries. For as long as their materials are in demand, repositories will have to pay. However, capturing scholarly and public interest is difficult. Even when a writer achieves acclaim, their status among scholars and the public must remain constant, or show signs of growing, to fetch a high price in the trade.

SCHOLARLY VALUE

Ironically, the value of contemporary literary archives to American repositories originally rose from their affordability. Acquiring contemporary writers' papers was a cheap way for university libraries to begin building collections of distinction for the benefit of their burgeoning number of students and scholars in the postwar period. As the market progressed after 1955, acquisition rates varied but remained on an upward trajectory. Furthermore, the market's growth did not depend on academic trends, such as New Criticism.

Following World War II, the first universities to recognize the teaching and research potential of contemporary writers' papers ignored naysayers who saw these writers, as well as their materials, as less prestigious subjects for study and chose instead to amass these collections. A growing number of students entered American higher education after Congress passed the Servicemen's Readjustment Act (more commonly known as the GI Bill) in 1944, swelling the size of younger universities.[16] These new students then enrolled in graduate school, eventually completing more dissertations on American literature between 1948 and 1961 than between 1891 and 1948.[17] University libraries acquiring the materials of contemporary writers could provide these students with more affordable sources for their research compared with the costs of building significant holdings in early modern books or medieval manuscripts.[18]

Even though traditionalists in English departments discouraged their graduate students from studying early twentieth-century authors[19]—C. S. Lewis famously derided the practice by staying "the student who wants a tutor's assistance in reading the works of his own contemporaries might as well ask for a nurse's assistance in blowing his own nose"—the discipline of contemporary literature caught on.[20] After all, as the Ransom Center's former director Thomas F. Staley noted, "It was natural that these expanding university libraries with burgeoning new graduate programs concentrated their rare book and manuscript buying in the area of the twentieth century, where materials were available, materials which were then not left to ripen but were quickly made available to dissertation students hungry for new topics."[21]

Now these authors are known as the "modernists." Those graduate students, interested in discussing evidence of new composition methods they discovered in writers' papers, became the New Critics. And the universities found a novel solution to their problem of providing affordable research materials for their students by establishing unparalleled collections, even if they must pay more now than they did then.

At least one scholar took advantage of the new field and the infant market to obtain James Joyce's papers for his exclusive use: Richard Ellmann.

Ironically, he would not be a New Critic. While New Criticism is predicated on the argument that literature stands apart from the author and therefore does not admit the validity of biographic influences, Ellmann insisted that the life informs the work. His academic approach would alienate him from his peers, yet it influenced their critical development nevertheless.[22]

Richard Ellmann wrote prominent biographies on such modernists as James Joyce, Oscar Wilde, and William Butler Yeats. He recognized the strategic advantage that presented itself when Joyce's papers remained uncataloged at the University at Buffalo, restricted at the National Library of Ireland, or in private hands and took it upon himself to write Joyce's biography.[23] Ellmann found the paucity of an accessible Joyce literary collection as a provocation to reach out personally to Joyce's living friends, family, and colleagues. Ellmann not only secured the transfer of some of these papers from private to university holdings but also managed to obtain the exclusive right to publish manuscripts from the collection.

This sleight of hand—making a valuable collection visible to others, but at the same time restricting others' ability to use the material—was a masterful coup. Ellmann achieved it by serving as the consultant for the sale of the letters of James Joyce's widow. Ellmann brought Nelly Joyce's letters first to the University of Kansas but finally sold them to Cornell University for $37,000 in 1956. This example is only one of the many times that Ellmann's connections to heirs or collectors benefited his scholarship.[24]

Although Ellmann's efforts to obtain modernist literary papers during the middle of the twentieth century for his own work took foresight, many library directors had the same impulse. They anticipated the direction of literary studies and wisely began seeking the archives of contemporary writers on behalf of their institutions. As noted earlier, the Ransom Center made a sagacious venture into the field, but two other libraries also founded collections in this moment: the University at Buffalo and Washington University in St. Louis.

The first library director of the University at Buffalo, Charles D. Abbott, began his collection by reaching out to living authors. Abbott asked Elizabeth Bishop, Allen Ginsberg, Marianne Moore, and William Carlos Williams to give his university the contents of their waste paper baskets.[25] Although Buffalo did not necessarily win all these writers' papers—which would go to Vassar College, Stanford University, the Rosenbach, and Yale University, respectively—Abbott achieved his objective.[26]

Washington University in St. Louis pursued a similar goal. Their head of special collections, William Matheson, convened a set of writers headed by Mona Van Duyn to advise the libraries' collecting in the field in 1964. Matheson's instructions to this committee were simple: they should "suggest the names of poets and novelists whom they considered critically underappreciated, but who stood a good chance of being important in fifty years."[27] Due to this unconventional method, Washington obtained papers at the onset from Robert Creeley, James Merrill, and May Swenson, among others.[28] As with those collected by the University at Buffalo, sometimes these authors' primary literary archives would wind up elsewhere. In Washington's case, most of Creeley's papers eventually went to Stanford.[29] However, Merrill, Swenson, and others would keep their papers with Washington University.[30] Matheson was successful because he had a good collecting strategy: he deliberately sought to collect underappreciated authors.[31]

Although institutions like the University at Buffalo and Washington University in St. Louis may not have the same footprint in the literary archives market that larger ones do, their activities nevertheless comprise a significant portion of the trade. The University at Buffalo Libraries now supports the Poetry Collection, one of the largest collections of materials related to twentieth- and twenty-first-century Anglophone poetry, while Washington University in St. Louis collects modern literature.[32] Together, these universities, and others not named, preserve the papers of an array of writers whose critical estimation may be high but whose lower popular recognition allowed their materials to warrant more accessible prices.

Overlooking contemporary academic prejudice and intellectual trends allowed library directors at diverse institutions to establish and grow holdings to benefit scholarship. At the start of the literary archives market in the middle of the twentieth century, the modernists were too new to be reasonable subjects of study. By the late twentieth century, papers of contemporary writers would be overlooked in favor of theory. The avant-garde method of the 1950s New Critics would atrophy in published criticism throughout the 1960s. Theory, such as structuralism, poststructuralism, and deconstruction, eventually replaced New Criticism during the 1970s, 1980s, and 1990s. Although literary archives continued to be used to illuminate editorial decisions, textual studies would remain out of vogue for over a generation in academia. Nevertheless, many library directors continued to collect writers' papers. The perseverance of these directors prepared their institutions for the renaissance generated by the archival turn, a rejuvenation of interest in literary archives and archives in general.

Jacques Derrida, a French theorist, precipitated this intellectual shift with the publication of his *Archive Fever: A Freudian Impression* (1995). In *Archive Fever*, Derrida encouraged scholars to consider the archives not only as a place where records can be found but also as a location for reflection. Derrida emphasized how archives are linked etymologically to government and theoretically to psychoanalysis. Pondering the etymology of the word "archive," Derrida found "the Greek *arkheion* . . . a house, a domicile, an address, the residence of the superior magistrates, the *archons*, those who commanded" as evidence of the archive's role as serving as the "passage from the private to the public."[33] Preoccupied with how archives are linked inextricably to power and how power is as tied to maintaining confidentiality as it is to educating the public, Derrida spurred his intellectual successors to reflect critically on how the administration of records shape how history is recorded. This book continues the academic inquiry spurred by Derrida's archival turn by analyzing how stakeholders in the literary archives market shape academic research through their management of these papers.

PUBLIC VALUE

Writers donate or sell their papers to gain financial stability, and literary scholars use literary archives to bolster their research. Yet there are also loyal readers who form a nonacademic audience for literary archives. Their enthusiasm justifies mass media coverage when a repository acquires an author's papers. Furthermore, when new texts by such authors are found in literary archives, fans eagerly buy them. It is this public enthusiasm, combined with academic interest, that supports the financial value of twentieth-century American literary archives.

The anecdotes shared at the start of this introduction regarding the papers of Gwendolyn Brooks, Billy Collins, Flannery O'Connor, and Toni Morrison begin to illustrate how broadly literary archives appeal to the public in popular news media. The insights they provide into a writer's creative process and the details of their everyday life alternatively charm and provoke readers. The diversity of content within and among these papers makes them ripe for news coverage.

Even more newsworthy is when new works from established authors appear in literary archives. These new titles offer publishers the opportunity to capitalize on a familiar name, a formula that nearly guarantees success. During July 2015, an example of this phenomenon occurred regarding the papers of Nelle Harper Lee.

In July 2015, Nelle Harper Lee, author of *To Kill a Mockingbird* (1960), controversially released *Go Set a Watchman*, an earlier draft of *To Kill a Mockingbird* that her publisher marketed as a sequel to her beloved classic that "continues to sell more than a million copies a year." Lee spent most her life in seclusion and denied researchers access to her papers. The sudden access to her manuscript, kept in what her estate described only as "a secure place," raised questions from her fans regarding her health as well as the motives of her lawyer, Tonja Carter. Lee had a stroke in 2007, and her sister, guardian, and lawyer, "Miss Alice," or Alice Lee, died in 2014.[34] Carter took over Lee's guardianship following Miss Alice's death for the short period before Lee herself died in February 2016. Although Lee was living when *Go Set a Watchman* was published in July 2015, Carter's sudden discovery of *Go Set a Watchman* seemed too well timed; Carter gained the legal right to sell the book just as Lee's health declined. Many loyal fans found the circumstances off-putting given that Lee had long portrayed her disinterest in publishing additional books.

But what publishers described as the "Mockingbird industrial complex" proved too hard to resist.[35] HarperCollins published the novel; a *New York Times* opinion piece went so far as to call it one of the most "epic money grabs in the modern history of American publishing."[36] Critics derided the book, declaring it only an earlier draft to the masterpiece that was to become *To Kill a Mockingbird*. These ethical concerns did not stop *Go Set a Watchman* from setting publishing records. The novel sold 1.6 million copies to become the "fastest-selling book" in HarperCollins's history.[37]

Why Lee decided to reverse her lifelong commitment to not publishing additional books just as her health began to wane became a controversy partially because Lee's literary collection remained in private hands. If Lee had transferred her papers to a repository, these papers, or portions of these papers, would either have been open to researchers or restricted for a set period. In other words, the rights regarding access would have been more clearly articulated. If Lee's manuscript for *Go Set a Watchman* remained in an open portion of her collection and was later found by a researcher, the repository would direct that person to the copyright holder if he or she wished to quote from it, photograph it, or encourage its publication.[38] Or, if the manuscript remained restricted, then the copyright owner's wishes would be enumerated legally and the manuscript would never have been a potential text for publishers. Although the literary executor would decide the outcome in either case, placing Lee's papers in a repository might have reassured the public that all proper steps regarding the management of her estate had been observed.

The interests of global audiences and publishers parallel their American counterparts. In January 2016, Jo Hanks at Random House released the news that he had found a new story by Beatrix Potter in her papers at the Victoria and Albert Museum. In April 2016, Copper Canyon released new poems by Pablo Neruda found in his papers at the Fundación Pablo Neruda.[39] Publishers realized that a simple way to generate profit is to maximize the return they can make on established authors. Writers' papers provided a relatively easy way to add margins by expanding an author's list of available texts.

Sometimes, publishers do not even need to find a new text in a literary collection. All they need do is create a new edition of an old favorite that represents details from a writer's manuscript. Facsimiles of handwritten drafts or reproductions of an author's line edits can prove just as enticing to readers—and just as profitable for publishers—in the United States and abroad. Consider how "an unexpected pilgrimage to the basement of a Canadian library became necessary" when Anthony Burgess's publisher, W. W. Norton & Company, wanted to rerelease *A Clockwork Orange* (1962) to celebrate the novel's fiftieth anniversary. At McMaster University, editor Andrew Biswell found the sole manuscript of the novel, which McMaster librarian William Ready bought for $250 in 1971. The manuscript showed how Burgess carefully refined his character's invented slang, wrote an additional chapter that provided a more uplifting ending to his dark portrait of teen culture, and even provided his own illustrations to accompany the text. These findings allowed Norton to publish a restored edition of *A Clockwork Orange* (2012) to lure new readers, old fans, and scholars keen to discover Burgess's thoughts without traveling to Hamilton, Ontario.[40]

CONCLUSION

Writers' papers show how acclaimed authors led everyday lives while creating works of exemplary merit. Visitors to Gwendolyn Brooks's papers at the University of Illinois can learn she tracked every meal she ate while also writing the sensitive depictions of black Chicagoans that would eventually win her the Pulitzer Prize. This combination of the commonplace and sublime fascinates scholars and the public, generating the monetary value of literary archives.

While such attention is critical for writers to capture if they wish to justify the highest financial value in the literary archives market, the interest writers can generate is dependent on their cultural capital. Cultural capital is determined by many factors authors cannot control, such as their race, sex, and age. Chapter 2 investigates how these variables influence authors' brands and therefore their market participation and reception.

CHAPTER 2

Brand

Authors and Families

We live in an age in which everybody's for sale, everything is for sale.
—Cornel West

Authors who gained high cultural capital through earning the respect of their peers, the attention of scholars, and the public's interest use their identities as brands to sell their literary archives. The higher their cultural capital, the more sought after their papers will be. Writers included in literary teaching anthologies such as *The Norton Anthology of American Literature* (*NAAL*) hold the highest cultural capital because their work has become canonical. However, who the canon includes constantly shifts owing to changing editorial prejudices and tastes. Nevertheless, using an anthology to delineate who is considered canonical at a certain point in time is a necessary boundary condition. The 102 writers in the seventh edition of *The Norton Anthology of American Literature* generate a data set of authors whose experience in the literary archives market provides the quantitative and qualitative perspectives on the trade used for the remainder of this book. Of these 102 writers, 79 placed their papers beginning in 1955. The first authors to find a repository were white men. Twenty-six years would elapse before a woman of color's brand inspired repositories to seek her collection. Furthermore, not all writers were alive when it came time to place their collections. If an author's literary estate was managed by a relative, these family members sought repositories that reinforced their relative's preexisting brand.

BRAND

In the poem "a reader," Charles Bukowski complains "my cat shit in my archives." Bukowski was frustrated not only because his cat created a mess but also because he made a mess of particularly valuable papers destined to reside at the Huntington, a private research library that promotes itself as "one of the world's great cultural, research, and educational centers."[1] Bukowski realized that his drafts would have archival value based on his cultural capital. As the introduction explained, cultural capital is a benefit of socioeconomic privilege. While Bukowski came from and lived his life within a working-class milieu, the public and academic interest Bukowski built over the course of his career allowed him to obtain the cachet he needed to make his papers of interest to collecting repositories.

Cultural capital does not necessarily indicate a highbrow cultural register. Bukowski warned his readers not to "get the idea I am a poet; you can see me / at the racetrack any day half drunk."[2] Instead, Bukowski's cultural capital came from his authentic perspective on lower-class life. As an alcoholic, gambler, and womanizer, Bukowski became an authentic spokesman for a type of hard-bitten existence that rejected the pretentions of art.

No matter where cultural capital comes from, it can translate into profit. John Martin from Black Sparrow Press discovered Bukowski's work in 1966 and decided to pay Bukowski $100 a month to supply the press with his manuscripts, which it then published.[3] Bukowski died in 1994, but Martin held Bukowski's rights until he retired in 2002. Martin made a solid investment; Bukowski was a prolific poet who attracted a large readership and supportive critics.[4]

Bukowski's readers were interested in his distinctive perspective, which became identifiable with his name. Thus, his name became a brand, what the American Marketing Association describes as "a name, term, design, symbol or any other feature that identifies" a distinct service or good that begins to accrue symbolic value.[5] That Bukowski's brand did not match the rarified milieu of his future repository did not matter. The Huntington wanted to use Bukowski's collection to expand its reputation rather than seeking an author who would simply fit in.

The formula of taking "a cool artist, associat[ing] that mystique with your brand, hop[ing] it wears off and makes you cool too" appears to be a straightforward marketing strategy. Yet not everyone can become a brand.[6] Cultural capital accumulates differently for individuals based on their sex, race, and age.[7] Recall how chapter 1 showed that the literary archives market began when regional universities needed inexpensive papers for students to study. At the time, the most affordable papers belonged to contemporary writers who had yet to enter the canon of mainstream literary studies, yet these writers were largely white men. The market might have been avant-garde for finding contemporary papers collectible, but it was not egalitarian. The trade diversified only when literary studies itself became more interested in hearing from a variety of voices, which eventually allowed papers created by women and people of color to gain visibility and thus monetary value.

The narrative of how the literary archives market diversified cannot be separated from how I chose which writers to track, for this book's data set cannot represent all American authors whose papers went through the literary archives market after 1955. Rather, it measures the placement decisions of writers who appear in the seventh edition of *NAAL*.[8]

The Norton Anthology of American Literature generates what sociologists describe as a "boundary condition," an easily perceived status marker that becomes a shortcut to verifying quality.[9] Many authors' works are of comparable or even greater cultural value than are those appearing in *NAAL*, but as "the teaching anthology is one obvious place where the academic world intersects with the marketplace," such a measure is an efficient verification of a writer's critical acclaim and broad readership.[10] Any text included in the anthology is "*reproduced* by being taught over and over again," making it—and its author—more canonical over time than when it was first collected.[11] As a result, pedagogical institutions, rather than writers, are the arbiters of cultural capital. The syllabus creates the canon; the canon does not determine the syllabus.[12] And the syllabi of most introductory undergraduate literature classes is prescribed by the class text—the anthology.

This point is critical because the most desirable acquisitions of the literary archives market are the papers of writers included in the *NAAL* anthology. Yet because anthologies are problematic, readers of this book should understand how predicating an analysis of the literary archives market on an anthology shapes what quantitative data and qualitative case studies emerge.[13]

Historically, anthologies have been sexist. M. H. Abrams, the editor of *The Norton Anthology of English Literature* (*NAEL*) between 1959 and 2006, confessed in 2004 that he had "not found ten lines worth reading in any of the women added" to the anthology. He saw *NAEL*'s inclusion of women because of the need to "be p.c." rather than the inherent merit of their perspective. The Irish were not as direct: the three volumes comprising *The Field Day Anthology of Irish Writing* (1991) simply forgot to include women. After Anthony Bradley, Edna Longley, and Colm Tóibín denounced the anthology, it would take eleven years to correct the mistake.[14]

American anthologies are not much better. In 1982, Judith Fetterley and Joan Schulz investigated women's representation in three American anthologies. They found *NAAL* provided the widest selection of women due to an editorial policy that prioritized including women's work. Nevertheless, only 29 of the 131 selected authors were women, leading Fetterley and Schulz to remark caustically that "anyone who is interested in seeing the 'canon' expanded by including neglected authors who are not white and male is bound to be disappointed."[15] In 1988, the debate continued to rage. Editors wondered who among women wrote timeless masterworks while feminists objected to their rhetoric of mastery.[16] Two decades later, although scholars finally agreed that women's writing should be considered a part of literary history, quantitative analyses showed that "gender still silently determines the canon of American literature" because women remained underrepresented in anthologies.[17]

To make matters worse, anthologies historically have also been racist. Genre policing is a common way an editor permits racial bias. Consider Selden Rodman's *New Anthology of Modern Poetry* (1938), which attracted critique for daring to include "selections not usually considered poetry, including African-American folk songs."[18] Yet Rodman included these works not out of respect for their quality but rather to meet a quota of African American authors. Rodman reflected that "when I was editing anthologies in 1933, and again in 1946, I remember going through the complete works of Countee Cullen, Claude McKay, Langston Hughes and the others, hoping desperately to find a poem, and falling back reluctantly on the spirituals and the blues."[19] All three African American men are poetic masters, now widely taught and acclaimed for their technique and vision. Rodman may have included Cullen,

McKay, and Hughes in his anthologies, but he did so without recognizing that his search for poetry contained a bias: that poetry should look how he expected it to look, which either was divorced from all musical traditions entirely or connected only to its European expressions.

Anthology editors also indulged in racial essentialism. Another editor from the same era, V. F. Calverton, remarked that black writers and artists had a physical propensity for jazz due to "a difference in the calcium factor in bone structure or conjunction, accounting for an exceptional muscular resiliency."[20] Alarmingly, Calverton not only edited the *Anthology of American Negro Literature* (1929) but also *Readings from Negro Authors for Schools and Colleges* (1931), a volume intended for educational purposes. Rodman's and Calverton's racist legacy remains in the largely white makeup of recent anthologies, including the seventh edition of *The Norton Anthology of American Literature*.

Sexism and racism occurred because anthology editors did not document literary history, they created it. Each editor promoted values determined by their subjectivity that included or excluded certain demographics. These choices say more about an editor than they do the field, for the intrinsic value of the works under consideration, and the rank of their authors, cannot be separated from the lens through which they are viewed.

Studies of anthologies prove this by examining how inclusion alone does not determine an anthology's message. Just as any one text can contain a plurality of meanings, so can any single author. Langston Hughes can represent "humanistic affirmations of black identity" or an attack "on white racism and on Christian hypocrisy." As editors typically prefer to subsume potentially fraught narratives into an impression of "timeless, uncontested, universal value," the former Hughes usually is preferred to the latter. Other writers also can be subjected to similar treatment as anthology editors prefer their nonpolitical writing to pieces that include social and political critiques. As a result, editors of anthologies can include women and minority authors without permitting their presence to change the tone of the volume.[21]

Once English scholars better understood how their own subjectivity shaped the canon, they began to reflect on what it meant to serve as the editor of these volumes during the so-called canon wars. Yet the authors they included in anthologies remained predominantly white and male.[22] Soon, counter-anthologies cropped up to expand who and what works could be considered canonical.[23] African American, Asian American, Native American,

TABLE 1. *NAAL* authors' demographic deposit rate by decade

Decade	Collections (n)	White men (n)	White women (n)	Minority men (n)	Minority women (n)*
1950s	1	1	0	0	0
1960s	7	7	0	0	0
1970s	4	3	1	0	0
1980s	17	8	6	2	1
1990s	21	13	2	4	2
2000s	18	8	3	3	4
2010s	10	1	3	3	3
Total		78	41	15	12	10

*Toni Cade Bambara does not have a placement date, so she is not counted.

and Latinx academics and authors produced their own identity-based anthologies, such as *Black Fire: An Anthology of Afro-American Writing* (1968), *Asian American Authors* (1972), *The Winged Serpent: American Indian Prose and Poetry* (1962), and *Barrios and Borderland: Cultures of Latinos and Latinas in the United States* (1994). Additionally, a competitor to *NAAL* emerged in 1990. The *Heath Anthology* included what was then an extraordinarily large number of editors—fourteen people equally divided between women and men, people of color and whites—to "achieve a more truly democratic literature through greater inclusiveness."[24] Despite the *Heath*'s widespread acceptance among literary scholars and the number of identity-specific anthologies now in circulation, *NAAL* remained a commonly used anthology in college classrooms.

As a result, to interrogate how literary history is "by white males for white males about white males," *Placing Papers* follows poet Elizabeth Alexander's exercise of counting when people of color are present—and when they are absent—in the literary archives market to portray how this depiction of the trade is based on a subjective canon.[25]

AUTHORS

The Norton Anthology of American Literature authors can be divided into two groups: those who have and have not placed their papers in an archival repository, defined by Linda M. Morra as "the literal establishments that hold material traces of an author's contributions."[26] As of January 2016, 79 of 102 *NAAL* writers had placed their collections. The remainder of this book will discuss the authors who found a repository for their papers as a data set, while the conclusion will consider the writers who have yet to locate an institutional home. Variables such as demographics (sex, race, age) provide the basis for quantitative assessments. Then key examples of these quantitative trends are explored through qualitative reflection.

When providing an overview of a variable in the literary archives market using quantitative analysis, the nearest whole number is reported if numbers or percentages are employed. But names will be preferred over numerical representation whenever possible to acknowledge this study's small sample size of 79 authors. Additionally, since one minority woman does not have a placement date attached to her collection, the sample size for quantitative analysis sometimes consists of 78 writers when acquisition date is under consideration.

Table 1 shows that authors with placed collections consisted mostly of white men, whose 41 sets of papers made up about 53 percent of the trade.[27] Accordingly, white men entered the market first, followed by white women, minority men, and minority women. This timing highlights that an author's race and sex determined when he or she would be able to place papers in an institution.

To give names and narratives to these numbers, the first author to appear in the market, Randall Jarrell, was a white man. He gave his papers in 1955 to the University of North Carolina at Greensboro (UNC-Greensboro). As his collection is the first to appear in the literary archives market, the placement of his papers marks the beginning of the *NAAL* data set and the period this book covers. Jarrell was not from North Carolina; he was born in Tennessee and attended Vanderbilt University with such contemporaries as Robert Penn Warren. Although both a poet and a scholar, he is better known for his criticism lionizing three poets who would become the figureheads of modernism: William Carlos Williams, Robert Lowell, and Elizabeth Bishop. Jarrell taught at Kenyon College and the University of Texas at Austin before he decided to spend the remainder of his career at the Women's College of the University of North Carolina in Greensboro, which later became UNC-Greensboro. Jarrell was living when he donated his collection. Without a historical precedent to draw on, he turned to the nearest repository rather than considering alternative institutions.[28]

Eighteen years later, Sylvia Plath became the first white woman to appear in the trade when her executors selected Indiana University's Lilly Library in 1973 rather than the repository affiliated with her alma mater, Smith College. Plath's collection at the Lilly provides an example of the interpretative choices embedded in transforming qualitative research into quantitative data. Although the bulk of Plath's papers at the Lilly arrived between 1973 and 1974, her Indiana collection includes eight total components: four manuscript collections; two manuscript collections of her husband, Ted Hughes; Plath's correspondence with Gordon Ames Lameyer, a former boyfriend; and the print collection. An alternative approach could count these papers as individual collections as each exhibits a unique provenance, content, and size.[29] If a literary archive is measured by when it first arrived at Indiana, the date assigned to Plath's collection would change to 1961, when she sold 130 pages to the university either by herself or through a London bookdealer named Ifan Kyrle. Then the elapsed time between Jarrell's placement of his papers and when Plath had a repository found for hers would shrink from eighteen years to six. In either case, the market would take more than half a decade to accommodate women; it would take even longer before it included the papers of people of color.

Twenty-five years elapsed between the start of the market and the market's first acquisition of papers by an author of color. Ishmael Reed and Robert Hayden, both black men, placed their papers in 1980. Reed, who was still alive as of 2018, had a manuscript dealer sell his papers to the University of Delaware. Hayden's were donated by his wife, Erma Hayden, to the National Bahá'í Archives in Evanston, Illinois, following his death. While both Reed and Hayden are African American men, their work differs sharply in form and content. Reed, who was born in Chattanooga, Tennessee, and grew up in Buffalo, New York, briefly attended the University at Buffalo. Although Reed did not graduate, the prominence of his poetry and nonfiction allowed him to teach at the University of California, Berkeley, as well as many other institutions throughout the United States. Reed's approach is informal and his language vernacular. He is well known for his protest writing; he believes "writing is fighting."[30] Hayden, Reed's elder by twenty-five years, grew up in foster care in Detroit, Michigan. Reed eventually became a professor of poetry at Fisk University and the University of Michigan in addition to serving as a consultant in poetry to the Library of Congress. Unlike Reed, Hayden wrote in a formalist style and downplayed his racial perspective in favor of cultivating a claim to universal interests. While critics now understand Hayden's orientation as deriving from his long-standing commitment to the Bahá'í faith, Hayden's fellow poets were less sympathetic. Peers felt Hayden avoided the responsibility to speak out against racial injustices, particularly during the tumultuous 1960s.

A full twenty-six years would elapse from 1955 before Maxine Hong Kingston, the first woman of color, participated in the market. Kingston gave her papers to the University of California, Berkeley, in 1981. She graduated from Berkeley with a bachelor's degree in English in 1962. After teaching briefly in Hayward, California, and at the University of Hawaii, Mānoa, and publishing *The Woman Warrior* (1976), a founding text in the field of Asian American literature, Kingston returned to Berkeley to serve as a lecturer. She would remain there as a lecturer until her retirement in 2003.[31] Kingston benefited from the convenience of donating her papers to the university where she both attended and worked, while the Bancroft Library at Berkeley gained a prestigious collection without needing to engage in expensive outreach.

Table 1 showed when *NAAL* authors placed their papers in repositories by decade to highlight the slow diversification of the market by race and sex; table 2 conveys how old writers were when they transferred their collections to institutions, separated by whether an author was living or dead at deposit. The data shows that on average, authors wait to sell or donate their papers until they are about 65 years old. On average, living authors deposit their collections when they are about 58 years old, whereas those who died prior to their deposit date would have been around 70 years old. White authors place their papers earlier in their life than minority writers, irrespective of whether the writers are living or dead at the time of deposit or if the authors are men or women. This finding results from the literary archives market's delayed interest in the papers of people of color.

Earlier market participation can be seen by age disparities at the time of deposit. Age disparities become more overt when comparing differences between living and deceased authors within each demographic. Although each demographic has a different number of placed literary archives, the pattern that emerges is that white men experience the quickest placements after death. White and minority men see the smallest difference between their elapsed time between birth and acquisition, indicating their historical higher collectability. On average, minority and white men experience about a 9-year difference between living and deceased authors' ages, while women

TABLE 2. *NAAL* authors' average, rounded deposit age by demographic and mortality

Placed	Collections (n)	Deposit average age*
White men	41	62
Living at placement	12	55
Dead at placement	29	64
White women	15	63
Living at placement	6	53
Dead at placement	9	71
Minority men	12	70
Living at placement	6	65
Dead at placement	6	74
Minority women†	10	64
Living at placement	6	58
Dead at placement	4	73
Total	78	65
Living at placement	*30*	*58*
Dead at placement	*48*	*71*

* Rounded to the nearest whole number.
† Toni Cade Bambara does not have a placement date, so she is not counted.

experience a longer lag of 15 years for minority and around 18 years for white women.

White women placed their papers earlier than any other demographic. Additionally, this result is skewed to make white women's average ages appear even older than they would be otherwise. Two contributing factors to the skew are this category's small sample size and the experiences of Lorine Niedecker and Flannery O'Connor. Each writer had her papers sit in private hands for more than thirty years after her death. As a result, the average deceased white woman's papers inflated to an average placement age of about 71 years, younger than any other demographic except deceased white men, whose executors transferred their papers when they would have been, on average, about 64 years old. Without Niedecker or O'Connor, deceased white women would have an average placement age of about 59 years old.

Lorine Niedecker's 12 linear feet of papers at the Fort Atkinson Historical Society/Hoard Historical Museum arrived gradually through donations by her friends and associates. The most significant addition came from Niedecker's friends Bonnie and Gail Roub in 2003, thirty-three years after her death. Since most of the collection consists of the Roub materials, Fort Atkinson uses their donation date to represent the year the entire collection was acquired on their website even though some Niedecker materials came earlier. Most of these additional papers originated with Niedecker's biographers. Jane Shaw Knox, author of *Lorine Niedecker: An Original Biography* (1987), and Margot Peters, who wrote *Lorine Niedecker: A Poet's Life* (2011), both gave their research files.[32] Niedecker's case, like Plath's, highlights that acquisition years used in this study are not definitive; rather, they are judged as the most appropriate date to record receipt of the collections in a repository.[33]

By placing her papers at Fort Atkinson, Niedecker's donors selected a repository that honors her regional identity at the cost of her researchers' ease of access. The museum is in Fort Atkinson, Wisconsin, close to the shores of Lake Koshkonong where Niedecker was born and lived near for most her life. Fort Atkinson is roughly halfway between Madison and Milwaukee. Niedecker did not reside in Fort Atkinson but lived in even more isolation on Blackhawk Island, located on a peninsula of Lake Koshkonong. By choosing to have her papers remain within the "lakeshore silence" in Fort Atkinson, Wisconsin, Niedecker's donors respected her life choices. Niedecker never sought a more cosmopolitan environment, preferring to maintain her myriad connections through the mail. Her poetry benefited from the focus and simplicity afforded by her rural location.[34] However, a researcher traveling to Fort Atkinson must contend with the town's distance from major airports and the fact that the museum that holds Niedecker's collection does not provide access to her finding aid online.

The decisions made by the executors of Niedecker's collection contrast with choices made by the executors of Flannery O'Connor's papers. O'Connor's executors determined that her papers should stay in a repository connected to a university that could facilitate greater access rather than honoring the local flavor of her work by keeping her collection in the closest available institution. As a result, O'Connor's collection came to Emory University rather than Georgia College.

Rosemary Magee, Rose Library's director, explained how Emory's conversation with the O'Connor family began in 1963, before O'Connor died of lupus in 1964.[35] Emory then spent decades attempting to convince her family that O'Connor's papers would be best cared for in Atlanta rather than in Milledgeville. Emory probably put forward four arguments that would eventually win them the right to make the purchase. First, Emory could attract more researchers to its campus than would Georgia College due to the former's location in metropolitan Atlanta. Georgia College is located nearly two hours by car from Hartsfield-Jackson Atlanta International Airport. Second, Emory could provide better access to its holdings through its research fellowships. While Georgia College possesses the manuscripts for O'Connor's novels and short stories, a finding aid is not available online.[36] Third, Emory had the advantage of already owning related collections. Rose Library holds the papers of O'Connor's friend Betty Hester, who donated her letters from O'Connor in 1987 with the stipulation that they be sealed until 2007.[37] Additionally, Rose possesses the papers of Sally Fitzgerald, O'Connor's editor, which Emory acquired through local foundations in 2008 and 2014.[38] And, fourth, Emory is internationally prominent in the field of literary archives. The university collected the papers of *NAAL* authors James Dickey in 1993, Lucille Clifton in 2006, and Alice Walker in 2007. Outlining the advantages of its location in addition to its commitment to access, supplemental collections, and holdings helped Emory make the case that it should be allowed to purchase O'Connor's collection.

Most *NAAL* writers have executors who placed their papers after they died. White authors and their executors find repositories sooner than their minority colleagues. These findings highlight the way the literary archives market developed to prioritize acquiring the collections of white writers over authors of color. This historical trend is particularly apparent when analyzing the reason behind the average age reported for deceased white women. Although this demographic of authors places its papers earlier than any other group except white men, the average appears much higher than it would have otherwise due to the over thirty years it took the collections of Lorine Niedecker and Flannery O'Connor to come to their respective repositories.

A majority of *NAAL* authors die prior to having their papers enter institutions, but men and women of color are less likely to place their papers posthumously. Families are more important when an author dies before an institution can acquire his or her collection, while professional executors are more prominent when writers are still alive. Executors will be discussed in chapter 3. The remainder of this chapter will consider how writers' families manage the responsibility of finding a home for their relative's collection.

FAMILIES

Family members who accept this role undertake a difficult task. They will be overshadowed by their relative's achievements while committing their life to stewarding the author's legacy. Furthermore, families often underestimate the knowledge they need to successfully steer their relative's literary estate. They may see themselves as protecting an author's reputation by shielding the writer from potentially unflattering coverage and may argue with other relatives for financial benefits without understanding the impact these actions will have on their relative's legacy.[39]

Consider James Baldwin's and Jack Kerouac's estates. Neither estate had straightforward management following the author's death. Both families weighed what was in their relative's best interest. Baldwin's family needed to navigate the complexity of his multiple collections, whereas Kerouac's estate suffered competing claims over his will.

When Nobel laureate Toni Morrison eulogized Baldwin, she recalled the encouraging words he said to her: "Our crown has already been bought and paid for. All we have to do is wear it."[40] Baldwin may have suggested to Morrison that their crown had been bought and paid for by the struggles of other African Americans, but Baldwin took on much of the battle himself, spending his life fighting discrimination as a black gay writer. The cultural capital he claimed for himself helped open the canon to such later writers as Morrison.

Baldwin grew up in Harlem, New York, as the eldest of nine in a poor family. He spent his childhood in libraries and much of his teenage years in the Pentecostal Church, where he began to preach. When he looked for more intellectual stimulation, he found Beauford Delaney, a black painter who came to artistic maturity during the Harlem Renaissance. Delaney mentored Baldwin, although the two men would find solace in different cities.[41]

Angry at the racism he encountered in New York, Baldwin saw an alternative path in the trajectory of Richard Wright, another artist he admired. Baldwin followed Wright to France. Baldwin remained there for most of his life as one of the many black American writers and artists who found refuge in the country. But leaving did not mean Baldwin detached from his homeland. In 1962, he became active in the civil rights movement after James Meredith integrated the University of Mississippi. United States Attorney General Robert F. Kennedy called the Mississippi governor, Ross Barnett, to support Meredith's case, which resulted in five hundred U.S. marshals traveling to Mississippi to protect Meredith during his arrival on campus. This show of force turned out to be necessary—the desegregation of the school prompted a riot, a nightmare that prompted Baldwin to write "Faulkner and Desegregation" and visit Meredith in Oxford, Mississippi, over New Year's 1963. Baldwin then conducted a lecture tour to address the issue, speaking across the South in places like New Orleans, Louisiana, and Greensboro, North Carolina. Owing to these activities, *Time* placed him on the cover of their May 17, 1963, issue.[42]

Baldwin's sexual identity also alienated him from American society. In France, he found a space for his bohemian lifestyle, a place that welcomed racial and sexual fluidity. In the United States, the hatred he endured as an African American was compounded by the derision he faced as a gay man. "For his editors in New York, publishing a black writer was fascinating, but publishing a black homosexual writer was impossible," recounted Colm Tóibín in the *London Review of Books*. Not only did an American editor recoil from his sexuality, so did a notable politician. President John F. Kennedy once described Baldwin as "Martin Luther Queen."[43] In response to this type of discrimination, Baldwin wrote pieces like "Freaks and the American Ideal of Manhood," in which he decried the infantile standards of American masculinity.

Until 2017, most of James Baldwin's papers resided at the Beinecke Rare Book and Manuscript Library at Yale University. Bart Kaplan, the man who donated Baldwin's collection to Yale in 1998, obtained the papers through eminent domain. Kaplan had taken possession of the old building of Baldwin's publishers in the 1960s and found the papers, long thought lost, inside a suitcase left in the structure. Once the Beinecke obtained Kaplan's find, Baldwin studies rapidly developed. In 1999, New York University Press released Dwight A. McBride's edited volume *James Baldwin Now*. In 2013, the *African American Review* dedicated a special issue to the author. In 2015, Douglas A. Field, Justin A. Joyce, and Dwight A. McBride founded the annual *James Baldwin Review*. In 2016, Raoul Peck directed the documentary *I Am Not Your Negro*, a retrospective of Baldwin's time working with Medgar Evers, Martin Luther King Jr., and Malcolm X. Samuel L. Jackson narrated the documentary from text culled from *Remember This House*, Baldwin's unfinished thirty-page manuscript about the era. *I Am Not Your Negro* enjoyed widespread acclaim; in its review, *Rolling Stone* regaled its readers with the power of Baldwin's "hooded eyes flashing as he speaks truth to pissed-off power."[44] Archives may not generate an author's cultural capital, but expanded opportunities for research grow a writer's brand by enlarging their academic and public audience.

The Beinecke's papers from Baldwin are not the only collections related to his life and work. One set of materials, 626 pages written by Baldwin between 1956 and 1968, lives at the Ransom Center. Another can be found in FBI records. The FBI gathered nearly 1,884 pages of evidence on Baldwin's activities between 1958 and 1974.[45] Although these materials add rich contextualization to Baldwin's life and writings, Baldwin's primary set of papers would not become available to researchers until 2017 when his family would find a repository willing to accept their terms: the Schomburg Center for Research in Black Culture.

The Schomburg Center, an affiliate of the New York Public Library (NYPL), which bills itself as "one of the world's leading cultural institutions devoted to the research, preservation, and exhibition of materials focused on African American, African diaspora, and African experiences," now has Baldwin holdings far exceeding any other repository. The location is appropriate. Baldwin visited the Schomburg as a child and found it a place of refuge. When he was dying, he asked that his papers be placed there. Unlike Yale's collection, the Schomburg's was bought from his family. While the center did not disclose what it paid for Baldwin's papers, it did acknowledge donations helped it acquire and process his collection. The Ford Foundation, Katharine J. Rayner, James and Morag Anderson, the John S. and James L. Knight Foundation, and New York Life supported the acquisition, while the Arcus Foundation financed its arrangement and description.[46]

Baldwin's family agreed to place his remaining papers at the Schomburg with one caveat: the library would agree to keep Baldwin's correspondence closed for twenty years. Kevin Young, the center's director, diplomatically remarked when pressed about the restriction, "Well, there's about 30 linear feet of material, and only about less than a foot is restricted."[47] By placing the restricted materials into context, Young highlighted the amount available to scholarship while honoring the Baldwin's family's request. After all, Young likely had no choice in the restriction. Honoring Baldwin's wishes to have his papers at the Schomburg was of more importance than immediate access to one additional foot of content. These materials probably remained restricted to protect Baldwin according to his family members' preferences.

Twenty years is not much for the family or for the Schomburg Center, but it frustrates scholars who wish to engage with the full breadth of Baldwin's work. Yet researchers could have predicted this outcome. Baldwin's family is notoriously protective of his legacy, though Baldwin himself realized that trying to control critical discourse was ineffective. Baldwin once said, "Things may be said which hurt, and you don't like it, but what are you to do? Write a White Paper, or a Black Paper, defending yourself? You can't do that."[48]

Perhaps Baldwin's sister, Gloria Karefa-Smart, should have taken his advice. In 2010, Karefa-Smart asked Ed Pavlić, a professor at the University of Georgia, to view the 120 letters Baldwin wrote to his brother David. She even asked him to compose a book about them. Pavlić agreed and came to her home in Washington, D.C., thinking he would have access to them for a few hours each day. When Pavlić arrived, Karefa-Smart allowed him to take the letters with him—not just to Maryland, where he intended to stay for the duration of his visits to Washington, but all the way back to Athens, Georgia. There, Pavlić explored letters depicting Baldwin's personas: the public James, the private Jimmy, and the family's Jamie.[49] Yet as soon as Karefa-Smart opened the door, she closed it. Once Pavlić finished his manuscript, she rescinded permission to quote directly from the letters. A potential reason, one that Pavlić himself did not mention in his own account of the incident, is that Karefa-Smart might not want Baldwin's letters to be made public due to how they portray Baldwin's sexuality and his stepfather—Karefa-Smart's father.[50] Without a statement from Karefa-Smart, it is impossible to know what made her decline Pavlić's project.

Baldwin's literary archive is split between three institutions, each of which has a set of papers with its own provenance. The provenance of Baldwin's collection at the Beinecke demonstrates that even highly acclaimed authors may have their papers lost for a period. Baldwin's FBI files show that the government can create its own record of a writer's activities that constitute a significant historical account for later researchers. But collections that come from families are more common occurrences. As Pavlić's experience highlights, families prove to be difficult for researchers to manage on their own. Yet once families place their relative's papers in a repository like the Schomburg, relatives can negotiate balancing their needs against researchers' desires in a way that better supports the objectives of both parties.

As families are the most common donors of collections after authors themselves, a second example helps further illustrate how important relatives can be in shaping the placement of an author's literary archive. The figurehead of the Beats, a postwar movement that grew out of discontent with 1950s conformity, Jack Kerouac represented rebellion in all forms. He rejected social conventions by using profanity, taking drugs, experimenting sexually, exploring Eastern religions, and flocking to counterculture zones in New York and San Francisco. Kerouac's fellow Beats included a range of now-famous names such as William S. Burroughs, Gregory Corso, Diane di Prima, Lawrence Ferlinghetti, Allen Ginsberg, and Gary Snyder. While Baldwin was watched by the FBI due to his race, Kerouac was protected. Even as a counterculture author, Kerouac's whiteness ensured that he remained marketable.

The combination of Kerouac's Beat persona and the success of his books, most notably *On the Road* (1957), generated an estate worth $20 million. This exceptionally high value derives from Kerouac's commercial appeal. Allen Ginsberg, himself a Beat icon, remarked that Kerouac's mystique alone "sold a trillion Levi's, a million espresso coffee machines, and also sent countless kids on the road."[51] Gap even put Kerouac in an ad in 1993 to sell khakis. When Christie's auctioned the original manuscript of *On the Road* on May 22, 2001, Jim Irsay, the owner of the Indianapolis Colts, bought it for $2.43 million. Irsay then sent the scroll on tour and allowed Penguin to publish a copy of it to honor the fiftieth anniversary of the novel's publication. Critical and public fanfare met both tour and edition.[52]

James Baldwin's papers were spread around when he died and surfaced through a myriad set of circumstances, including eminent domain and the FBI; only in 2017 did his family step forward with his full literary archive. In contrast, all of Jack Kerouac's papers were in the hands of his relatives. Still, Kerouac's relatives contested who had the right to be his estate's executor, whereas Baldwin's family remained united in protecting their relative. When Kerouac died, he left his estate to Gabrielle Kerouac, his mother, rather than to Stella Sampas Kerouac, his wife. When Gabrielle Kerouac died in 1973, she supposedly left the estate to Sampas, rather than her two grandchildren—Paul Blake Jr. and Jack Kerouac's only child, Janet "Jan" Kerouac.[53]

When Stella Sampas Kerouac died in 1990, Kerouac's estate passed to her youngest brother, John Sampas. John Sampas began to sell off Kerouac's belongings with the help of Jeffrey Weinberg, owner of Water Row Books in Marlborough, Massachusetts. But John Sampas soon recognized that it would be more financially lucrative to keep Jack Kerouac's estate intact, rather than sell it piecemeal. He ended up selling the papers to the New York

Public Library's Henry W. and Albert A. Berg Collection of English and American Literature in July 2001 for an undisclosed sum.[54]

But in 2008, a judge declared Gabrielle Kerouac's will a forgery. By this point, who was the rightful owner of the estate had little bearing on the literary archive, as it had already been sold to NYPL. John Sampas profited by placing the papers where they would generate the highest possible price and by acting before a judge could make a final decision on the will's legitimacy. The finding aid for the Jack Kerouac collection at the NYPL noted only that the papers previously were owned by "John Sampas, executor of the Kerouac estate." This record may be diplomatic, but the metadata fails to account for the complexity of the provenance of Kerouac's papers.[55]

While Baldwin's papers reside in three institutions that reflect happenstance (the Beinecke Library), oppression (the FBI archives), and personal preference (the Schomburg), Kerouac's papers dwell together in a repository that fits his life experience. Even though Kerouac's career started at Columbia, his work is more tied to the New York City than to the university, which makes the NYPL a sensible place for his papers. Very little information remains about alternative institutions that might have been interested in Kerouac's papers. Jack Boulware, writing for the *San Francisco Weekly* in 1998, hinted that Anthony Bliss, curator of literary manuscripts at the Bancroft Library of the University of California, Berkeley, might have been interested.[56] The Bancroft also would have been a good place for Kerouac's papers, for it holds the records of City Lights Books, as well as the papers of fellow Beats of varying stature such as Lawrence Ferlinghetti, Ted Joans, Philip Lamantia, John Montgomery, and Philip Whalen.

James Baldwin's and Jack Kerouac's literary archives share the same institution, but their lived experiences differed sharply based on race and sexuality. As a black gay man, Baldwin was pushed to the margins. He moved to France to escape racism and homophobia. The distance helped him critically reflect on the United States, allowing him to generate the novels and essays that earned him a spot at the Schomburg, NYPL's Harlem location. By comparison, as a white straight man, Kerouac felt free to roam America. His travel would be reflected in the syntax and style of his novels, which expanded into Whitmanesque monologues. His papers came to rest at the Henry W. and Albert A. Berg Collection in the main Manhattan branch, the Stephen A. Schwarzman Building. Baldwin's papers took a long time to come into institutional hands, but when they did, they were placed and managed carefully.

Kerouac's literary archive experienced a more contentious afterlife, one fueled by economic interest more than by literary guardianship. These results illustrate the effect families have on the literary archives market.

CONCLUSION

How a data set is created shapes the narrative its numbers can tell. Anthologies are problematic historically as well as limited in the sample size they generate, but they continue to be the best way to determine which authors are considered canonical. The authors listed in *The Norton Anthology of American Literature*'s seventh edition showed that it took twenty-six years for the literary archives market to include women and people of color. Once women and minorities participated in the market, a pattern appeared. White authors still placed their papers at earlier ages than did writers of color, a result of the amount of time it took for their cultural capital to rise.

Families also shape the timing and placement of a literary archive. Relatives seek to protect their family members' legacy either by opening or by selectively closing these papers. Jack Kerouac's family chose the former, while James Baldwin's chose the latter. However, Kerouac's family contested among themselves the rights to his legacy, whereas Baldwin's family did not debate who would become his representative. In the end, both Baldwin's and Kerouac's papers found their home in the New York Public Library. Only the branches in which these collections reside show the impact of their life experience: Baldwin found his home in Harlem's Schomburg Center, with Kerouac inhabiting Manhattan's Schwarzman Building.

Professional executors, literary agents and manuscript dealers should have only a financial, rather than an emotional, stake in where authors' literary archives reside. Yet as chapter 3 will illustrate, agents' and dealers' interest in maximizing profit on behalf of their clients is considered uncouth in a market that prefers to keep financial details private.

CHAPTER 3

Profit

Agents and Dealers

———

If you are going to represent the best, you must represent a preponderance of the best. You've got to be very aggressive about representing the right people.

—Andrew Wylie

As discussed in chapter 2, authors most often represent themselves or employ their families to help them place their papers. But professional executors—manuscript dealers or literary agents—have become an increasingly prominent feature of the literary archives market in recent decades. Manuscript dealers and literary agents, hereafter referred to as "agents" and "dealers," are not interchangeable. They both have the same motive: to ensure the survival of their business by looking out for writers' best interests. However, they are viewed very differently by repositories. Institutions find agents problematic and dealers acceptable owing to their discourse. Agents profess that they care only about profit, whereas dealers weigh the value of their relationships with repositories. Although attitudes are rhetorical rather than substantive differences, they result in divergent experiences in the trade.

PROFIT

Stephen Enniss, director of the Harry Ransom Center at the University of Texas at Austin, advanced his preference for dealers over agents at the annual gathering of the Rare Books and Manuscripts Section (RBMS), a division of the Association of College and Research Libraries (ACRL), in 2014. There, Enniss described that dealers understand the culture in which they interact and seek to establish long-term relationships, whereas agents seek the highest payout and do not see themselves as part of the market. As a result, he believes that agents have become predatory, pitting universities and their limited budgets against one another, something that did not occur when the trade was limited to dealers.[1]

But verifying Enniss's claim is difficult as the data do not seem to match his statements. Within the set of authors included in *The Norton Anthology of American Literature* (*NAAL*), table 3 shows 12 *NAAL* authors opted for the help of manuscript dealers and 6 writers used agents out of a group of 79 *NAAL* authors with placed papers.[2] Such data do not appear to justify such a complaint. But these numbers are misleading.

The reason that repositories likely underreport this information is that finding aids are not required to include executors, so writers' affiliations to dealers and agents are often left out. The Society of American Archivists (SAA) determined that custodial history and immediate source of acquisition, the closest fields to executor, are added value elements only within the finding aid section devoted to acquisition and appraisal. "Custodial history" is determined to be the time a collection "left the possession of the creator until it was acquired by the repository," while "immediate source of acquisition" is intended to identify "the source from which the repository directly acquired the materials being described, as well as the date of acquisition, the method of acquisition, and other relevant information." The recommendations do suggest recording "any other information considered relevant (e.g., address

TABLE 3. *NAAL* authors' executors as reported by institutions

Demographic	Collections (n)*	Author	Family	Dealer	Agent	Other
Total	74	33	18	12	6	5

* Five *NAAL* collections have unreported executors: Saul Bellow, Billy Collins, Fanny Howe, Toni Morrison, and David Ray.

of the source/donor, agent, price, source of funding), if this information is not confidential." Although these definitions would give the necessary information, it is recorded inconsistently because such input is optional.[3]

The SAA *Glossary* only adds to the confusion. "Executor" and "dealer" are not included in the *Glossary*, and "agent" is defined as "an individual who acts on behalf of another individual or an organization."[4] While intermediaries are acknowledged in finding aids as likely participants in a collection's deposit, users are not provided with definitions that delineate the work of executors, dealers, and agents. Verifying Enniss's claim using metadata provided by finding aids is not possible. Institutions could be contacted individually to try and collect this information, but repositories often cannot provide this data either due to privacy restrictions or because they did not retain it.

In his RBMS talk, Enniss portrayed the ideal market of the past, the one that he would like to reinstate in the future, as organized by competition "for the offer itself, the opportunity to buy." Once a repository could secure the ability to make a bid, negotiation would then proceed without outside interference.[5] His preference is for institutions to negotiate among themselves for the opportunity to make an offer. Only the winning repository would approach the dealer. Institutions would create a single buyer scenario by controlling the market. But as chapter 4 will show, Enniss's portrayal of the past does not reflect reality. Occasionally, institutions have discussed acquisitions with one another, as when both the Ransom Center and the Beinecke wanted Ezra Pound's papers—discussed at more length in chapter 4—but these occurrences are exceptions rather than the rule.

Even though it cannot be determined if agents raised market prices and trade was never as orderly as Enniss describes it, he is not the only director to make this complaint. In 2000, Lisa Browar, at the time director of the Lilly Library at Indiana University Bloomington, addressed the issue of literary agents increasing the prices of writers' papers at the Fleur Cowles *Flair* Symposium, a biennial conference.[6] In her talk and subsequent paper for *Libraries & Culture*, Browar described how special collections are nonprofits that pay for their holdings once and do not gain revenue from their materials, unlike publishing's expectation of continuous profit.

A decade before Enniss made his comments, Browar proposed a different strategy to manage the emerging situation. Browar wanted to control the market's suppliers, rather than such institutions as hers that provided the demand. She sought to convince agents to adapt their new business model by lowering rather than raising their prices and argued that agents thought of repositories like publishers. But publishers generate profit and repositories do not, which changes what repositories realistically can pay.[7] Browar expected agents to undercut their financial best interest to better support repositories. While Browar's point is correct—repositories do not generate a profit—her solution was not convincing. Agents cannot discard their responsibility to their clients' financial interests. Enniss's solution is more feasible as it would not require agents to undercut their clients' profit. After all, the profession of literary agents arose because authors required representatives to advocate on their behalf.

AGENTS

Literary agents became a profession in England during the late 1800s when shifts in law and technology began to hurt authors' ability to make a living. Steam printing in the 1840s, the abolition of the newspaper penny tax in 1855, the elimination of the paper duty in 1861, and the invention of linotype machines in 1886 radically increased the number of available publications. As competition increased, publishers began to experience revenue losses and needed to find a way to retain their profit; what worked best was paying authors less.

Authors wanted to better represent their interests, so they created professional associations to address the problem. A crop of organizations dedicated to authors' rights appeared in England throughout the late nineteenth century, including the Guild of Literature and Art (1851), the Association to Protect the Rights of Authors (1875), the Society of Authors (1884), and the Authors' Syndicate (1890). But authors were not experienced negotiators and lacked knowledge of the publishing environment. Even working together, writers could not bridge the gap between their trade and their new responsibilities.

The era's authors then turned to literary agents. As observed in the introduction to this book, professions sustain themselves by generating specialized knowledge, controlling access to that knowledge through education, enforcing how educated workers apply their knowledge, and espousing a service ideal that justifies the profession publicly. Literary agents found their niche by interpreting the law for the financial benefit of authors rather than publishers. Technically, literary agents are not a profession as the field does not require specialized education that must be completed to obtain the right to work. By contrast, attorneys must attend law school to learn how to pass a bar exam that provides the certification enabling them to practice. However, literary agents resemble a profession because they have specialized services that appeal to authors, a previously underserved and exploited demographic.

A. M. Burghes, A. P. Watt, and Curtis Brown were the first literary agents. Burghes defrauded his clients. But Watt and Brown had more character and became successful in a new profession that required them to be "one-third lawyer, one-third editor, and one-third schmoozer, with a little bit of psychologist thrown in."[8] Watt would go on to represent Arthur Conan Doyle, Thomas Hardy, and Rudyard Kipling. Brown became the most famous of the three. As an American who had moved to England, Brown's ability to negotiate caused English publisher Frederick Macmillan to describe him as "a most objectionable man, who emanates, I am afraid, from your side of the Atlantic."[9] Another publisher, Henry Holt, expanded the complaint to the whole profession, describing all agents as "contemptible interlopers" and "pests."[10]

These complaints arose because previous business conventions benefited the publisher. Agents forced the power dynamics to become more equitable. Instead of admitting that agents threatened their bottom line by advocating on behalf of writers, publishers focused their attention on the behavior of agents and criticized them for acting in an ungentlemanly manner. Revealing that literature was a commodity like any other violated the discursive norms of publishing—a mindset that sociologists would describe as a *habitus*—that required treating literature as if its profit margin did not matter. Agents dispensed with this protocol by buying and selling "copyrights much as a cotton broker bought and sold cotton."[11] As agents saw copyright as a good, they were not inclined to indulge in polite behaviors suggesting that publishing literature was anything more than just another business. But this attitude cost them social capital.

Even agents' own clients underappreciated their work. While writers needed agents, they did not always wish to understand their value. W. H. Auden moaned, "What goes on in that office and what they do for the 10% of my hard earned money I cannot imagine."[12] Raymond Chandler concurred: "Technically, you can fire your agent; it is a sticky operation, but a determined man can achieve it. It really ends nothing."[13] Like publishers, authors preferred to see literature as more than a good bought and sold in a market. After all, they wanted to endow themselves with artistic cultural capital. But literary agents thrived as a profession because writers' financial needs outweighed their psychological demands. Chandler recognized he could fire his agent, but he still needed a representative to oversee the management of his copyrights. One agent could be replaced; avoiding representation entirely would damage his career rather than help it.

Published advice for new agents recognized the thanklessness of their role. Books written for aspirants recommended accepting the criticism as a part of the job, presenting it simply as a "drawback of the occupation." These books even counseled that as future agents grew their business, they would be likely to incur more outrage.[14] Experienced agents recognized that low social capital was an indication of success rather than failure.

Criticism directed at literary agents compounded after 1976 when the United States decreased the tax benefit authors could claim from donating their collections. The 1969 Tax Reform Act had allowed full tax deductions for literary estates in paragraph 1221, which specified that "a literary, musical or artistic composition, a letter or memorandum, or similar property held by . . . a taxpayer whose personal efforts created such property" could "leave such papers in his estate; and heirs can claim a full tax deduction for them."[15] Accordingly, authors and their executors often were persuaded by these benefits to donate rather than sell their papers. When the law changed in 1976, authors had less incentive to donate.[16]

With more authors choosing to sell their papers, there came a greater need for executors who understood how to get the most profit from repositories. Authors favored agents over dealers because agents optimized profit, whereas dealers also considered placement of the collection. As a result, the profession continued to grow. Recent numbers show that between 2004 and 2008, the number of agents increased to 1,018 from 811, while the number of agencies increased from 471 to 569.[17]

Andrew Wylie is the most well-known agent in the literary archives market. Wylie grew up in a family of publishers and bankers. He drew from these two fields when he founded the Wylie Agency in 1980 in New York City.[18] In 1996, he opened a second office in London, England. Wylie's successful business model depended on acquiring the rights to authors and then protecting these rights domestically and internationally. He is uninterested in popular authors or genres, which provide the most profit in publishing.[19] Wylie is not the first to represent only established writers. Paul Revere Reynolds, the first American literary agent, "refused to take on unproven talent." This decision cost him the opportunity to represent Upton Sinclair and Gertrude Stein.

Reynolds also only took on genres that paid well, which led him to reject poets.[20]

Wylie's approach paid off. His client list reads like an international who's-who of artists, fashion designers, musicians, politicians, and royalty. Thirteen *NAAL* writers appear in his client list: Donald Barthelme, Saul Bellow, Raymond Carver, Ralph Ellison, Allen Ginsberg, Jack Kerouac, Louise Glück, James Merrill, Arthur Miller, Philip Roth, Leslie Marmon Silko, Hunter S. Thompson, and John Updike.[21] His means of obtaining these authors earned him the nickname "The Jackal."[22]

Since Wylie is uninterested in emerging authors, he must seduce established writers away from their current representation. Such activity hurts the businesses of other agents.[23] For example, Wylie wrested Saul Bellow away from his longtime literary agent Harriet Wasserman. Wasserman served as Bellow's agent at her own company between 1981 and 1995. Before then, she managed his intellectual property at Russell & Volkening from 1948 to 1980.[24] Bellow's letters to Wasserman acknowledge her devotion to his career. On one occasion, Bellow thanked Wasserman for throwing him a party "with champagne, Chinese food, big surprises and Roman splendor" and expressed his gratitude by writing "I was touched. It's seldom that anyone takes so much trouble over me."[25]

Bellow would drop Wasserman for Wylie in 1995. Wylie first became interested in Bellow in 1994. Bellow agreed to work with Wylie, allowing Wylie to ask Wasserman for Bellow's backlist and foreign rights. Wasserman rejected this proposal by writing "there's one author and one agent. You don't divide up lists." Bellow persisted, asking for Wasserman to work "under Wylie's supervision." When Wasserman turned down this idea too, Bellow decided to go with Wylie entirely.[26]

After years of devotion to Bellow's career, Wasserman keenly felt Bellow's decision to move to Wylie. Her memoir *Handsome Is: Adventures with Saul Bellow* (1997) recounted her time with her client in what a reviewer described as "embarrassingly personal" rhetoric. She included memories of when Bellow leered at her and one incident when the two slept together.[27] Despondent after Bellow's departure, Wasserman neglected her other clients and mismanaged their funds. Authors then sued her agency to regain their lost royalty payments, leading to its closure in 2007.[28]

How Bellow came to prefer Wylie to Wasserman illustrates that representing writers is a business. Bellow wanted the agent who would be the best advocate for his estate. Wasserman might have been a literary agent, but she saw a greater value in relationships—in loyalty—while Wylie found his calling in maximizing profit. Wylie won Bellow because his view of the profession better aligned with his client's needs. Therefore, Enniss, and the directors and curators of many American repositories, are up against some of the most ruthless agents in the market.

DEALERS

Wylie eliminated much of his competition within his profession, but he did not jettison all professional executors. A few manuscript dealers adjusted and succeeded despite the trade's dynamics. Ken Lopez and Glenn Horowitz maximized their profit and ensured the survival of their businesses, but they did so through opposing tactics. Lopez emphasized relationships, following the tradition of his trade, whereas Horowitz, like a literary agent, downplayed relationships to concentrate solely on connections that generated profit.

Ken Lopez began dealing books in 1976 and became an executor of literary estates in 1981. In 1999, he reflected on why his business came to focus more and more on papers rather than books. Lopez described how, in the 1990s, private collectors flooded the market looking for high spots, which are first editions of well-known titles bought for investment purposes rather than pursuing personal interests for nonmonetary rewards. In-demand items incurred a rapid increase in their price while less popular books experienced "tremendous competitive pressure driving prices downward." Lopez noticed that the market bifurcation influenced curators collecting for institutions. In the early 2000s, curators shifted their focus to literary archives from rare books. To continue to be viable in the market, Lopez widened his reach to include such archives but also maintained his business in modern first editions.[29]

By 2013, the *Wall Street Journal* advised: "Authors, take notice: remember those crates of scratch pads and tax returns in the garage? The trunkful of hotel bills and childhood doodles in the garden shed? Don't junk any of it—not before you call up somebody in Ken Lopez's line of work. . . . He sells to rich research libraries." As the *Wall Street Journal* is a newspaper for those interested in business, not creative writing, the article's provocation to save manuscripts probably did not reach its presumed audience. The *Wall*

Street Journal was more likely informing investors indirectly about a lucrative investment opportunity.[30]

Lopez presents himself as valuing relationships. He wrote that he strives to find suitable repositories for the authors he represents, which include N. Scott Momaday, Gerald Vizenor, Gwendolyn Brooks, Sylvia Plath, and Leslie Marmon Silko.[31] Lopez observed that collaborating with institutions allows authors and institutions to develop relationships that extend "beyond the mere financial transaction."[32] His rhetoric, which acknowledges but downplays money, is a result of his training in the rare book world. When one hopes to not sell just one book but many over the course of a career, connections represent repeat customers. It would make sense that as Lopez moved into literary papers, he would see his new offerings in the same way. After all, his institutional clients were the same. Their interests may have changed, but the connection—the idea of the repeat customer—is historically what provided Lopez's business with stability. However, the literary archives market does not depend on repeat customers in the same way that the rare book trade does; chapter 4 does shows how top repositories buy multiple collections, but most manage only one.

Unfortunately, Lopez's impeccable rare book world credentials did not allow him to skirt criticism. In a review of *Book Talk* (2006), an edited volume to which Lopez contributed a chapter, Michael Ryan claimed that Lopez could afford to be benevolent: "New money, new collectors, and the Web have been a profitable brew for him." Ryan goes on to contrast Lopez's perspective as a "market orientation" rather than a "bibliophile focus."[33] According to Ryan's analysis, recognizing and adapting to market trends revealed an overinvestment in the financial aspects of the trade. Once again, violating the social norms of the habitus—the requirement to ignore or downplay financial realities—prompted critiques.

If Ken Lopez has a market orientation, then his colleague Glenn Horowitz is even more attuned to its demands. Glenn Horowitz began his business in 1979, only three years after Lopez. But while Lopez started in Massachusetts, Horowitz immediately settled into New York. He wanted to combine his family's history of "selling things" with his interest in literature. Horowitz's big break came in 1983 when he helped W. S. Merwin transfer his papers to the University of Illinois for $185,000. At this point, Horowitz found the benefit of targeting buyers with "deep Champagne pockets."[34]

By 2016, Horowitz would represent nine *NAAL* writers, some of whom also were represented by Wylie: Bernard Malamud, James Merrill, W. S. Merwin, John Updike, John Cheever, Amiri Baraka, Philip Levine, Thomas Pynchon, and Hunter S. Thompson.[35] He also managed the papers of authors not included in this data set. Horowitz transferred Vladimir Nabokov's papers to the New York Public Library for $1 million in 1991, David Mamet's to the Ransom Center for $1.7 million in 2007, Alice Walker's to Emory University for $1 million in 2007, and Bob Dylan's to Tulsa, Oklahoma, for between $15 and $20 million in 2016. The profits from these sales allowed Horowitz to expand to a second location in East Hampton.[36]

As with Lopez, Horowitz's success came with detractors. Marvin Taylor, of the Fales Library at New York University, claimed Horowitz inflated prices. Yet when the United States Securities and Exchange Commission investigated one of his sales, the commission was concerned not that he marked up the papers of Franklin D. Roosevelt from $3.5 million in 2003 to $8 million in 2004 but that his buyer purchased the papers with his employer's money.[37]

Although he rarely discusses his philosophy as a dealer, Horowitz said in 2000 that he does not see the literary archives market "conform[ing] to the classical model animated by a willing seller and a willing buyer dynamic" portrayed by Stephen Enniss.[38] Instead, Horowitz argues that literary archives are valuable because they are nonfungible and nonliquid assets. Nonfungible assets are goods that are unique and cannot be exchanged. Writers' papers are nonfungible at both a micro and macro level. Each manuscript is a unique item, so it is nonfungible because one manuscript cannot substitute for another. The entire collection is then nonfungible because that set of papers cannot be found anywhere else. Nonliquid assets are those that cannot immediately be translated into currency, which is correct as the financial value of writers' papers is predicated not on their intrinsic worth but on the ability to convince a buyer to pay a certain price. Repositories' interest and ability to buy fluctuates depending on broader circumstances, which highlights the status of collections as nonliquid assets.

As a dealer, Horowitz stated that his role is "to broker a marriage between an uninformed seller (the generator of the papers or the party who has inherited the papers) and a likely but unsuspecting purchaser (a research library)."[39] This statement appears derogatory, but it communicates a common and fundamental problem that economists describe as "asymmetric information."

After all, if both sides knew the same amount of information, negotiations could proceed so rationally that intermediaries would become unnecessary.[40] The value of negotiation, and the need for a go-between, emerges when one party, or both, holds incomplete information. Authors need help because they are selling their life's work. Few institutions would consider themselves to be unsuspecting, as curators are experts in their field. However, curators may need to be made aware of the unique qualities of the collection on offer. Horowitz's purpose is not to emphasize either party's ignorance. Rather, he emphasized the value he adds to these negotiations to justify his commission.

Ken Lopez and Glenn Horowitz are outliers among manuscript dealers. Both men value relationships, but neither does so to the degree that he espouses beliefs that undercut the need to ensure the largest possible profit. Yet not all dealers can afford to resist the pressure to undercut their profit to capitulate to institutional expectations. Consider that when Robert A. Wilson suggested in 1992 that "friendly relationships between a dealer and a customer are common," the friendship he describes is predicated on an unequal status between dealer and institution, as the institution receives the value of friendship while the seller retains the right to remain friends.[41] After all, friendship between dealers and institutions should be charted in consistent, reciprocal recognition of each other's roles. However, this pattern cannot be observed consistently. In 2006, Michèle Kohler observed, "one sign of the close relations between booksellers, their customers, and the books and manuscripts they sell is the public recognition that a library sometimes gives its supplier."[42] *Sometimes*, but not all the time. An institution retains the right to choose whether to acknowledge a dealer, highlighting a power dynamic that looks less like friendship and more like business.

Fair enough; the literary archives market is a business. Nevertheless, should institutions begin to doubt booksellers' intentions, dealers are quick to reassure them. For example, in 2013, Howard Rootenberg of B & L Rootenberg Rare Books & Manuscripts wrote in *RBM: A Journal of Rare Books, Manuscripts, and Cultural Heritage*, the journal of record for special collections librarians, that dealers are not "out to hammer the libraries for as much money as possible." Rootenberg then reiterated his point: "It isn't about the money! Honestly!"[43] Of course, Rootenberg did not stop charging for his offerings, but neither did he feel he could dispense with the performance that relationships come before profit.

CONCLUSION

When Stephen Enniss complained about the predatory nature of agents within the literary archives market, he refrained from naming names. Instead, he concentrated on a type of agent—one whose activities disrupted the trade in writers' papers, those who moved behavioral norms from cooperative to competitive. With such a distinguished client list, it would not be a stretch to imagine that Enniss intended to critique Wylie. Yet by complaining about agents like Wylie, Enniss obscures his intended goal to control the prices of literary papers himself.

Enniss seeks what is in his repository's best interest. Each side of the market naturally has opposing needs. If the writer is the supply side, the executor is a convenient scapegoat acting as an author's representative. Rather than targeting the writer—telling authors that they are greedy would be unlikely to go over well—repository leaders can choose to push their agenda by vilifying agents, who accepted their low social capital in return for their financial success as a profession. Dealers largely escape judgment owing to their rhetoric, which professes a close tie to institutions. Although dealers do not devalue their relationships with authors, that they need to espouse a nonprofit narrative when they run a for-profit business suggests that maintaining this discourse is necessary to their habitus.

The problem with this account of executors within the literary archives market is that it is based on anecdotal evidence. Verifying how much or how little executors shape the institutional collecting of literary archives is difficult to determine quantitatively because of incomplete finding aid data and inconsistent self-reporting. Therefore, chapter 4 asks if higher institutional funding levels help repositories compete on the literary archives market. With more resources at their discretion, presumably wealthier institutions would be better positioned to make acquisitions.

CHAPTER 4

Competition

Directors and Curators

―――

Manuscripts and archives are no longer cheap, virtually every research library buys on some level, and there is intense competition for the most desirable collections.

—Stephen Enniss

Stephen Enniss's complaint that literary archives are too expensive in his plenary at the 2014 Rare Book and Manuscript Section (RBMS) conference shows how institutions need to keep prices accessible so they can seek more highly regarded acquisitions. The fact that it was Enniss who made this complaint is important. Political scientists note that well-positioned stakeholders with high cultural capital "can use their authority to change the 'rules of the game,' increasing their own capacities for political actions while diminishing the power and authority of their institutional rivals."[1] Enniss's behavior adheres to this insight. As the director of the most active repository in the literary archives market, he is the most likely person to attempt to— and potentially succeed in—shifting this market to ensure that sales practices benefit the demand rather than the supply side of the trade.

COMPETITION

Enniss's solution organizes repositories to counter the strength of literary agents. As chapter 3 showed, agents and dealers, who represent the supply side of the market, have a responsibility to maximize their clients' profit, as authors have only one literary archive. As a result, the demand side of the market holds a weaker position, for institutions that miss the opportunity to buy a writer's papers permanently lose the chance to acquire that author's works.

Enniss's idea to have repositories agree to limit competition among themselves to lower prices in the literary archives market is provocative because it requires institutions to place higher priority on the collective good (the good of all institutions to keep prices down) rather than the private good (the good of the institution to own an author's papers if it can pay). An outside observer might not see this as a problem; all collections would end up in a repository where papers of equal caliber reside. But then only one repository and its parent institution would be able to claim the cultural capital of owning that author's papers.

The Ransom Center at the University of Texas at Austin benefits from the historical advantage it gained during the initial postwar period. By using its "deep pockets and hefty endowments" to gather relatively cheap literary manuscripts before others saw their value, the Ransom Center was well situated once demand increased and prices rose.[2] The Ransom Center's combination of financial power and cumulative cultural prestige makes it nearly unbeatable today. Due to these early investments and continuing funding advantages, the center justifiably seeks to continue to reap the benefits. Yet because it could pay high sums for collections does not mean it wants to continue doing so.

Unfortunately for the Ransom Center, writers now know that at least one repository is prepared to pay top dollar. Olivia Manning, a British writer, recommended that her friend sell her manuscripts to Texas with the following words: "Those arrangements with Texas are very elastic & I have twice received sums long before they were due to arrive. Try & see if I am not right!" And authors rebuke their peers who elect to donate, rather than sell, their papers. Another British writer, Evelyn Waugh, complained to his brother, Alec, in 1965 that "your gift of archives" to Boston University "will cause a painful precedent."[3]

If authors succeed at ensuring the continuation of today's competitive market, at some point even Texas's resources will be strained.[4] Yet without a monopoly, even a pace-setting institution cannot control a market. Simply paying less would allow another institution to step into the vacuum. Accordingly, Enniss recognized that the key to managing his market position is to limit his competition by placing barriers to entry.

Enniss encourages leaders of other institutions to see the literary archives market as their market too. Then he asks them to consider how they can act to stop prices from continuing to rise. The solution he puts forward to his peers is to suggest that they should refuse to bid against one another, which drives the prices up at their collective expense. In effect, what he is asking for is for other repositories not to bid against the Ransom Center.[5] Which institutions are peers remains undefined, although Enniss outlines it would be the research library that has faculty with similar interests and a long-standing relationship with the author. These variables are not measurable—they are abstract representations of cultural capital. Most top research institutions have faculty interested in twentieth-century American literature. And the connections of libraries to authors, as well as for how long they have courted a writer to show interest in his or her papers, are not documented. The variable that remains, and the one that is the most easily compared, is repositories' funding levels.

Funding levels do influence collecting rates for papers of *Norton Anthology of American Literature* (*NAAL*) authors. While Enniss would like to direct attention to the qualities of the literary archives market that are not financially quantifiable, the institutions that can afford to court a writer with the goal of acquiring his or her collection and thus wind up in a competitive position are limited. The annual Library Investment Index published by the Association of Research Libraries (ARL) provides a ranking system identifying which libraries have the most funds.[6]

Table 4 displays the number of *NAAL* authors' papers placed each decade and then compares that amount to the average ARL rank of institutions making these acquisitions. This averaged rank is then rounded to the nearest whole number. The table shows that the 1990s were most competitive decade on the literary archives market, as institutions that collected papers in the 1990s have the lowest average, rounded ARL ranking of 12 (e.g., the highest amount of library funding). Prior to these decades, collecting institutions that

TABLE 4. *NAAL* authors' average, rounded ARL rank by decade

Decade	Collections (n)*	ARL Library Investment Index (n)	ARL rank average†
1950s	1	0	—
1960s	7	5	25
1970s	5	3	37
1980s	16	14	22
1990s	22	13	12
2000s	18	15	22
2010s	9	9	20
Total		79	23

* Toni Cade Bambara does not have a placement date, so she is not counted.
† Rounded to the nearest whole number.

belonged to ARL varied significantly in their average funding levels. In the 1970s, a recession era, ARL libraries' average, rounded rank climbed to 37, which means that collecting institutions experienced their lowest average funding levels in the 1970s. As a result, even when these repositories could acquire collections, they were much less likely to do so.

While the 1950s and 2010s have lower amounts of placed collections, these decades are not representative of the market. The trade started in the 1950s, and only one *NAAL* collection found a repository in this decade—and this repository does not belong to ARL. *Norton Anthology of American Literature* data recorded in the 2010s include only the first half of the decade, from 2010 to 2015, as data collection ended in January 2016. Although the 2010s show a relatively low average, rounded ARL rank of 20, the limited number of years counted in this decade restricts what conclusions can be drawn from the most recent data.

To view the market holistically, including both ARL- and non-ARL-affiliated institutions, return to table 1.[7] This table shows that the number of literary archives placed in institutional repositories varied widely among the measured ten-year intervals. The 1990s were the market's most active acquisition period with 21 placed *NAAL* collections. The 1980s and the 2000s were the second most active eras in the trade; in the 1980s, authors donated or sold 17 collections to repositories, while in the 2000s, 18 sets of papers came into institutional hands. On average, the market saw an average of 11 sets of papers placed per ten-year period.

With these upward numbers in mind, return to table 4. A wide range of regional institutions participated in the market during the its early period, the 1950s through the 1970s. As a result, the average ARL rank of *NAAL* institutions remained high. Universities active in this era were less likely to come from the highest echelon of American universities. On average, the market in the 1980s, 2000s, and 2010s decreased to ARL average, rounded ranks between 20 and 22. Only the 1990s broke this pattern. During this high-activity decade, the average, rounded ARL rank of institutions participating in the market rose to 12.

These acquisition patterns occurred due to the market's diversification in the 1980s as well as the overall economic strength of this decade, which continued into the 1990s. By 1981, the trade had finally embraced the papers of women of color. Yet a more inclusive literary archives market did not parallel a more inclusive academia, as seen in chapter 2's depiction of how slowly anthology editors confronted their sexism and racism. Bolstered by decades of civil rights protest, legislation, and consciousness-raising, in the 1980s editors began to acknowledge the value of work by minority authors and their predecessors. Some faculty resisted shifts in the curriculum, but overall, libraries and English departments realized the importance of teaching and studying the writing of minority authors. As a result, top authors of color netted high market prices from well-funded schools.

During the 1980s, library directors also enjoyed the expanded collecting opportunities granted by generous endowments. Although university endowments do not have to contain a set amount of money allotted for libraries, university endowment levels and library funding levels have a close relationship. On average, between 1977 and 2009 universities devoted 2.75 percent of the overall budget to their libraries.[8] When college and university endowments experienced a 14.1 percent return on their endowments in 1989 according to the National Association of College and University Business Officers, the growing wealth of academic institutions enabled library archives budgets to grow as well. The 1990s saw both a higher number of *NAAL* collections available for purchase or sale and a more competitive market that favored higher-ranked ARL libraries.[9]

In contrast with the 1980s and 1990s, the economy weakened in the 2000s, which is reflected in institutions' lower collecting rates.[10] With the value of diversity in the curricula mostly embraced by the 2000s, *NAAL* authors experienced a more active market regardless of their race and gender. Yet universities did not have a steady economic climate on which to consider acquisitions. The average return on endowments was negative in 2001.[11] Higher education's endowments would gradually improve through the 2000s, but the decade would end as it began: poorly.

In 2008, the American housing bubble burst, miring the end of the decade and much of the next in a general recession that affected libraries due to their "relative dependence on endowments." A year later, over 79 percent of ARL libraries suffered from reduced or flat budgets. Charles B. Lowry, executive director of ARL at the time, reminded his audience to "definitely not take heart" at early reports of an economic turnaround in 2010 for "the de-funding of North American research libraries, I believe, is the 'new normal.'"[12] By 2013 and 2014, the financial future looked brighter; universities witnessed record giving to higher education and an average return of 11.7 percent on their endowments.[13]

Nevertheless, Lowry's warning appeared prophetic. American research libraries did see a funding decrease. In 2012, university endowments devoted only 1.5 percent of their annual budgets to libraries.[14] The University of Michigan–Flint library director Robert Houbeck Jr. half comically, half seriously wrote that "even the most generous-spirited library directors, on occasion, imagine university administrators as restless Saronic eyes, searching for pots to plunder. But if their reddened gazes are directed anywhere, in my experience it's not toward us. They think about us a lot less than we believe they do—and that is a problem."[15] If Houbeck is correct and libraries are simply of lower priority to university administrations, they may not be either a target for budget cuts or a beneficiary for increases.

As library directors allot their portion of university endowment funds, curators find their financial and intellectual support critical if they are to advance an active archive development program.[16] However, as literary papers can be the most expensive acquisitions a library makes, who decides whether to purchase an author's collection varies by institution. Sometimes directors act as curators of literary archives while also managing their libraries, while in other circumstances curators operate under the supervision of the director. Therefore, in the three case studies that follow, one depicts directors acting without curators, and two show curators working underneath directors. But in all three examples, directors and curators rise to their position owing to their combination of subject knowledge and administrative ability, which allows them to balance their repository's need to make newsworthy acquisitions with their institution's priority to manage archive development budgets strategically.

DIRECTORS

Identifying which repositories are the most active in the literary archives market is necessary to understand which directors and curators to study. Table 5 provides the five most active repositories in the American literary archives market: Texas, Yale, Stanford, Emory, and Harvard. Together, these five institutions managed about 41 percent of the placed papers from *NAAL* authors, or 32 of 79 collections.

Among this elite set of institutions, Texas is the most substantial collector, demonstrating Enniss's role as the leader among directors of libraries that specialize in twentieth-century American literature.[17] As of 2017, Yale's E. C. Schroeder, Stanford's Robert G. Trujillo, Emory's Rosemary Magee, and Harvard's Thomas Hyry complete the cohort. But these individuals were not necessarily the ones who were responsible for their university's place in this ranking. Enniss was appointed in 2013, Schroeder in 2011, Trujillo in 1982, Magee in 2012, and Hyry in 2014.

Each library exhibited different collecting patterns. Institutions built their holdings in distinct ways rather than following similar acquisition policies.

TABLE 5. *NAAL* authors' top 5 collecting repositories by decade

Decade	Collections (n)	Texas (n)	Yale (n)	Stanford (n)	Emory (n)	Harvard (n)
ARL rank	-	*12*	*2*	-	*19*	*1*
1950s	0	0	0	0	0	0
1960s	2	2	0	0	0	0
1970s	0	0	0	0	0	0
1980s	6	2	2	0	0	2
1990s	11	2	2	5	1	1
2000s	8	2	3	0	2	1
2010s	5	2	2	0	1	0
Total	32	10	9	5	4	4

Table 5 shows that Texas acquired papers earlier and more consistently than its peers. The Ransom Center acquired two collections in the 1960s and then kept the pace of accepting two *NAAL* collections per decade through the 2010s, except for the 1970s. Emory did not join the literary archives market until the 1990s. Once Emory entered the market in 1993, it made a significant collecting commitment. Stanford, on the other hand, only participated in the trade during the 1990s. The Ivies, Harvard and Yale, demonstrated parallel collecting patterns. Both did not begin acquiring papers from authors listed in *NAAL* until the 1980s.

These libraries' unique funding histories explain their differing *NAAL* collecting patterns. The University of Texas's money comes from oil, so its lack of acquisitions in the 1970s coincides with the national energy crisis that affected oil prices and likely limited the university's spending. Emory took a long time to enter the trade because it did not have the financial capacity to participate until Robert W. Woodruff donated $100 million to the university's endowment in 1979. Stanford suddenly started collecting *NAAL* authors when a curator seized the financial opportunity provided by a change in leadership. Yale acquired more than did Harvard, which reflects Yale's greater emphasis on literature and the arts. Yet both schools show a conservative collecting strategy: recall that they were among the institutions whose initial lack of interest in modern literature allowed Texas to gain an upper hand in the field following World War II. Once Harvard and Yale decided to pursue more contemporary American writers, their choices reflected a slower pace. After all, such newer institutions as Texas and Emory needed to establish their status quickly, whereas Harvard and Yale were only required to maintain theirs by expanding their coverage.

Examining the institutional histories of Texas, Stanford, and Yale helps situate how they became among the most significant repositories in the American literary archives market. Texas's early investment in contemporary literary papers allowed it to remain in the trade's lead position. Yale is an example of the Ivy League approach, which enters the market late but then heavily invests once it commits. Stanford demonstrates an alternative strategy: one that depended less on institutional goals and more on the quick thinking of a curator during an era of institutional transition.

Harry Ransom, an English professor and assistant dean, realized that Texas's "upstart library could never match the antiquarian collections of European and Ivy League universities." Instead, he thought of a new vision:

The University of Texas at Austin should collect the papers of contemporary authors. To sell his idea, he gave a lecture in which he proposed the need for a research institution in Texas that could serve as the "Bibliothèque Nationale of the only state that started out as an independent nation." Ransom's speech proved convincing. In 1957, the University of Texas at Austin formally established the Humanities Research Center (HRC).[18]

Ransom's pitch to the state of Texas was successful not only because Texas wanted to prove that it had international cultural capital but also because the United States as a nation was engaged in the same struggle. During the Cold War, the United States needed to portray itself as a more attractive option than was the Soviet Union, culturally as well as militarily. The problem was that Europeans were wary of Americans' "shallow, business-dominated culture" and felt more sympathetic to communist values. American governmental agencies exploited the global appeal of homegrown modernism to showcase how free speech led to higher artistic achievement. American artists and writers became the subject of international propaganda.[19] Ransom's bid to make Texas more visible as a culturally rich state was one example of a larger-scale campaign in the United States to win the Cold War through hard and soft power.

Ransom's timing was perfect and his approach novel, as he used business to support the literary arts at a previously unseen scale. Ransom initially needed the help of private donations to support his new center, but the university soon created a more sustainable funding model: its Permanent University Fund (PUF). The PUF was established with the proceeds from the 2.1 million acres of land deeded from the State of Texas to its two university systems, the University of Texas, which receives two-thirds of the proceeds, and Texas A&M, which receives one-third. When oil was found on this property in 1923, the state university systems suddenly became much richer. The Austin campus became abundantly so, for until 1984, it would be the main beneficiary of the seventeen oil wells placed on the land. As the state decreed that the PUF must be spent half on general maintenance and half on construction, recruitment, or library collections, the HRC was authorized "to spend abundantly on collection materials."[20]

Affluence allowed the HRC to dominate the American literary archives market through a succession of seven directors—Harry Ransom, F. Warren Roberts, John Payne, Carlton Lake, Decherd Turner, Thomas Staley, and Stephen Enniss—who collectively created an aggressive acquisition legacy.[21]

However, each of these leaders had his own collection priorities because of his unique personality, interests, and career. While an institution may appear to be a single stakeholder in the market, it is represented by individuals whose decisions over time generate the holdings seen today.

University historians named Harry Ransom the most influential person in the University of Texas's history.[22] Ransom had taught at North Dakota State Teachers College, Colorado State College, and the University of Texas at Austin before he completed his PhD at Yale. Upon graduation, Texas offered Ransom an assistant professor position. During World War II, Ransom took a break from academia to serve in the Air Force. When the war concluded, he returned to Texas with the rank of major and a driving ambition that would lead him to engage in research, take increasingly high-profile administrative roles, and found the institution that bears his name and legacy.

Ransom's research focused on "copyright law, bibliography, Texas History, and eighteenth- and nineteenth-century literary history."[23] The fact that he did not study twentieth-century American literature is not a surprise, for it was Ransom himself who helped make this field a legitimate subject of study.[24] Ransom ultimately wrote fourteen books, including publications of his speeches and other occasional writings in addition to five more books he coauthored with his wife, Hazel Ransom. Ransom also edited four volumes of Texas Folklore Publications; served as an associate editor of *Southwestern Historical Quarterly* between 1952 and 1957; and founded *Texas Quarterly*. While managing this scholarly activity, Ransom served as associate professor (1946), full professor (1947), assistant dean (1951), vice president and provost (1957), president (1960), and finally chancellor at the University of Texas (1961–71) as well as becoming the first director of what became known as the Harry Ransom Humanities Research Center between 1957 and 1961.[25] Due to his short tenure, Ransom's legacy would be the institution, rather than any particular set of papers.

F. Warren Roberts served as the leader of the Ransom Center between 1961 and 1976. Roberts obtained his PhD from the University of Texas at Austin in 1956 and came under Ransom's tutelage during the course of his doctoral studies. As he shared Ransom's frustration about the paucity of papers dedicated to early twentieth-century authors like D. H. Lawrence, on whom he focused his scholarly attention, his academic interests fit nicely with Ransom's vision for the center. When he became a faculty member and then the center director, Roberts sought papers related to Lawrence's career with the center's blessing. Roberts then wrote a series of pieces documenting how these materials were dispersed among the authors' friends and family in Italy and the United States.[26] Ransom and Roberts together managed the acquisition of two *NAAL* collections: those of Arthur Miller and Thomas Pynchon. While both acquisitions are significant, Roberts's era at the Ransom Center is more known as the period when the library moved from the Academic Center at the University of Texas to its new building designed by the Jessen Associates.[27]

When it came time for Roberts to step down, he hand-picked his successor: John R. Payne, who held the position from 1976 to 1978. Before Payne took over the Ransom Center as interim director, he worked for Roberts as a bibliographer. Roberts commissioned Payne to work with Adrian H. Goldstone, a major donor, to coauthor a bibliography of Goldstone's collection of John Steinbeck materials.[28] The result of that collaboration, *John Steinbeck: A Bibliographical Catalogue of the Adrian H. Goldstone Collection* (1974), fell out of print "more quickly than any previous publication by the HRC," yet now is valued highly on the antiquarian book market.[29]

Payne was not very successful on the job, but the economy was the problem. His era was the only time the Ransom Center failed to add any *NAAL* collections to its holdings. During the recession that stretched from November 1973 to March 1975, the Ransom Center lost $300,000 from its budget. The recession occurred, in part, because of an oil embargo placed on the United States. The Organization of Petroleum Exporting Countries (OPEC) issued the embargo in retaliation against the American support of Israel during the Arab-Israeli War. Although the United States produced its own oil, primarily in Texas, the American economy heavily relied on external sources. Although President Nixon attempted to negotiate out of the crisis, he sought to return the United States to a greater reliance on domestically produced product through what became known as "Project Independence." Even though the embargo lasted for a relatively brief period, it triggered years of economic stagnation and lower federal investment in public universities. The glory days of the Ransom Center seemed over.[30]

Carlton Lake took over the Ransom Center from John Payne in 1978 and served in the role until 1980. Like Payne, Lake caught the eye of a former director—in his case, Harry Ransom—due to his other skills. While Payne's skill was bibliography, Lake's asset was his personal collection of French literature. Ransom not only wanted Lake to come to the Ransom Center but also he wanted Lake's collection. Ransom offered Lake the invented title of "lifetime curator" in 1969. Lake had begun to sell and donate his materials to the Ransom Center in 1966, but he did not accept a job there until 1976 when he became the curator of French literature, a role he would later hold alongside acting director and then executive curator (1980–2003).[31] Under his tenure, Anne Sexton's papers came to the Ransom Center. However, like Payne, Lake is better known for his writing rather than his leadership.[32] Payne's and Lake's strengths as independent appraisers and collectors and their relative weakness as directors is a symptom of how the lingering 1970s economic depression affected the Ransom Center.

Once the 1970s ended, the Ransom Center began to regain its economic vitality. With a more robust flow of funding came a renewed commitment to building its collections. An indicator of the Ransom Center's increasing dominance in the literary archives market was that its directors were no longer required to perform multiple roles. To recall, Harry Ransom also was an English professor; F. Warren Roberts was the British literature bibliographer; John Payne was the librarian; and Carlton Lake was the French literature curator, all while acting as director. Decherd Turner would be the first director who focused solely on one position.[33]

Born in Missouri, Decherd Turner studied at the University of Missouri and Vanderbilt, where he became a Presbyterian minister. He then decided to expand his professional horizons to librarianship and became the first director of the Bridwell Library in the Perkins School of Theology at Southern Methodist University (SMU) in 1950. At the Bridwell, he oversaw the dedication of the library and its enlargement, which owing to his efforts became one of the foremost rare book collections in the state.[34] Turner came to the University of Texas at Austin in 1980, lured by a starting salary of $50,000 and a $2 million annual acquisitions budget.[35] Yet once he arrived, Turner had difficulty adjusting. At SMU, Turner focused on early theological texts. At Texas, he invested in the HRC's rare book collection over its literary manuscripts, although he can claim the acquisition of Robert Lowell's papers.[36]

While the Roberts, Lake, and Turner years sustained the Ransom Center, the institution truly hit its stride again in 1988 when Thomas Staley began as director. Staley, called "the second reincarnation of Harry Ransom," would stay until 2013. Perhaps he came prepared to be a collector of literary archives given his background, which combined a mother with "means" and a father whose wealth came from the manufacture of embalming fluid.[37]

Staley's tutelage in money and preservation was compounded by his rigorous intellectual training; he represented the Ransom Center's return to director-scholars. Like Ransom, Staley started his career as a James Joyce researcher. After receiving his PhD from the University of Pittsburgh in 1962, he became a professor at the University of Tulsa. There, he rose to become chair of modern literature and provost and founded the *James Joyce Quarterly*.

But it was not Staley's intellectual achievements that captivated commentators. Journalists preferred to emphasize Staley's physicality. Grasping for a metaphor for his personality and activity level, reporters at the *Economist* described Staley as "recruiting authors as aggressively as other Texans recruit football stars," while those at the *New Yorker* thought the Ransom Center "operate[d] more like a college sports team, with Staley as the coach—an approach that fits the temperament of Texas." Staley did not disagree with this portrait of himself. He thought Turner's mistake had been to focus on preservation rather than acquisition. "Acquisitions are what people like," he says. "They like to be a part of it."[38] In other words, Staley knew what built a team and kept it motivated.

Facing the literary archives market like a football recruiter, Staley's strategy was to maintain lists of contemporary authors to pursue. His list was extensive; 600 or more writers were divided into three tiers, with the A tier made up of the most desirable authors. Ian McEwan grabbed an A spot, David Foster Wallace was on the B list, and Dave Eggers resided on the C tier. To illustrate how successful Staley's strategy was, all three of these authors would have their papers in Texas by 2014. Wallace's collection came in 2010, Eggers's McSweeney's Archive arrived in 2013, and McEwan's papers were sold to the center in 2014. Eventually, Staley acquired over a hundred literary archives, including such *NAAL* authors as Sam Shepard, Ronald Sukenick, David Mamet, and Julia Alvarez; grew the Ransom Center's endowment to over $30 million; and supervised the center's renovation in 2003. These materials, and those acquired by his predecessors, would be collectively insured "for a billion dollars."[39]

Such a successful track record created detractors. As chapter 1 began to depict, global institutions became angry as their cultural heritage increasingly began to come to the United States. English novelist A. S. Byatt based *Possession* (1990), which won the Booker Prize, on the international tension in the literary archives market. The antagonist of the book was a curator from New Mexico named Mortimer Cropper—a close doppelgänger of Tom Staley.

When Staley retired in 2013, Stephen Enniss took his place. Enniss began his career as a curator at Emory and was promoted to director in 2003. While employed at Emory, Enniss earned his doctorate in English from the University of Georgia. He also built Emory's Irish literary holdings. But Enniss supercharged his career with his acquisition of Salman Rushdie's papers in 2006. Two years later, Enniss moved on to Washington, D.C., becoming the Eric Weinmann Librarian (that is, director of) the Folger Shakespeare Library. When Staley retired in 2013, he recruited Enniss to head the Ransom Center. In Texas, Enniss has been eager to follow in his predecessor's footsteps, collecting a wide range of authors—including *NAAL* poet Billy Collins—in the past four years.[40]

CURATORS

After the University of Texas at Austin, Yale is the second most significant institution in the literary archives market. Yale was not an early adopter in the market for contemporary literature. Unlike Texas, which began its acquisitions in the 1960s, Yale did not begin seeking the papers of authors listed in the seventh edition of *NAAL* until the late 1980s. Understanding how and why Yale's Beinecke Rare Book & Manuscript Library decided to shift its priorities to include those previously covered by the Ransom Center requires understanding how its curators' approach to the market evolved over time.

Yale's prominence in the field of American literature began with early American literature. Owen Franklin Aldis donated his collection of first and rare editions of early Americana to Yale in 1911. His intent was to establish "a nucleus for a thorough and complete collection for the advanced study of American literature, its History and Bibliography." Due to the stipulations of the donation, Yale agreed to keep the Aldis materials in a separate space and provide the collection with its own curator. Aldis's gift came with an unusual request. He did not want the collection named after him, for he felt doing so would limit others' interest in adding to its holdings.[41] As a result, the collection did not become a separate set of materials but the seed to a greater vision.

First held in the College Library built in 1846, the collection was moved to the newly built Sterling Library in 1931, where it inhabited the Rare Book Room under the auspices of Keeper of Rare Books Chauncey Brewster Tinker. Tinker, who had graduated from Yale and served as Sterling Professor of English Literature in addition to maintaining his role in the library, recognized that the quality of rare books and manuscripts held at Yale would determine whether the university could aspire to become one of the world's principal libraries. He cautioned the alumni of 1924 that "if we are not willing to compete with the best libraries in this country, it is folly for us to attempt to be one of the great universities."[42]

Tinker meant what he said. By 1938, Gaillard Lapsley, Edith Wharton's literary executor, formally offered Wharton's papers to Yale as long as the following conditions were met: her holdings would be accepted as a permanent addition, content related to her personal life would be closed for thirty years, and even manuscripts earmarked as open would become "accessible only to bona fide students of literature."[43] Today, Wharton's bequest would be problematic. Contemporary curators seek to ensure rather than restrict access. But in the late 1930s, Wharton's demands did not register as an ethical challenge. As a result, her papers became the university's forty-second manuscript collection; in 1973, scholars lined up to see the formerly restricted papers.[44]

Tinker then developed Yale's strength in early twentieth-century authors on the reputation generated by Wharton's presence in the repository, even though his personal interest was eighteenth-century literature. Tinker maintained his ambitious acquisitions in American and British literature by combining Yale funding with the support of major donors Paul Mellon and John Hay Whitney. Soon, Tinker's collecting would be documented in a catalog of its own, *The Tinker Library* (1959), and his legacy would be recognized by an anonymous gift to be given to each year's top English undergraduate as well as in his own manuscript collection at Yale.[45]

In 1946, Donald Gallup replaced Tinker as the curator of American literature, a title he would hold until his retirement in 1965. Gallup was an internal hire; he knew Tinker from his undergraduate and graduate days at Yale. As an undergraduate, Gallup thought of Tinker in hyperbolic terms. Tinker was "awe inspiring," "frightening," and even "unsettling." Nevertheless, Gallup pursued his doctorate under Tinker and followed in Tinker's footsteps. He, too, spent most of his career at Yale; his only detours were a few years teaching composition at Southern Methodist University and a stint in the military during World War II.[46] Gallup developed Yale's collection of modernists by purchasing Ezra Pound, Gertrude Stein, and William Carlos Williams's papers and famously identifying the manuscript of T. S. Eliot's *The Waste Land* long after it had been thought missing.[47]

Gallup's work was not always easy. Wanting to buy Ezra Pound's papers, Gallup worried that he would not be able to find the $200,000 required to purchase the collection. Texas had the upper hand due to its deeper pockets. Gallup wondered, "Where were we, who owned no oil wells, to find $200,000?" Yale's primary donors, E. J. Beinecke and F. W. Beinecke, "had little concern for the papers of twentieth-century authors and no particular interest in Ezra Pound." Gallup eventually did find the money, thanks to an anonymous donor, but Texas itself had to consent to the acquisition. Yale's president, Kingman Brewster, petitioned Harry Ransom on Gallup's behalf, asking him to defer to Yale's earlier claim on the papers. Ransom ceded his interest and allowed Gallup to make a successful bid in a relatively rare case of institutional collaboration.[48]

Another complication arose in Gallup's career when Gertrude Stein recognized how to exploit the literary archives market in her best interest. She placed her papers at Yale on deposit rather than give them outright because she wanted to retain the ability to sell if the need arose. Stein proved herself not only an avant-garde writer but also an astute judge of the financial opportunities within the trade in writers' papers. Thankfully for Gallup, Stein never needed to raise additional funds and decided to keep her papers at Yale.[49]

The most monumental event that occurred during Gallup's tenure as curator came in 1963 when Edwin, Frederick, and Walter Beinecke created an endowment to commission a new library for Yale's expanding rare book and manuscript collections. Edwin and Frederick became interested in Yale's infrastructure needs as both men collected rare books. Edwin was interested in Robert Louis Stevenson and early printed books, whereas Frederick liked Western Americana. Together, they commissioned Gordon Bunshaft to design the building as "not just the biggest but the best of its kind."[50]

Gallup's dedication to Yale helped what became known as the Beinecke transition from Tinker's earlier "treasure room" to a contemporary research library. But his single-minded determination came at a personal cost. Gallup led an ascetic lifestyle which allowed him "to spend all his time, day and night, in service to Yale and its collections." But Gallup was devastated when his efforts were not met by corresponding internal interest. "The failure of most of the English department faculty properly to appreciate and make use of the resources of the collection for research" was a truth that Gallup found "too painful even to think about."[51]

However, Gallup could take comfort in the fact that his successors augmented his legacy. Patricia C. Willis took over the job of curator of American literature in 1987 and held it until 2008. Willis believed that an "author's personal papers . . . are of far more interest than the fair copy of a poem."[52] As a result, she acquired seven of Yale's eight *NAAL* authors: Annie Dillard (1986), Robert Penn Warren (1986), Leslie Marmon Silko (1992), James Baldwin (1998), Gerald Vizenor (2000), C. D. Wright (2007), and Louise Glück (2008).

While Willis built her collecting profile on a wide range of midcentury to contemporary authors, her own scholarship focused on modernist writers. She wrote on Ezra Pound but was particularly focused on the work of Marianne Moore.[53] Pound's papers are held at the Beinecke; Moore's belong to the Rosenbach in Philadelphia, where Willis spent fifteen years as curator. Willis's ability to assert that Moore was "not a peripheral member of the coterie but an architect of the movement" helped bring Moore's texts to contemporary audiences, even if Moore's collection was not one that fell under her stewardship.[54] Willis wrote a series of exhibition catalogs, books, and edited volumes on her favorite author and even manages a website dedicated to her work.

Willis's intellectual contributions at the Beinecke and elsewhere remain underdocumented. For example, Adrienne Raphel, a staff writer for the *New Yorker*, chose to quote biographer Linda Leavell, editor Heather White, poet Robyn Schiff, and professor Bonnie Costello rather than Willis in her article dedicated to the resurgence of critical interest in Marianne Moore. However, the Marianne Moore society published "Hummingbird—for Patricia C. Willis" by Jeredith Merrin, which compares the bird's labor to the curator's efforts. A portion of it reads:

> They work hard at what they do—
> . . . .
>
> And this requires,
> the ornithologist I'm reading says,
>
> the most energy-demanding flight,
> the relatively largest heart
> of any bird, of any sort.[55]

Willis "worked hard," hovering, deeding, and heading for more of what she needed—the literary papers with which to stock the Beinecke. Merrin suggests that Willis's labors, like Gallup's, were extensive. Unlike Gallup, Willis did not write a memoir documenting her decisions. As a result, her influence on the Beinecke's collections is more difficult to trace.

After Willis, Nancy Kuhl and Melissa Barton shared the role of curator of American literature. Nancy Kuhl served as the assistant curator of American literature between 2002 and 2006, after which she was promoted to associate curator, a title she held until 2008, when the Beinecke divided responsibilities for the collection by genre. Kuhl became curator of American poetry, the title she holds today. Kuhl also briefly held the title of acting curator of prose and drama between February 2012 and May 2013, which she ceded when Melissa Barton obtained the position in 2013.[56] Kuhl's titles demonstrates the scale and pace of Yale's activity in the literary archives market. As with how the Ransom Center began to have directors who took on only one role after 1980 due to the increased number of acquisitions, the Beinecke's decision to split curatorial positions into more specialized areas demonstrates the repository's rapid expansion in its holdings. Kuhl carried on Willis's legacy by acquiring N. Scott Momaday's collection in 2012 and Yusef Komunyakaa's papers in 2014.

Kuhl's and Barton's backgrounds as creative writers and researchers demonstrate how institutions value curators who engage both academically and artistically with the content they manage. Although both Kuhl and Barton maintain creative and scholarly presences in their field, Kuhl holds a more substantial record given her longer career. While serving as curator, Kuhl wrote six scholarly articles and two book chapters, four chapbooks and three collections of poetry, three exhibition catalogs, and served as coeditor of Phylum Press. Barton, who holds a PhD in English from the University of Chicago, is the author of two exhibition catalogs and a contributor to a compilation of images from the Beinecke's collections.

A century's worth of library donors, directors, and curators built the Beinecke by steadily developing their institution's prominence around twentieth-century literary archives. Once the market began to prove the intellectual value of contemporary papers and Gallup decided to compete, Yale moved confidently into this postwar scene.

Along the way, Yale's high endowment bolstered its interest in literary manuscripts. In 1985, Yale's assets were $1 billion, considered by some to be a high amount, yet one that financial experts assessed as underperforming on its returns. Because of this estimate, the university took on a riskier investment strategy that year, guided by its new endowment manager, David F. Swensen. Yale's approach paid off when, by 2012, this new strategy helped the university's endowments rise to $19.3 billion. Yale's endowment now stood second only to Harvard's ($30.7 billion), although its growth outpaced Harvard's. Yale's risky approach did hurt it eventually. In 2008, their endowment sank 25 percent, generating a $150 million budget shortfall.[57]

Yale still had money for the Beinecke, which spent a year, and $73 million, to renovate the library in 2015. The building's façade was cleaned, its technical capacity updated, and its spaces made more inviting for students. And this expenditure did not cut into the Beinecke's acquisition budget. Each year, the library adds 1,000 linear feet of archives, 10,000 to 15,000 books, and between 2,000 and 3,000 manuscripts and other materials.[58]

Texas and Yale provide contrasting examples of the history of the literary archives market. Texas began the trade with its early interest in contemporary American literature; Yale, a latecomer, steadily moved into more recent writing as it grew from a repository that concentrated on nineteenth-century American literature due to the Aldis donation to a repository that embraced the modernists under Gallup and the postmodernists under Willis, Kuhl, and Barton.

Stanford provides an alternative to both collecting models. According to *NAAL* data, Stanford neither showed an early nor a late commitment to the field but rather a brief interest. Stanford grew its collections faster than any other repository by acquiring five sets of papers in the space of two years: Denise Levertov (1993), Robert Creeley (1993), Fanny Howe (1993), Allen Ginsberg (1994), and Robert Pinsky (1994). Stanford's acquisitions showcase the power of a single curator, William McPheron, who acted quickly during a time of institutional transition.

William McPheron's career stretched across the tenure of three library directors: David C. Weber (1969–92), Robert Street (1992–93, interim), and Michael Keller (1993–present).[59] After twenty-three years under David Weber, Stanford took a year to find the leader it would keep for the next several decades. McPheron's experience helped him capitalize on the opportunities presented during the brief period of leadership change during 1992 to 1993, which led to the five collections he acquired in 1993 and 1994.

When David Weber retired in 1992, McPheron was an active researcher, having written two of his three books, all six of his bibliographies, and two articles on collection development. Although McPheron discussed a variety of American writers, stretching from lesser-known authors such as William Eastlake to those widely known like John Steinbeck, his overarching intellectual interests focused on the Black Mountain College, an avant-garde art school that educated twelve hundred students between 1922 and 1957.

Black Mountain College employed John Dewey's model for progressive education by allowing students to participate in curricular design and to learn through hands-on experience. While the college initially emphasized the visual and performing arts, Charles Olson, its leader between 1948 and 1957, shifted the focus to creative writing. In 1954, Olson established a journal to profile student work titled *The Black Mountain Review*. Unfortunately, Olson's time at Black Mountain would see the close of the visionary school.[60]

The demise of the Black Mountain College did not deaden its long-term influence in American artistic circles. The college's faculty, as well as their students and those inspired by their example, would go on to inhabit the canons of American painting (Josef Albers), music (John Cage), performance (Merce Cunningham), and poetry (Charles Olson, Robert Creeley, and Denise Levertov).

Black Mountain College's success contributed to the allure of authors' papers associated with the school. To give examples of how collectible college-affiliated artists became, Albers's papers primarily stayed with his foundation, the Josef and Anni Albers Foundation in Bethany, Connecticut, but also were sought by the Smithsonian, the Frick, the State Archives of North Carolina, and Yale University. Northwestern University and Wesleyan University acquired Cage's works. The New York Public Library proudly accepted Cunningham's materials, and the University of Connecticut purchased Olson's papers. Although Connecticut bought Olson's collection before McPheron obtained his position at Stanford, McPheron could seek the papers of Olson's colleagues, Denise Levertov and Robert Creeley.[61]

Denise Levertov was born in England in 1923. Her family educated her mostly at home. When World War II broke out, she worked as a civilian nurse in London. After the war, she came to the United States, where she met and married Mitchell Goodman. Goodman introduced Levertov to Robert Creeley, Charles Olson, and Robert Duncan—the Black Mountain poets—and Cid Corman, who would go on to publish her poetry in *Origin*. Her work immediately gained critical acclaim, faltering only once she became more politically active during the Vietnam War. As a result, Levertov was less read at the end of her life than she was earlier in her career. However, her place in the canon is stable; she was the only woman included in the pivotal Donald Allen anthology, *The New American Poetry, 1945–1960* (1960).

Robert Creeley was three years Denise Levertov's junior and born in Massachusetts. Creeley lost an eye at only two years of age; it was a brief trauma amid an otherwise privileged life that lead him from the Holderness School to Harvard, where he would meet John Ashbery, Kenneth Koch, Donald Hall, and Frank O'Hara. However, among them Creeley felt restless. He dropped out and spent a two-year interlude in India and Burma with the American Field Service. When he returned to the States, Creeley contacted Ezra Pound, William Carlos Williams, and then Charles Olson, who asked him to teach at the Black Mountain College and edit *The Black Mountain Review*. Afterward, he lived in San Francisco, New Hampshire, and then Mallorca, Spain, before traveling back and forth between Mallorca and the college. In 1956, he received a bachelor's degree from the college and moved to New Mexico, where he would earn a master's degree at the University of New Mexico in 1960. In 1967, he joined the faculty at the University at Buffalo, a location he would come to call Black Mountain II for its heavy emphasis on radical poetics. There, he protested the Vietnam War, but Creeley's work did not become as tied to the era as Levertov's did; as a result, his critical reputation remained stable.[62]

William McPheron demonstrates that a university's successful collecting strategy often is the result of a curator's passion dovetailing with institutional support. McPheron's long-standing interest in the Black Mountain School not only helped Stanford acquire the papers of Denise Levertov and Robert Creeley but also allowed them achieve renown with an even more significant acquisition: the papers of Allen Ginsberg.[63]

A leader of the Beat movement, Allen Ginsberg attended Columbia University, where he met Jack Kerouac and William Burroughs, a fateful encounter that set all three authors' careers in motion and was documented in the film *Kill Your Darlings* (2013). After Ginsberg graduated from Columbia in 1948, he eventually moved from New York to San Francisco. There, Ginsberg joined the San Francisco Renaissance and wrote his best-known book, *"Howl" and Other Poems* (1956). "Howl" depicted Ginsberg's impressions of an America degraded by war and consumerism. The poem begins with the now-famous line "I saw the best minds of my generation destroyed by madness, starving hysterical naked," and then unrolled a vision of "angelheaded hipsters" battling drug and sexual addiction, racism, poverty, communism, and capitalism.⁶⁴ Ginsberg's perspective proved contentious. The U.S. Customs and San Francisco police accused *"Howl" and Other Poems* of obscenity. The book's publisher, Lawrence Ferlinghetti, was even sent to trial. Although Ferlinghetti was acquitted, the incident set in place Ginsberg's reputation as a counterculture character at odds with the government. Ginsberg built on his standing through his participation in Vietnam War demonstrations, drug use, and experience of being expelled by two countries—Cuba and Czechoslovakia—in the same year.

Ginsberg's lengthy poetics are matched only by the size of his papers. At 1,000 linear feet, his collection is the largest of all *NAAL* authors' holdings. Steven Mandeville-Gamble's 1,059-page finding aid meticulously records the span of Ginsberg's materials, which include the obligatory journals and correspondence—the latter series alone taking up 380 boxes—alongside more surprising items, like a pair of sneakers Ginsberg saved to demonstrate the harshness of communist Czechoslovakia. They looked worn even when new due to being poorly manufactured.⁶⁵

What is notable about the Ginsberg archive is its provenance, not just its size. Columbia kept Ginsberg's materials before Stanford acquired them. While this fact is not well advertised, Stanford's finding aid does offer a clue to the papers' history. In the Scope and Contents note, Mandeville-Gamble wrote, "Wherever Ginsberg's original arrangement of materials was encountered, the order was retained. However, materials previously housed at Columbia University show signs of having been rearranged significantly. As a result, several series show evidence of conflicting intellectual arrangements, one imposed by Ginsberg and his staff, another by third parties."⁶⁶ Ginsberg's papers moved from Columbia to Stanford in 1994 because Columbia could not pay the $5 million assessed value. No university could. Ginsberg had to decide whether to split his papers or accept a lower value for his holdings.⁶⁷ Ginsberg chose the latter, deciding that he would obtain the most profit by selling his papers to whichever institution could keep them together while paying the most. Stanford won when it offered Andrew Wylie, Ginsberg's agent, $1 million. Although this price was one-fifth of Ginsberg's assessed value and he had no connection to the institution, he accepted it on the advice of Wylie and his bibliographer, Bill Morgan. Ginsberg recalled that "Stanford was dominated by a very conservative, formalist poetry that very much rebelled against the kind of ecstatic, apocalyptic, William Carlos Williams–based naturalistic poetry we wrote." The university had never even invited him to give a reading. Ginsberg did not hold a grudge. He surmised that he could "have a kind of osmotic influence" on the university's conservative Hoover Institute.[68]

The deal came with a catch: Ginsberg was supposed to keep the purchase price a secret. Ginsberg was controversial. Liberals disliked his willingness to pose for a Gap khakis ad—it paid $20,000 and seemed too crassly commercial—while conservatives were repulsed by his homosexuality and membership in the North American Man/Boy Love Association. Even his counterculture friends found his success hard to swallow. One would call him "just a rich Jewish merchant." The price Ginsberg received might have been substantially less than he was owed—Ginsberg himself described the sale as going for "bargain-basement rates"—but his reputation meant that any payment would likely remain politically problematic.[69] To carry off these major acquisitions, McPheron would need to have strong collection support from his library and his university.

Stanford was not in a strong financial position in the early 1990s owing to the general national recession that occurred between 1990 and 1991. In March 1991, Stanford reported that it was expected to incur a shortfall of $20 million in 1991 and $30 million in 1992. To save money, the university planned a new budget, one that included slowing the rate of monograph acquisition. Stanford's administrators also thought it could address the shortfall by creating a stronger investment portfolio. Accordingly, Stanford established the Stanford Management Company to manage its funds, appointed a new chief financial officer, and committed to the goal of raising $1.1 billion in donations.[70]

Stanford's actions succeeded, and the university passed its fund-raising target by June 1991. Its financial health slowly returned thereafter. Thus, when McPheron began to purchase literary papers in 1993 and 1994, Stanford was well into its campaign to pull itself out of its deficit. Yet the university was still not back to normal. In 1994, Stanford reported that its library would need to cut $405,000 from its allocations for the following years. Nevertheless, it managed to provide the $1 million necessary to fund the acquisition of Allen Ginsberg's collection, to advance, as Director of Collections Anthony Angiletta put it, "Stanford University Libraries' efforts to develop distinguished collections in support of the study of twentieth-century culture."[71] Stanford became one of the market's top repositories because it made the decision to support distinctive collections even amid a recession, although it has not recently acquired any more authors listed in the data set generated by the selection of writers included in the seventh edition of *The Norton Anthology of American Literature*.

CONCLUSION

Texas, Yale, and Stanford are three of the top five collecting repositories in the literary archives market, but how they acquired writers' papers varied significantly based on their institutional history and culture. Although all three institutions hired directors and curators who combined subject expertise with administrative savvy, Texas saw itself as a leader in the new field of contemporary literary studies, giving collecting responsibilities to directors rather than curators. Except for the recession of the 1970s, Texas's oil investments allowed the university to remain fiscally healthy for most of the market's timeline. In contrast, Yale began to collect contemporary literary papers much later. Its curators slowly worked their way from late nineteenth- and early twentieth-century holdings into the modernists before expanding their interest into more recent works. Along the way, Yale would acquire top papers in its designated field, benefiting from a high endowment that was invested aggressively to achieve higher returns. Stanford, unlike Texas and Yale, was neither a regional institution that struck it rich nor a conservative Ivy. Instead, Stanford gained from a single curator who transformed his own interests into an area of distinction for his repository, even when his library faced budget shortfalls during a recession.

The 1980s saw a blossoming of the market to include more voices and more money, leading to more highly ranked ARL libraries successfully acquiring literary papers. The 2000s, on the other hand, featured a greater volume of archives in the trade, but libraries faced a riskier financial climate. In the 2010s, the economy in the United States began to recover from the 2008 recession, but the effect of renewed wealth did not result in greater financial equality between institutions. Rather, the 2010s resulted in a wider gap between greater and lesser funded institutions. Now, the literary archives market largely reflects interests of the top two—not even the top five—schools. These trends demonstrate that Enniss's suggestion to limit competition among institutions participating in the literary archives market is unnecessary. Already, the market has begun to contract around a few well-endowed universities, namely, his own repository at the University of Texas at Austin and the Beinecke at Yale University.

The Ransom Center and the Beinecke led the trade in literary archives because the identity of an institution determines the demographic profile of the writers it can collect. The more prestigious the authors an institution acquires, the stronger its legacy as a collecting repository becomes. Cultural capital does not apply only to authors but also to institutions. As literary papers have become a luxury good within the university environment, they invoke both research value and symbolic prestige. Once a repository can capitalize on its prestige, its position within the market becomes stronger, leading toward the consolidation of the trade in writers' papers to benefit a few institutions that can afford to collect widely rather than according to narrow regional or aesthetic preferences.

No matter which institution they reside in, all literary archives eventually undergo arrangement and description, which is when an archivist takes an author's papers and organizes them into a usable resource. Often, this process is completed before collections become accessible to scholars and the public. While the timing of this workflow means that archivists are a part of the papers' provenance and a stakeholder in the literary archives market, the presence of archivists frequently remains undocumented in finding aids and uncited in research. To address this oversight, chapter 5 recounts how archivists' management of paper-based, digitized, and born-digital collections shapes the trade and informs later academic inquiry.

CHAPTER 5

Provenance

Archivists and Digital Archivists

In the digital environment, records don't just happen. With word processing, many—if not most—of the drafts Ransom would have wanted are lost.

—Richard Pearce-Moses

Archivists organize writers' papers, taking an author's materials from how it looks in their home to how it will appear to researchers in a repository. Yet their work remains an undiscussed aspect of the trade in writers' papers, largely because their names are not recorded in contrast to the library directors and curators, whose names define institutional eras. Following the precedent established in the digital humanities to foreground all collaborators' contributions, as well as research in citation studies highlighting how an author's demographics shape how frequently he or she is studied, chapter 5 examines why finding aids rarely name the archivists who arranged and described collections and then illustrates how this practice predisposes scholars to recognize only archivists' reference support rather than their supervision of a collection's arrangement and description. Scholars are not solely to blame, for archivists do not advocate for their significance owing to professional norms that deemphasize individual contributions. As a result, this chapter concerns how archivists create literary archives through their management of these writers' physical, digitized, and born-digital documents.

PROVENANCE

An item's provenance is its record of ownership. So far, this book traced literary archives from the authors themselves and/or their families to literary agents and book dealers. Once these papers are sold to a repository, the collection's provenance includes its institution, represented by directors and curators. But institutions also include archivists who process collections by arranging and describing them for ease of use. Molly Schwartzburg, formerly curator of American literature at the Ransom Center, explained that by the time a finding aid is created, an archivist "has touched and arranged every item and [finding aids] represent his extensive knowledge of the collection."[1] However, finding aids do not consistently include the name of the archivist who wrote them, even though records are accessible for research only if they are determined by archivists to be of historical value during arrangement and description.

The need for institutions to credit archivists parallels the way in which the "digital humanities"—an umbrella term for a diverse set of emergent methodologies that include but are not limited to the production of digital archives, global information systems, online editing and publishing, text mining, quantitative analysis of cultural data, and visualization—grappled with questions regarding the recognition of and value accorded to its practitioners' labor.[2] Within university settings, research often is presumed to be the domain of faculty. Yet many digital humanities practitioners who contribute to or direct projects do not have faculty appointments. Digital humanities now recognizes that ethical projects must extend credit to every individual who contributes. Optimistic observers argue that this field offers individuals the opportunity to "renegotiate professional status."[3]

Citation analysis examines patterns regarding who gets cited when, where, and why. Although traditionally practiced as a methodology in linguistics, the history of science, and information science, citation studies now is more likely to appear in journals dedicated to academic or library administration as a way to better understand an individual's productivity, a journal's impact, or a discipline's scope and direction.[4] Citation studies reveals a bias toward

American-centric sources and a preference for white male authors over content written by women or people of color. Scholars who are white males can then accrue higher prestige.[5] Recent investigations reveal that these citation patterns partially result from the preference of citers for writers from more prestigious educational backgrounds and the propensity of male researchers to cite themselves.[6] Additionally, the contributions of women researchers are more likely to be overlooked if they work in a team setting.[7] To remedy this problem, inclusive citation asks researchers to evaluate the diversity of their sources and address unequal representation by seeking out and adding more underrepresented voices to their syllabi and publications to amplify research by women and minority writers.[8]

This chapter expands arguments for inclusive citation practices to request that institutions include who processed a collection in its metadata so that researchers can cite these archivists correctly. Doing so recognizes archivists as part of papers' provenance, accepts arrangement and description as a mode of research, and acknowledges archivists' influence on the shape of later scholarship.

Finding aids are not required to include archivists' names.[9] Not all institutions omit names; the practice varies by repository. The Ransom Center consistently names who worked on an aid, but the Beinecke rarely does. As a result, researchers can learn that Micah Erwin and Grace Hansen processed Julia Alvarez's papers; Katharine Mosley managed Billy Collins's; Jennifer Patterson and Joan Sibley organized Robert Lowell's; Joan Sibley arranged Arthur Miller's; Stephen Mielke oversaw Thomas Pynchon's; Chelsea S. Jones and Stephen Mielke worked on Anne Sexton's; and Liz Murray processed the papers of both Sam Shepard (with Daniela Lozano) and Ronald Sukenick. In contrast, the only credited finding aid among the Beinecke's seven collections belonged to James Baldwin, whose papers were processed by Timothy G. Young.

Table 6 highlights that the number of *Norton Anthology of American Literature* (*NAAL*) collections with unattributed finding aids is inconsistent over time. Archivists were most likely to be cited in the 1990s, when—rounded to the nearest whole number—86 percent of finding aids mentioned who arranged and processed the collection. Other decades' finding aids included the name of archivists from 47 to 75 percent of the time. An average attribution rate of 65 percent shows substantial improvement is still necessary, but at

TABLE 6. *NAAL* authors' finding aids with named archivists by decade

Decade	Collections (n)*	Named archivist (n)	Finding aids with named archivists (%)†
1950s	1	0	0
1960s	7	4	57
1970s	4	3	75
1980s	17	8	47
1990s	21	18	86
2000s	19	13	68
2010s	9	5	56
Total		78	51	65

* Toni Cade Bambara does not have a placement date, so she is not counted.
† Rounded to the nearest whole number.

least this improvement can build from a practice seen in the finding aids of most *NAAL* collections.

Repositories that do not name their archivists ascribe to corporate authorship. Kathleen Feeney, head of archives processing and digital access for the Special Collections Research Center at the University of Chicago Library, explained the policy in this manner: "Processing and finding aid creation and revision is usually the work of several staff members, so our policy is not to assign authorship credit to individuals, but rather to the Library as a corporate author."[10] While Chicago cites corporate authorship as an outcome of collaborative workflows, other universities defend the practice of not naming archivists as stemming from their desire to protect their employees: it has been used as a tactic to prevent patrons from contacting a paraprofessional who aided in processing, a staff member whose responsibilities shifted over time, a person who is no longer with a repository, or an archivist whose focus is on arrangement and description rather than reference. Omitting proper names can be a way to direct questions to the appropriate reference account rather than to an individual who might not be able to respond to the query.[11]

These justifications for corporate authorship focus on the collection's users, not its provenance. Paraprofessionals have the right to be named if their analysis shaped the literary collection. Rather than assuming paraprofessionals are less-skilled archivists, many paraprofessionals are trained archivists who must take lower-tier positions because of a difficult job market. Jackie Dooley, the 2013–14 president of the Society of American Archivists, identified labor as a "mega-issue" for the profession. Entry-level jobs are scarce, 21 percent of the field is under thirty, and 19 percent of those paying dues make under $20,000 a year.[12] And even if paraprofessionals are not trained archivists, their work should be accorded equal value; the collections they arrange and describe still are shaped by their hands. Additionally, staff members who changed jobs internally or who moved to a new employer do not have their history of processing papers eliminated. Overlooking a name to prevent a researcher from contacting that individual assumes that institutional workflows should matter more than careful provenance.

Archivists did not advocate for their labor and research to be counted as part of a collection's provenance because they believed they were objective processors. Once historian and political scientist Howard Zinn challenged this precept in "Secrecy, Archives, and the Public Interest," the talk he gave at the 1970 meeting of the Society of American Archivists, archivists began to recognize how their decisions regarding collection management reflected their own identities. But they did not see how their broader cultural capital operated to create practices that obscured the value of and implications of their role processing papers. Archivists became aware of how the historical record they created was devoid of the voices of women, of people of color, and of the working class and rushed to address their oversight.[13] But, in their attempt to improve the diversity of their collections, they overlooked how arrangement, not just acquisition, shapes the historical record.

Archivists also did not advocate for themselves because they lacked a professional identity. Archival science began when it split from the discipline of history in the early twentieth century; in this early era, archivists trained as researchers before choosing to pursue alternative employment. Eventually, archivists began to organize. In 1936, they established the Society of American Archivists (SAA). By 1938, SAA began its journal of record, *The American Archivist*, which continues to publish both practical and theoretical research in the field semiannually.

Yet one of the hallmarks of professional status, formal training obtained through specialized education, took decades for archivists to establish. Independent graduate archival programs did not exist; students entered the profession by obtaining either a master of arts (MA) degree in history or a master's in library and information studies (MLIS) at a university with a specialization in archival education.[14] While the MA socialized archivists to think of themselves as researchers, MLIS programs rarely focused on this attribute. These bifurcated tracks led to disagreement as to what an archivist's identity and skills should include, namely, whether archivists should be trained as researchers like their peers in history or should imagine themselves as belonging to an entirely separate field. And these disagreements led to the postponement of a standard archival education. Although SAA set training standards in 1973, updating them in the following decades, the late curricular development set a confusing precedent. The first master's program solely devoted to archival studies would not be launched until 1981, at the University of British Columbia, Canada.[15] Because of the confusion regarding what archivists were and what they did, in the eyes of many historians, archivists became a "species of mere technicians and higher grade file clerks." Now, the SAA's specifications for graduate curricula are extensive and include research methodologies, but this detail came too late to dispel this reputation among scholars.[16]

Archivists recognize that researchers overlook their labor. Stacie Williams told the following anecdote on her blog, *On Archivy*: "Last fall, I had an engaging lunch discussion with a visiting historian about her research, during which she revealed that she had not previously paid much attention to who (or what) was doing actual work in the archives until she found her book at a standstill because much of the material she needed was in archives that were severely underfunded and understaffed. She said at times, she was given boxes that had not even been surveyed, let alone arranged or described, and with no finding aids available in analog or digital format. Almost none of the collections she needed had been made available via digital means (including metadata). That was the first time, she said, that she had ever even considered that there are people who do this work daily so that she could conduct her research in an orderly, efficient manner." Williams continued: "As a researcher, it's easy to take all of those things for granted. . . . But how would we expect people to know? Archivists do a terrible job of advocating and informing people about our labor and the overall contributions of our labor to society."[17]

What Williams identifies as a problem is comprised of two components. The first factor is researchers' ignorance of the service element of the archival profession. Recall the characteristics a job must have to qualify as a profession: education, access, monopoly, and service. Service is what justifies the maintenance of the profession. As scholars do not understand what archivists do to support their work, they are not able to identify it. The second factor is that this service is not valued. As discussed in chapter 3, literary agents accepted a lower cultural capital for the survival of their profession and personal financial success. Archivists did not have to defend their profession to the degree that literary agents did even though they also are employed in a recently developed field. But archivists generally do not find the financial success that top literary agents enjoy.

Even academic conferences that attempt to remedy this professional oversight fall victim to their own inbuilt bias. Kate Eichhorn recounted that a 2009 conference at Columbia University devoted to the theme of women in the archives field with an explicit agenda to bring together scholars and archivists included only one archivist/librarian—her colleague Jenna Freedman, founder of the Barnard Zine Library.[18] While Eichhorn's narrative does not examine why archivists largely were absent from this particular conference or delve into the general reasons why archivists do not present alongside scholars more frequently, her point stands. Practitioners are omitted from archival discussions because their role is seen as supportive of rather than central to the academic enterprise.

Yet many well-intentioned scholars argue that archivists are not overlooked; academic etiquette suggests acknowledging those who supported a research project, including librarians and archivists, in an introductory paratext to the monograph. But giving credit by courtesy rather than by practice reveals a power differential, a point previously made in chapter 3's discussion on whether manuscript dealers received acknowledgment for their contribution to the literary archives market.

Consider the contrast between how a scholar and an archivist describe the value of acknowledgments. Aptly named James F. English explained at the start of his acknowledgments for *The Economy of Prestige* (2005) that "too much acknowledgement can ruin the whole noble ceremony of exchange, subjecting it to an overly scrupulous accounting and laying bare the messy truth of cultural debts and gifts: the fact that they are unending, coterminous with society itself."[19] Nevertheless, English endured listing the conventional types of people who helped him: his research assistants, university colleagues, professional contacts, readers, and family. As English's monograph is not based on archival research, no archivists are mentioned. The only librarian he names is Bob Walther, from the University of Pennsylvania's Van Pelt Library, despite "research trips to Rome, London, Los Angeles, and elsewhere."

Presumably, many more librarians had direct contact with English or indirectly supported his inquiry, but their names and places of work go unstated.

Archivists find acknowledgments crucial; they read them to check whether scholars remembered their contribution. Maarja Krusten pointed out "that as an archivist and historian, I always read acknowledgments in academic and popular history books. They give me a sense not just of research, but also of the author's sensibilities. Whom he or she thanks, words used, order, etc. A place to see generosity of spirit or lack of it."[20] Krusten recognizes it is a scholar's choice whether to include an acknowledgment of archival labor, rather than his or her responsibility, revealing the power differential between gratitude and citation.

Furthermore, the problem with acknowledgments is that they almost always rely on archivists' role as providing reference and research help rather than recognizing what is for many archivists their primary duty—processing collections. Many times, these roles may even be undertaken by different people. A scholar may see the reference archivist but not the processing archivist, so the person acknowledged in published work often is not the same person who originally created the finding aid and/or organized a collection's contents. Acknowledgment rather than citation also obscures the work done on literary collections when they arrive at the archivist's desk in their penultimate stop through the literary archives market.

Repositories inconsistently report which archivists create finding aids for *NAAL* authors' literary papers. As seen in table 6, the 1990s show a high level of attribution—86 percent. Yet institutions in the 2010s did worse than those in the 1960s and 1970s; in the 2010s, archivists are named 56 percent of the time, whereas in the 1960s and 1970s, they were cited 57 and 75 percent of the time, respectively. These numbers show that corporate authorship is a common, although not dominant practice among repositories active in the literary archives market.

This finding is encouraging considering that archivists' arrangement and description practices shape scholar's research outcomes. Eliminating corporate authorship on finding aids will help researchers recognize the value of citing, rather than acknowledging, archivists and will bolster the likelihood that they will dedicate time to understanding archival workflows for paper-based, digital, and born-digital records to generate more informed analysis of the literary papers they encounter. The next section begins to rectify this knowledge gap by exploring the methodologies and mindsets archivists bring to their management of literary collections.

ARCHIVISTS

Authors listed in the seventh edition of *NAAL* possessed primarily paper-based literary collections. Archivists who appraise physical collections can conduct either an item-level review or follow the "more product, less process" (MPLP) method. Item-level review requires each item to be examined before duplicate materials or those of lower artefactual value are removed, such as copies of periodicals an author collected but did not annotate. Then, remaining items are organized and described in detailed finding aids.[21] The MPLP method, invented by Mark A. Greene and Dennis Meissner in 2005, is a more general assessment that allows archivists to save time by focusing on generally summarizing holdings. To better understand the impact of size on processing speed, both size and speed findings from the *NAAL* authors' collections are represented to the hundredths place whenever possible. Size findings are given as precisely as possible in table 7, while speed is summarized in the following discussion.

Item-level review is slow, so MPLP began to speed up arrangement and description. As item-level review is the most commonly used method, 52 processing studies undertaken between 1976 and 2012 show that this approach takes 4.64 hours on average per linear foot, although speed varies by holdings' complexity. Greene and Meissner argued that the slow processing rates generated by item-level review could be rethought to allow more collections to be delivered to researchers sooner—a critical point as backlogs remain nationally endemic. Backlogs occur when repositories acquire papers but leave them unprocessed and inaccessible to scholars. As of 2015, 44 percent of cultural heritage holdings in the United States are unavailable to researchers because of backlogs.[22] With limited personnel and funding, acquiring a collection that cannot be organized is preferred over refusing it and potentially allowing it to be lost to history.

Proponents of MPLP not only espouse the backlog-clearing intent of the method but also note these collections are more likely to retain their creators' original intent. The technique decreases archivists' intervention in the records, as those who follow this principle spend less time sorting materials for description. Proponents also argue that MPLP releases archivists from tedious workflows, allowing them to invest more heavily into documenting, theorizing, and publicizing archival labor, activities that would increase their research output and enhance their academic status.[23] Opponents protest that such measures will deskill archival labor into assembly-line techniques.[24]

Most archivists who manage literary collections do not opt for MPLP. Literary archives' high cultural capital means that their housing institutions are more willing to commit the large amount of time and money required for archivists to produce detailed finding aids. Seventy-one of seventy-two placed *NAAL* collections have been or will be processed at an item level.[25] Furthermore, MPLP was not introduced until 2005. Although 16 collections were deposited by *NAAL* authors after this year, none were processed with this now-famous method. These numbers highlight how much repositories invest in literary collections.

The time and cost required to arrange and describe writers' papers is substantial owing to the size of these collections. Table 7 shows that *NAAL* writers' papers stretch to 72.65 linear feet on average. White men's collections are the largest, being 105.06 linear feet on average. In contrast, the smallest collections belong to white women, whose holdings include only 40.74 linear feet of content. Accordingly, within the *NAAL* data set, archivists spend the most time arranging and describing white men's papers, which is important to consider as not only have institutions dedicated more resources to white men's holdings over time but also archivists have intervened more in the final presentation of these archival bodies.

Whether a literary archive is digitized, in part or in full, is an indicator of a repository's financial health. Due to the expense required to digitize

TABLE 7. Average size of *NAAL* authors' papers by demographic

Demographic	Collections (n)*	Collection size range (linear feet)	Collection size average (linear feet)
White men	39	0.84–1,000	105.06
White women	15	8.50–159	40.74
Minority men	12	0.83–219.50	63.68
Minority women	10	30–180	81.11
	Total: 76	Overall range: 0.84–1,000	Overall average: 72.65

* The collections of Toni Cade Bambara, Billy Collins, and Kurt Vonnegut do not have sizes affiliated with their holdings.

documents, if institutions have internal funding or can locate external support for digitization, they are much more likely to provide this service. But the papers themselves may make digitization easier or more difficult, for a collection's contents and copyright influence whether materials can be placed online. Thus, the presence or absence of digitized content provides an important clue as to the provenance of a collection and what provisions are required for its ongoing management.

Digitization is the process of taking preservation-quality photographs of papers and then loading these photographs into a platform that allows users to browse the collection off-site. To be more specific, archivists coordinating a digitization project would take photographs of documents and then sort them into files labeled with which box they originally came from. Afterward, archivists would run these files through an automated optical character recognition (OCR) system to make them keyword searchable. Finally, archivists would place these on a server as a digital master, with the physical boxes stored off-site in ideal environmental conditions. That way, the originals would be referred to only as necessary. Archivists would load access copies of the master images into access software for users.[26]

As digitization allows documents to be accessed by off-site researchers, the step is now considered an optimal component of twenty-first-century processing.[27] Although scholars often assert that working in person with the manuscripts is the gold standard for research, traveling to see items in person can be prohibitively expensive.[28] Research fellowships sometimes exist to support visiting scholars, although when they are offered, they can be competitive and may not cover all costs.

To provide the convenience of off-site access, papers usually undergo the expensive, item-level review described earlier. But many researchers assume all papers either are or will be digitized because they do not recognize that item-level review is not always possible. Leslie Perrin Wilson, curator of the Concord Free Library, outlined that such factors as budget woes and staffing shortages prevent many desired digitization projects from coming to fruition. The best way to cope, Wilson asserted, "is to follow a selective, interpretative approach based on our intimate familiarity with the content and strengths of our collections."[29] In other words, Wilson argued that archivists are better situated to determine what to digitize after they conduct item-level reviews. The implications of Wilson's point are twofold. First, collections that merit item-level review, like literary archives, are more likely to have some of their contents digitized. Second, the subjective assessments archivists bring to their paper-based processing work are magnified in their later decisions regarding which materials should be digitized. Accordingly, researchers working with digitized documents should consider how these materials reflect the judgment of archivists.

Not all digitization has to be conducted after item-level review; recently, MPLP practices expanded into digitization workflows. More product, less process digitization occurs immediately after acquisition, rather than after arrangement and description. Accordingly, MPLP digitized collections do not have comprehensive finding aids. Advocates argue that losing finding aids would not be a problem, for researchers often believe finding aids are confusing and must be taught how to use them. Contemporary researchers find keyword-searching OCR records more intuitive than analyzing how archivists use finding aids to organize information.[30]

While MPLP digitization appears transformative, it is unlikely to be employed for literary archives. Writers' papers do not undergo MPLP processing. Even if they did, this cost-saving approach to digitization still requires a prohibitive level of funding. When Google Books pioneered the idea of mass digitization, it presumed scanning at black and white with resolutions optimized for text over image. Literary archives often include content with color and image, factors that inflate costs.[31] Anne R. Kenney, writing on behalf of the Council on Library and Information Resources (CLIR), a key funder of digitization projects, highlighted this point in her report under the heading "Institutions Should Not Expect to Recover Costs Incurred in Digitization": "Scanning figures for graphic materials represents an order-of-magnitude increase in cost over scanning text. Steve Puglia of the National Archives has completed a comparative analysis of digital imaging costs, the results of which have been presented in *RLG DigiNews* (1999). His findings offer a sobering reminder that imaging is not an inexpensive proposition. In the National Archives' Electronic Access Project, which included manuscripts as well as graphic and photographic materials, image acquisition costs averaged $7.60 per image. These figures go up when one considers high-end imaging projects of museum holdings; the reported production rates to create 70–100 megabyte files range from 15 to 70 images a day."[32] A community of governmental, private, and organization-based funders have stepped in to help repositories as they recognize that the costs of digitization is significant and ongoing, but the need for their generosity highlights the problem. When external funding is required, these projects are less likely to be systematically adopted, because initiatives must compete against one another to win grants, leaving losing proposals without the money to proceed.[33]

Whether a project is conducted through a typical workflow or through MPLP-style methods, all digitization projects require the consent of copyright holders. Copyright regulates the reproduction, adaptation, distribution, performance, and display of all creative works for the life of an author and seventy years thereafter. Copyright is granted automatically to all works, even if they are unpublished, and is not automatically transferred with physical property. A repository usually owns a writers' papers without owning his or her copyright. The Copyright Act of 1976 allows archives and libraries to reproduce and distribute copies, but it does so only if they are for transformative and/or noncommercial use.[34] Despite the burden of digitization's costs, copyright is the more important element to consider when managing literary archives. While some authors may consent to digitization when they still hold copyright, most writers prefer to keep their papers offline owing to privacy concerns. Although donor agreements can stipulate only on-site use by restricting access to designated IP addresses, committing archival labor to digitize resources that can only be accessed on-site makes less financial and intellectual sense.

All *NAAL* authors are protected by copyright. The first writer to leave copyright protection will be Theodore Roethke, who died in 1963. His copyright will end in 2033. As fifty-eight *NAAL* authors are still living as of January 2016, it is impossible to know exactly when all twentieth-century authors will leave copyright protection, but a prediction is feasible. The youngest author in the data set, Jhumpa Lahiri, was born in 1967. As a result, all seventh edition *NAAL* authors should have their copyright opened by around 2130.[35] The 113 years between now and then demonstrates that copyright will continue to perpetuate the need for in-person access except in unique circumstances, such as in the case of Gabriel García Márquez's papers.

García Márquez is best known for his masterpiece, *One Hundred Years of Solitude* (1967). As a Colombian author, he is not included in *NAAL*. The Ransom Center bought García Márquez's collection for $2.2 million in November 2014. As of the time of the collection's acquisition, García Márquez already had twenty-eight books in English devoted to his work. Twenty-four were written after García Márquez won the Nobel Prize in 1982, and six were written in 2010.[36] The Ransom Center accordingly devoted significant resources to managing García Márquez's work by obtaining a bilingual archivist who provided item-level appraisal before a substantial portion of his papers were digitized with the consent of his estate.

To process García Márquez's collection, the Ransom Center found the archivist best suited to the task: Daniela Lozano, who is fluent in Spanish. Lozano is one of seventeen individuals at the Ransom Center whose employment is devoted to archival management. Lozano arranged and described the papers' 33.18 linear feet over the course of 2015 and 2016. As García Márquez died in 2014, the Ransom Center then obtained the permission of his estate to digitize 27,000 pages of his papers, which forms half of his overall collection. The extent of the digitization is considered "highly unusual" as García Márquez's collection is still under copyright. To complete the project, titled "Sharing 'Gabo' with the World," the Ransom Center sought a grant to support its Digital Collections Services department.[37]

The Ransom Center was successful in obtaining funding, for CLIR awarded it $126,730 to finish the proposed project in eighteen months.[38] Celia Shaheen, a digitization technician, took on this stage of the work. She described her process as follows: "Unlike the manuscripts and photographs in the archive, which were digitized using Epson flatbed scanners, the scrapbooks were photographed in the Ransom Center's photo studio using a Nikon D800 and studio lighting. The images were then processed through Adobe Bridge and Photoshop for re-formatting, cropping, and appending metadata. All of the scrapbooks that weren't spiral-bound were removed from their covers and unbound, so that each page, spread, and piece of ephemera (such as loose stickers, posters, and press release items) could be individually photographed. After I photographed them, the bolted scrapbooks were re-bound with better-fitting bolts by the Ransom Center's preservation and conservation division."[39] Shaheen summarized the technical aspects that go into imaging scrapbooks, including the types of scanners, photography equipment, setting, and software needed. But the most important aspect of Shaheen's narrative is that digitization does not necessarily mean taking one photograph per page; any items including mixed media require additional photography and conservation work.[40]

Digitization offers users greater access in return for more archival labor, as shown in Shaheen's description of her process. Jullianne Ballou, the project librarian who supervised the collection's digitization, remarked triumphantly in a 2017 Ransom Center press release that García Márquez's papers could now be accessed by anyone on the internet.[41] But this off-site access can be undertaken only if authors grant permission and if repositories are willing to commit their archivists' time to do so, which often requires obtaining substantial external funding. Furthermore, digitization, at least for literary archives and other materials requiring item-level review, involves more archival management, not less.

DIGITAL ARCHIVISTS

Born-digital content, content created on digital devices, can pose an even more fundamental intellectual and financial challenge to processing than does digitization. Born-digital files require decades-old principles to be reconsidered, such as when to preserve papers, how their integrity is maintained, how they are accessed by researchers, how they are organized by genre, which processing method is used, and how they are preserved. Therefore, it is most important for researchers to consider and cite archivists' role in preserving, organizing, and providing access to born-digital content.

Fully born-digital collections are not yet common. Hybrid collections, those consisting of both physical and digital content, are more frequently seen, but hybrid collections are only a stopgap to fully born digital records. To see how this shift will occur, *NAAL* authors can be divided by their sociological generation or when they deposited their papers. Generations depict how younger authors are more likely to create partial or fully digital collections. Deposit decades determine how this shift in composition practice is reflected in institutional holdings. After all, writers do not deposit their papers at the same point in their life. Generations demonstrate long-term trends in the authors' adaptation of technology, whereas deposit data indicates how quickly this change will arrive.

In the United States, generations are demarcated in roughly twenty-year intervals: the Greatest Generation (1901–24), the Silent Generation (1925–45), baby boomers (1946–60), Generation X (1961–80), and Generation Y, also known as the "millennials" (1981–2000).[42] As depicted in table 8, *NAAL* authors were born between 1903 and 1967, spanning four different generations: Lorine Niedecker is the oldest writer, and Jhumpa Lahiri is the youngest. Based on these generational definitions, 28 writers in the data set belong to the Greatest Generation, 50 to the Silent Generation, 22 to the baby boomers, and 2 to Generation X. No writers from Generation Y are included in *NAAL*, the first cohort of digital natives, because the seventh edition of the anthology was published in 2002, when the oldest members of Generation Y would have been only twenty-one years old. By generation and rounded to the nearest whole number, 93 percent of Greatest Generation and 90 percent of Silent Generation authors placed their papers in comparison with 36 percent of baby boomers and 0 percent of Generation X writers.

Already-acquired literary archives show a trend toward the increasing inclusion of digital content. Yet the holdings of people born prior to Generation Y contain significant digital content. Although only about 8 percent of placed Greatest Generation holdings include digital content, the proportion spikes in the collections belonging to the Silent Generation, the era with the greatest number of writers in *NAAL*. About 27 percent of the Silent Generation authors included digital materials in the content they gave or sold to repositories. Digital content already is a significant presence in repositories, and it will only continue to become more ubiquitous.

Examining the market by generation demonstrates that even those born early in the twentieth century used digital technologies; deposit decades depicted in table 9 show that these formats begin to appear in repositories during and after the 1980s. The first two decades of acquisitions with digital content showed very few incorporated this type of material into their collections. Rounding to the nearest whole number, 12 percent of writers who deposited their materials in the 1980s and 14 percent of authors in the 1990s

TABLE 8. *NAAL* authors' deposit rates with born-digital content by birth generation

Birth Generation	Collections (n)	Collections placed (n)	Collections with born-digital content (n)
Greatest Generation (b. 1901–1924)	28	26	2
Silent Generation (b. 1925–1945)	50	45	12
Baby Boomers (b. 1946–1960)	22	8	5
Generation X (b. 1961–1980)	2	0	0
Generation Y (b. 1981–2000)	0	0	0
Total	102	79	19

TABLE 9. *NAAL* authors' deposit rates with born-digital content by decade of deposit

Deposit decade	Collections placed (n)*	Collections with born-digital content (n)
1950s	1	0
1960s	7	0
1970s	4	0
1980s	17	2
1990s	21	3
2000s	18	8
2010s	10	6
Total	78	19

*Toni Cade Bambara does not have a placement date, so she is not counted.

had digital content. The percentage steadily increases across time. Forty-four percent of writers selling or donating their papers in the 2000s and 60 percent of authors active in the market in the 2010s included digital materials in their papers.

Other studies place these findings in context. For example, Beinecke Library archivist Michael Forstrom estimated that fifty-five collections at the library belonging to first-generation computer users included digital media.[43] These numbers demonstrate that while born-digital content is far from ubiquitous, its presence is already significant enough to change archival policies today.

Archivists recognized that born-digital content would change their profession as early as 1994. Australian archivist Adrian Cunningham argued that because file types become dated so quickly, archivists should establish software and hardware standards for incoming material. He then wrote a follow-up article five years later decrying the lack of the attention to this issue. Others tried to amplify his critique. In March 1996, Paul Conway, an archivist and associate professor at the University of Michigan, wrote a white paper on the preservation of digital image files and weighed the difficulty of doing so given "the mathematics of compression and communication."[44]

Nearly a decade later, Drexel University archivist and associate teaching professor of archival studies Susan E. Davis observed that, unfortunately, Cunningham's and Conway's warnings continued to be ignored in higher education. Government archivists remained the specialty's innovators because they were required to manage these materials, while those employed by colleges and universities could choose whether to accept them or not. Although avoiding born-digital content often seemed to be an ethical way to evade stewarding materials a repository felt it could not manage, recently archivists have begun to argue that such neglect leads to digital records' destruction. Like it or not, the present and future record depends on facing these challenges.[45]

To catch up, academic archivists created a variety of venues to discuss best practices in the management of born-digital materials. Archivists who need to obtain advice online can view the recommendation of the Online Computer Library Center (OCLC) that processing born-digital content should be done on a clean workstation without access to the internet to limit the possibility of viruses. This workstation should have a write blocker to prevent metadata from being altered on original files. Additionally, archivists should create project directories; document procedures on readme files; assign checksums, algorithmically generate numbers that record if changes have been made to a file's content; and review sensitive content. Archivists also can visit their professional organization, the Society for American Archivists, which has a more extensive checklist of steps to engage in digital preservation. Additional working groups document recommendations for considering decryption and file recovery as well as how and why to provide emulation, discussed further below, of born-digital content.[46]

Specialized professional organizations have appeared on both sides of the Atlantic as another way to meet these needs. In 2002, the Digital Preservation Coalition (DPC) was founded in England and Wales. The DPC wishes to create a social climate that understands the needs of digital preservation, provide a workforce trained to respond to these challenges, foster better techniques for preservation, and engage in collaborative enterprises outside the coalition. In the United States, the SAA supports the Electronic Records Section, which "functions as a locus of expertise, leadership, and information sharing for SAA regarding management and preservation of records in electronic form." The Electronic Records Section created a blog in 2015 which posts once per month at minimum on topics related to news and resources on the subject. The society also manages publications for archivists engaged in digital records preservation, with venues including a press, the *American Archivist* journal, and a newsletter (*Archival Outlook*).[47]

Those who want certification for their expertise in managing digital content can seek a digital archives specialist (DAS) certificate from SAA. The Association of Research Libraries (ARL) believes the DAS is the best way to retrain its workforce to manage born-digital holdings. Obtaining a DAS certificate requires nine courses and a comprehensive exam. Courses are divided into four tiers: foundational, tactical and strategic, tools and services, and transformational. Foundational courses include such topics as introduction to email preservation; tactical courses incorporate subjects such as accessioning and ingest of digital records; tools and services courses offer content like preservation formats in the context of PDF; and transformational sessions focus on such concerns as user experience design and digital archives.[48] After five years elapse, DAS holders must take four continuing education courses to maintain their certification. To accelerate reskilling, ARL also wants to create an intensive one-week workshop based on this course content.

Yet the future of the archival profession requires new educational tracks, not just additional information for professionals already in the field. Among the fifty-nine American Library Association accredited master's programs in library and information studies, which include those in both the United States and Canada, students can choose among specializations focusing on digital content, including archival studies, digital libraries, and information systems design and analysis.[49] Roles associated with digital content management on average earn a 10 percent higher salary than do archivists and librarians with more traditional responsibilities.[50] Mary Kendig, a 2017 graduate of the University of Maryland's College of Information Studies who now works as a research administrator at the same university, notes that if you "interview current MLS [master's of library science] students and those who received their degree in the last 5 years . . . they quietly confess their degree did not adequately prepare them for the electronic record influx." As a result, employers often prefer to hire applicants with business, computer science, and engineering backgrounds.[51]

Digital archivists' challenges remain substantial despite the recent growth in born-digital training options. Born-digital materials must be acquired earlier in a content creator's life because creators are likely to lose content if it remains in their sole possession, accessed through not one but a variety of delivery technologies, appraised for its originality and type, processed through electronic batch methods, and delivered to patrons through migration or emulation. The decisions digital archivists make at each stage in the workflow will determine the content and structure of literary collections, expanding or limiting the range of interpretive possibilities.

Digital archivists must determine when born-digital content should be preserved. Before, records could be collected once creators finished using them. Now, a substantial portion of content will disappear if this practice continues. Richard Pearce-Moses explained the problem: "In a paper environment, records were an unintended by-product of other activities; records just happened. . . . [But with digital,] each time a document is opened, revised, then saved, the previous version disappears unless consciously preserved. Few database systems are designed to be able to roll back data so that it is possible to see the state of the data at any given point in the past; data is added, changed, and deleted, with no thought to preserving older data for future reference. The challenge of paper documents is an excess of irrelevant memory captured in piles of paper. The challenge of electronic records is incremental amnesia."[52] Pearce-Moses suggested that as born-digital content becomes more ubiquitous, literary collections increasingly will hold only final drafts. As a result, the utility of literary collections in depicting an author's compositional process could diminish. In 2009, the National Endowment for the Humanities (NEH) validated the concern voiced by Pearce-Moses. In a survey of major contemporary authors, the NEH found that when born-digital content was not harvested early, significant content was lost. For example, Zadie Smith simply saved over earlier versions of her writing. In 2013, the British Library developed the idea of enhanced curation to correct this problem. Under enhanced curation, archivists began acquiring content from authors while they are still working to preserve and allow researchers access to digital content sooner. That same year, Stephen Enniss used the occasion of his appointment to the directorship of the Ransom Center to endorse this method.[53]

While the industry advocates for enhanced curation, early intervention in a writer's career alters the content and structure of materials in a way inorganic to the writer. This intervention does not mean that the writing itself is changed. Write blockers prevent documents from external intervention. Rather, the problem occurs when writers unconsciously shift their behavior because they know their materials will be observed sooner rather than later. What makes a collection interesting is what it reveals about an author. An author who chooses to write over his or her files and thus not leave drafts of the process is making a choice, even if it is embedded in the technology.[54] Furthermore, enhanced curation relies on determining who is worth collecting early in an author's career. Writers who achieve critical acclaim later in their lifetime will leave fewer records. The NEH accepts that if an author chooses to engage in benign neglect—allowing the loss of drafts and other content—the literary archive should reflect the writer's preference accordingly.

Once digital files are acquired, they must be accessed, but most repositories do not own the correct delivery technology for the media in question. In fact, "it is highly unlikely that any single organization (even the Library of Congress or the British Library) will be able to keep in operation the entire physical history of computing and its requisite media."[55] This point is critical as the history of recording technology shows what happens when machines are not collected alongside their content. Many repositories hold wax cylinders, the oldest form of recording music, but few acquired players. As a result, users are left with boxes of antiquated recording technology with no way to access their contents.[56] Floppy disks, zip drives, and other formats could easily be subject to similar loss. Outsourcing materials to third-party service providers poses its own costs.[57] Although such providers can capture content on obsolete formats due to their extensive inventory of hardware types, their work does not come cheap.

The OCLC proposed to manage this problem by creating locations that provide software and workstations for antiquated technology (SWAT), which would be available to repositories that need to access content in obsolete formats. Instead of asking institutions to independently hold their own hardware or completely outsource their born-digital content to third-party vendors, SWATs could be nonprofit solutions to the problem. Repositories could self-select to be SWAT sites that either specialize in a wide range of platforms or in one specialized area. The SWAT site would only transfer content to the updated format: the institution would need to manage it through its chosen methods of arrangement, description, and preservation. The objective would be to meet the challenge of managing born-digital content in a flexible way, rather than requiring institutions to find external funding or by abrogating responsibility to for-profit enterprises.[58]

Digital archival appraisal also is challenged by how records that previously had stable genres, for example, journals and correspondence, now occur together on new platforms. Facebook, Twitter, and Instagram generate feeds that resemble diaries while fostering epistolary connections. Of these platforms, Twitter receives the most attention from authors because it emphasizes words over images, unlike Instagram, and encourages a wider audience than Facebook, which began as a way in which to connect people who already knew each other.

In the *New York Times*, Adam Kirsch and Anna Holmes pondered that Charles Dickens and Oscar Wilde "would surely have loved Twitter."[59] However, contemporary authors' feelings bifurcate. For example, Margaret Atwood is fond of Twitter, whereas Jonathan Franzen dismisses it. Scholars have already begun to comment on both writers' approaches to the platform. Lorraine York dedicated a chapter of her book, *Margaret Atwood and the Labour of Literary Celebrity* (2013), to Atwood's use of Twitter. York applauded Atwood as an "interactive technology trendsetter" who realized early on that the key is for authors "to engage with new media promotional tools while carefully guarding the high-culture atmosphere of the transaction."[60] By contrast, commentators critiqued Franzen for dismissing social media. As Alison Flood in the *Guardian* pointed out, Franzen is a white male author who won the National Book Award and writes for the *New Yorker*. As such, he has the cultural capital to choose to avoid venues that women, people of color, and more up-and-coming writers use to create an audience.[61]

Social media could become a problem within the literary archives market because twenty-first-century authors will have their internet use reflected in their content. More writers are likely to be Atwoods than Franzens. To continue to use Twitter as an example, Twitter aggregates content from different genres into its one space. Although Twitter feeds can be scraped—extracted from a platform to be preserved and analyzed—this practice omits rich contextual details. Furthermore, not all social media platforms allow scraping: Facebook currently blocks the process.[62]

Once digital archivists overcome the hurdle of preserving digital content, they must choose how to arrange it. One proposed technique is batch archival processing, which uses digital tools, rather than humans, to examine collection contents, speeding up processing time at every stage "from creating the file catalog to ingesting files into a digital repository." Notably, a literary collection served as the test case for batch archival processing. A British playwright named Arnold Wesker, whose papers the Harry Ransom Center began to acquire in 2000, contained "75 3.5-inch floppy disks and one Zip disk" that together represented "more than seven thousand text files, for a total size of 100.01 MB." But completing batch processing required creating a disk inventory and file catalog as well as refreshing all content into current file types before preparing the metadata and performing the ingest. Even ingest, that is, pulling files into an archival backup, required several considerations, such as that of file extensions, passwords, corrupted content, original order, and duplicates.[63]

Lastly, digital archivists must choose the interface which delivers content to researchers. Born-digital content may be collected and even preserved, but it frequently remains closed as archives cannot always provide access through the two options currently available: "migration" and "emulation."[64]

Migration involves "the process of moving data from one information system or storage medium to another to ensure continued access to the information as the system or medium becomes obsolete or degrades over time."[65] In practice, migration in an archival setting results in transforming content and then moving it into a searchable database of PDFs. Researchers gain access to the content in an easily searchable format, but their experience is compromised by the loss of the information's original environment, which may contain contextual clues as to how and why that content was created. However, this loss is not enough to override the option's benefits, namely, that migration offers digital archivists faster and cheaper processing.

Alternatively, emulation gives researchers the media-rich environment they prefer by allowing contemporary machines to "imitate the functionality of obsolete computer platforms" by providing users with a copy of the original content and user interface.[66] As early as 1988, Jeff Rothenberg argued that emulation was the only workable solution for digital preservation.[67] Five years later, Anne Gilliland-Swetland began to consider the importance of the "evidential value of the system as a whole" and reflected on how computing environments required their own provenance.[68] Factors such as the size, shape, and provenance of a sheet of paper; the type of pen or pencil; the quality of ink or lead; the presence or absence of later revisions by the author or others; or even the type of desk on which the writing occurred contribute to how physical writing unfolds. Similar factors constrain authors who chose to write on digital devices. The ergonomics of an author's machine, which word processing program is used, the font style and size selected, if revisions were made by creating subsequent documents or if amendments to the original text were noted through an option like Microsoft Word's Track Changes feature, and even how an author arranged his or her files, programs, and apps:

these choices give researchers clues as to how a writer works. But these clues require emulation.

Emulation is not a typical delivery service due to its cost. Few repositories can provide the resources necessary to create emulations of literary collections. To date, Salman Rushdie's collection at Emory's Rose Library provides the most famous example of how emulation simulates an author's original digital environment for the benefit of researchers. Rushdie's Series 11, dedicated to born-digital contents, contains the contents of "one Macintosh Performa 5400/180, one Macintosh PowerBook 5300c, two Macintosh PowerBook G3 models, and one SmartDisk WFL60 FireLite 2.5-inch FireWire Portable Hard Drive." And, "at present, only the Macintosh Performa 5400/180" has been processed.[69] Rose Library both migrated and emulated the Performa in 2010, but the emulation is what obtained national recognition.

The *New Yorker*, *New York Times*, and *Atlantic* all reported on the emulation. Dan Rockmore for the *New Yorker* wrote, "The experience of poking around in an early computer environment, with its block fonts, file icons, and backdrops, can inspire a special sort of nostalgia, especially for those nerdy and old enough to remember their own first computer." Want to find out what games Rushdie "was playing while working under a fatwa"? If so, the emulation provides an answer. Yet Patricia Cohen for the *New York Times* suggests that while emulation seems "to promise future biographers and literary scholars a digital wonderland . . . this digital idyll has its own set of problems," for born-digital content is difficult to preserve. Devyani Saltzman for the *Atlantic* suggested that preservation is difficult not only for technical reasons but for ethical ones too, as "the hidden data makes it clear how thin the line is between Rushdie's literary legacy and private thoughts, particularly because he's an author who is still living."[70] This voyeuristic impression is amplified by the fact that the intent of the emulation was not to increase the ease of information access but rather to simulate the "look and feel" of Rushdie's machine. An emulation helps researchers understand Rushdie not from the perspective of the content in his born-digital files but from how they experience navigating his digital space.[71] Ironically, Erika Farr, who managed the programmers and archivists who created the emulation, found that the users preferred to work with migrated materials rather than those that were emulated, as the former provided a smoother research experience—one devoid of the annoyances which occur when using dated software.

An earlier example of emulation comes from a simulation created for fans of the late 1990s teen television show *Dawson's Creek*. The WB, the television network that created the show, provoked its viewers with the question: "Ever wish you could see inside someone's computer? . . . Someone like one of your favorite characters on Dawson's Creek? Well, here's your chance! Each week one of four different desktops appears here—Dawson's, Joey's, Pacey's, or Jen's! Between the episodes, you can delve into their journals, emails, instant message chats—even their trash cans! Just click 'Go' to enter."[72] Since the characters of *Dawson's Creek* are fictional, the WB did not need to emulate anything. What fans viewed was made from scratch and therefore worked better than what researchers confront with the real Rushdie emulation.

That the WB used emulation as a marketing strategy years before archivists adapted it for their preservation protocol poses the intriguing question of why the WB used the construct in the first place. The answer is that the WB saw curiosity about the digital lives of the show's characters as a natural outgrowth of watching the show. As *Dawson's Creek* ran between 1998 and 2003, teenagers in this era were more likely to leave evidence of their private thoughts on their computers, rather than in print journals or letters. The show's marketing team knew that a digital interface could retain clues as to the character's personality just as physical objects like diaries that would have been more common in earlier eras. With different backgrounds, applications, organization, and writing styles, each machine could be tailored to its user. Plus, the variety of communication tools on a computer could showcase how the character supposedly acted in different settings. Outward-facing thoughts, such as those that would be expressed in a regular conversation, could be found in instant messages, while private ruminations could be in journals. The contrast provided a wider range of information about the characters than would otherwise be expressed in the television show.

Researchers exploring emulations of literary papers made by digital archivists are not dissimilar to fans exploring a character's computer created by marketers. But what seems acceptable for curious teenagers interested in fictional lives can become potentially problematic for scholars. Digital archivists, as well as their colleagues managing paper-based and digitized content, must not only arrange and describe literary archives but also anticipate what ethical quandaries may occur. In the process, these professionals shape what researchers can see and what outcomes they determine.

CONCLUSION

Although corporate (anonymous) authorship is not ubiquitous, the fact that archivists are rarely named in finding aids prevents scholars from citing archivists, diminishing the value of their professional work as processors while amplifying their reference role and obscuring the history of how archivists shaped the literary archives market. But institutions and scholars are not solely at fault. Archivists need to assert their impact on literary collections, whether they are born digital or paper based, by embracing their value as professionals and educating scholars about how archival workflows influence researchers' conclusions. After all, a literary archive's provenance includes not only the author but also all others whose hands manage the transfer, acquisition, and arrangement of a writer's papers.

The final chapter of *Placing Papers* explores why scholars and the public seek access to literary papers in the first place, thus creating the demand that generates the literary archives market that begins with an author and ends with the archivist. A hint: it is not just television fans who like to see behind the scenes. Voyeurism may appear unseemly, especially for scholars, but that does not lessen its allure—or its risks.

CHAPTER 6

Access

Scholars and the Public

It is in the rough drafts, the handwritten documents of the writing process, that one concretely glimpses writing in the act of being born.

—Pierre-Marc de Biasi

Authors engage in the literary archives market to gain financial benefits and ensure their legacy. Yet living authors who deposit their papers face the problem of how to manage the personal access scholars and the public gain from these archival bodies. Even though repositories work with writers to explain what will be seen and negotiate, when necessary, to close sensitive content, some authors feel that their privacy is breached after depositing their papers. These writers may then seek to protect their privacy by preventing scholars from directly quoting their open collections. But authors who choose to sell or donate their papers must accept that they elected to provide access to their archival body. After all, those who die before deciding if and where to place their papers are even more susceptible to intellectual exploitation, especially when the writer in question suffers an untimely death. Such an archival body is likely to be fetishized as one of the market's most enticing commodities and subject to the most academic and popular interest.

ACCESS

A literary archive's scholarly value is based on fame, whereas its public value derives from celebrity. On first approach, this statement appears redundant. After all, "fame" and "celebrity" are synonymous. Yet each term has a distinctive connotation: "The object of celebrity is the person; the object of fame is some accomplishment, action, or creative work."[1] While authors who participate in the trade for writers' papers earn the interest of repositories through their fame, they are acquired owing to institutional desire to access their celebrity.

Celebrity authors loom larger than their art. At the turn of the century Americans needed artists who they could believe were of equal stature to those found in Europe. Henry James fit the bill, as his novels demonstrated sophisticated prose and cosmopolitan milieus. The problem was that the public did not read his novels. In the end, his cultural appeal "far exceeded his sales."[2] More recent literary celebrities suffered similar results. In 2000, Ronna C. Johnson complained that Jack Kerouac's artistic achievements were undervalued because "his writing has been overshadowed by his mass culture image," such as when his likeness, along with Allen Ginsberg's, was used to sell khakis for the Gap. Presumably, the company thought these writers portrayed their ideal San Francisco cool as bohemian Californians with critically acclaimed, yet accessible books.[3]

Even though "commodified hip" can overshadow an author's reputation, many current authors rationally decide to gamble their legacy on a wider public audience.[4] By engaging in self-branding, they bolster their chances of being remembered. Susan Orlean wrote *The Orchid Thief* (1998), a nonfiction book that became the film *Adaptation* (2002). In the film, Orlean was played by Meryl Streep. Orlean is also a staff writer for the *New Yorker*, composed the story "Life's Swell" for *Outside*, which became another movie, *Blue Crush* (2002); and is a frequent judge of nonfiction awards. Despite her success, Orlean devotes a significant portion of her time to online engagement to drive additional public interest. In an interview with Manjula Martin, Orlean confessed that what she was doing, "which I cringe at, but it's a reality, is *branding*." After all, without widespread name recognition linking her to a certain type of lifestyle or perspective, she is likely to be forgotten. Orlean knows that literary celebrities must become archetypes known for their identity as much as their art.[5]

Literary celebrity studies are a rapidly expanding field. Thirteen academic books were published on the topic in the last seventeen years, with subjects spanning American, British, and Canadian literature from the nineteenth to the twenty-first century. Most of these volumes are dedicated to historical surveys of celebrity authors from a specific period and emphasize the outsized importance of individuals as a hallmark of media culture.

Yet learning about notable individuals without said individual learning similar information about oneself is voyeuristic, because we are "get[ting] our pleasure from watching others' lives without having to interact with them."[6] Simply reading scholarship about literary celebrities can be voyeuristic, but directly interacting with primary sources—such as an author's literary archive—is even more so. Scholars relish learning intimate details of a writer's life, but few will admit that the pleasure of research is supported by the comfort of not having to engage that person face-to-face. Furthermore, scholars decline to acknowledge that the fetishization of literary manuscripts is based on their desire to have physical contact with a writer. In turn, authors who place their papers may recognize that they are agreeing to become research subjects, though they do not accurately predict how they will feel about this transformation in identity. A worst-case scenario is that authors will seek to protect their privacy by pursuing legal means to restrict scholarship resulting from their collections.

Consider how Dana Gioia, the chairperson for the National Endowment for the Arts from 2003 to 2008 and poet laureate of California from 2015 to 2018, describes viewing literary manuscripts. In his widely recirculated article on the power of manuscripts, "The Hand of the Poet," Gioia quotes Walt Whitman—"who touches this, touches a man"—before pondering why the collection of literary manuscripts is rarely considered as a topic for critical inquiry: "Thousands of librarians, curators, dealers, and scholars—as well as numerous private collectors—are currently building huge archives of primary materials. No other culture in history has even approached the level of activity now routine in America. Our institutions spend vast sums to acquire and house manuscript materials. . . . Without fully articulating why, the culture has agreed that, even in an era of shrinking resources, collecting and preserving literary manuscripts is a priority." Gioia then poses a question: why does American culture engage in such systematic financial investment in a field that it has thought so little about? He finds his answers in the physical body of the author, which gives literary manuscripts what he calls their magical (intangible) value. The magical value is what attracts scholars to study a manuscript; a document's meaningful value is what scholars do with that manuscript.[7]

A manuscript's magical value makes it a fetish. Even though the word "fetish" occurs only once in "The Hand of the Poet," when Gioia calls literary manuscripts' ability to generate a "direct and unmediated physical link between the viewer and author" like "a holy relic or shamanistic fetish," Gioia uses language that closely parallels how fetishes are described. For example, he explains that handwritten papers possess an "aura of total authenticity" that exceeds what can be found in digital copies. What matters is that a literary archive is an expansion of the writer's body, not just his or her mind.[8]

The scholarly discussion defining fetishism and its presence in contemporary culture is extensive. Most theorists begin their analysis from Karl Marx's definition. Marx described fetishism as a secret, explaining how objects take on fetishistic qualities when they are transformed from "an extremely obvious, trivial thing" to items "abounding in metaphysical subtleties and theological niceties." The metaphysical and theological aura Marx detected is but a remnant of "the definite social relation between men themselves which assumes . . . the fantastic form of a relation between things."[9] In other words, Marx saw fetishized objects as representing connections between people—a critical point as Gioia locates manuscripts' magical value in their ability to link author to researcher through a physical object.

Scholars who revere a particular writer can come to treasure a manuscript so much that they see it not as a fetish, an object that links them to an author, but as a part of that author. Consider Chauncey Tinker of Yale University, whose career was summarized in chapter 4. Tinker's former student Maynard Mack reflected that Tinker had an "undisguised love for these documents" and treated such papers "as if it were a person in the room."[10] Pierre-Marc de Biasi opined that writers' papers give concrete "glimpses [of] writing in the act of being born," whereas Susan Howe depicted her time in archives "as a séance" where she spent time summoning and mourning dead authors.[11]

Occasionally, embodiment became literal rather than figurative. Jacqueline Rose called this literal embodiment the *corps morcelé*, the "body in bits and pieces." After all, papers can include realia connected to the body, such as Walt Whitman's glasses or T. S. Eliot's waistcoat, or items taken from the body. For example, Victorians used to exchange hair as a sign of attachment; hairwork, the practice of creating art, jewelry, and wreaths out of hair would remain popular until the mid-1920s. As a result, many archives and museums collected notable people's hair. Harry Ransom derided the practice in 1956 by saying "only morbid curiosity seems to justify the preservation anywhere—much less in Austin, Texas—of miscellaneous locks of hair from the heads of statesmen like Napoleon and poets like Shelley." He continued: those "haircut museum[s] will never, never contribute to learning." Nevertheless, some archives and museums continue to preserve bodily specimens within their archival bodies. Stanford chose to preserve William Saroyan's mustache.[12] And, as Andrei Codrescu recounted in *Bibliodeath* (2012), Richard Brautigan's papers at the University of California, Berkeley, contain remnants of his brain. Brautigan committed suicide over his final manuscript, which meant that anyone who came to see the papers would be handling materials stained with his cerebellum. Musing on this grisly fact, Codrescu described the documents as blending "the flesh and the word made flesh."[13] Sometimes literary collections become archival bodies figuratively in the mind of researchers, while other times embodiment is made literal.

SCHOLARS

When scholars admit to their interest in the bodies of authors, they acknowledge their fetishization of literary manuscripts. By conducting research, they are engaging in voyeurism, for they are taking pleasure in seeing these archival bodies. But openly acknowledging such an emotional connection to their subject of study is discouraged; maintaining—or at least appearing to maintain—critical distance is necessary to guard against what Matthew Kirschenbaum calls "vulgar author worship."[14]

Some scholars do resist this requirement. Linköping University professor Margrit Shildrick embraces her archival encounters as she believes they help her gain greater understanding of her research. She finds that "to touch and be touched speaks to our exposure to, and immersion in, the world of others, and to the capacity to be moved beyond reason, in the space of shared vulnerabilities."[15] Shildrick engages emotionally with her scholarship through her awareness of a document's physical properties, which help her become more empathetic and thus more sensitive to the interpretative complexities of the materials. Catherine Bates imagines that scholarship does not need to come from a cool remove from its subject. Rather, she believes deep study can consist of recognizing and exploring connections, even when it exceeds the boundaries academics try to maintain, arguing that "when a personal, intimate engagement is made," scholars are more likely to touch, listen, and question, thereby moving "beyond reductive thinking."[16] In effect, Bates reveals that scholars are likely to feel emotions while in the presence of manuscripts on which their careers are based. Feelings cannot be taken out of academic work; scholars simply decide whether they should behave in a way academia deems appropriate.

Some scholars attempt to ameliorate this problem by peppering their narratives with scientific terminology that focuses on either the senses of sight (optic) or touch (haptic). Feminist researchers first argued that those who wish to avoid "false claim of neutrality and universality" should consider the scholar's body.[17] Shildrick's description of her archival work fits this mode of analysis, which has become increasingly popular in literary studies over the past five years. Jamie A. Lee used this tactic when she investigated how repositories structure encounters with their collections. Lee became sensitive to the "certain piqued, unnamed and unknown affective and haptic responses within the visitor to the archives" and advocated for a greater awareness of the way in which "embodied understandings of the archives themselves" can help transform inquiry.[18]

Repositories know that using voyeuristic language based on the fetishistic properties of manuscripts lures scholars and the public alike. Consider how the New York Public Library promoted its exhibition *Original Manuscripts by 100 Masters from John Donne to Julia Alvarez*. The library enthused that manuscripts provide "an intimate view of the creative process," inviting viewers to ogle papers in terminology that combines the stimulation of seeing with the value of feeling.[19] The view emphasizes optics, whereas the papers themselves, presumably written by hand, provide haptic value. While on display, the manuscripts cannot be touched, but visitors remain interested due to the opportunity to see physical traces of the author.

Scholars value the optic properties of documents, but haptic access is even more important. Recall the common parental warning to look, not touch. After all, only authorities, whether they are simply adults or curators in an institution, are empowered to touch or invite others to touch important objects. The entreaty not to touch manuscripts is based on the presence of hand oil, which degrades what it contacts. But who can touch materials historically is less based on preservation practice than on class differences. Nineteenth-century British museums allowed their patrons to touch their objects; doing so was understood to be necessary for full understanding and enjoyment. As visitors became more working class, museums slowly withdrew the privilege to touch their holdings. Physical access to manuscripts remains a highly prized asset for both magical and meaningful reasons, although repository restrictions have lessened in recent years. Educators invite students to touch manuscripts, a reversal of decades of practice that not just discouraged such proximity but also forbade it entirely.[20] Now the primary reason to ask students to avoid touching manuscripts concerns when materials are especially fragile.

Digitization seems like a solution for delicate papers as well as to broaden access for students and scholars who cannot visit collections on-site. However, examining digitized documents rather than originals can be problematic. Michelle Moravec, an associate professor at Rosemont College, argues that digitization obscures an item's material qualities and provides a different mode of access than working with original documents. April Hathcock, a former lawyer who is currently New York University's scholarly communications librarian, asserts that digitization without the consent of all contributing parties can violate personal or community boundaries, especially in the case of texts authored by marginalized people and groups.[21] Thus, working in person with materials is seen as preferable whenever possible, once again instantiating the value of haptic over optic access.

The scholar's engagement with the author's archival body assumes that the author, if he or she is living, will accept objectification. After all, writers agreed to donate or sell their papers to a repository and thus to transform their life and work into an archival body. But some authors recoil once scholars begin to show an interest in their papers, because they are disinclined to share their private life or are afraid of what scholars might see. In her many articles dedicated to the topic, former Huntington Library curator Sara S. Hodson summarized authors' concerns with evocative images of researchers pillaging the library stacks and digging in the archives to find salacious details.

Although public and scholarly interest cannot be rebuffed just because a "voyeuristic thirst for details of others' private lives" appears to be a motivating factor, repositories can attempt to prevent such scholarship by imposing privacy regulations. Archivists adopted an ethical standard to manage how researchers access the donor content when, in 1992, the Society of American Archivists recommended valuing "the privacy of individuals who created, or are the subjects of, documentary materials of long-term value, especially those who had no voice in the disposition of materials."[22] Accordingly, the council suggested that those who deserve the most protection are people who appear in collections yet who did not make the choice to place their papers in the repository. This situation could occur in literary archives when an author writes to a colleague, that colleague replies, and then the author keeps the reply. Decades later, when the letter goes into an author's literary archive, which is then deposited at a repository, the colleague might be surprised to find his or her materials as a part of the collection.

Currently, donors can decide which records are most likely to be sensitive, but a donor's choices can lead to disagreements between the author and the repository's archivist or curator. A donor may opt to restrict papers to preserve his or her relationships, while archivists and curators advocate for access whenever possible. While representatives of repositories wish to observe a donor's needs, often archivists and curators believe that sensitive papers should be reviewed as to if they are appropriate for deposit rather than placed in a repository and then restricted.[23]

Solutions to this problem include either observing the copyright of the contact's papers or approving researchers' requests on a case-by-case basis. As copyright ends seventy years after death, open papers—those that could be both accessed and cited—might be limited to those attributed to persons who either approve or no longer hold a copyright claim. Case-by-case approval, granted either by an author or his/her executor, is a more common solution. However, this policy automatically restricts collection contents to anyone with the wherewithal and time to make a personal request, privileging some researchers over others. Furthermore, case-by-case approval can quickly become onerous for authors who underestimate how time-consuming managing researchers' requests can quickly become.

An archivist cannot simply approve all researchers' requests once an author places his or her collection in their repository. Although the institution may own a writer's papers, the author or his/her executor still possesses copyright. The United States uses automatic copyright to protect individuals who create "original works of authorship." For example, a folktale without an original author, like "Snow White," can become the intellectual property of a contemporary writer when it is transcribed under his or her name using new language. Donald Barthelme wrote the novel *Snow White* (1967), and Anne Sexton composed the poem "Snow White and the Seven Dwarfs," which was published as a part of *Transformations* (1971).[24] Both Barthelme and Sexton's estates hold copyright to their written version of Snow White, but these estates cannot claim ownership of the tale itself.

Authors hold copyrights, not trademarks. Copyright applies to art and literature, whereas a trademark is meant for companies. Officially, trademarks are "a word, phrase, symbol, and/or design that identifies the source of the goods of one party from those of others." As a result, Walt Disney can claim the profits from the film adaptation *Snow White and the Seven Dwarfs* (1937), while Universal owns proceeds from another, *Snow White and the Huntsman* (2012). However, as Disney owns the trademark to "Snow White" as a phrase, Universal must pay Disney to use the name. Barthelme and Sexton did not have to pay Disney as their work fell under copyright instead of trademark. This example shows how intangible properties of shared cultural heritage are privatized through copyright or trademark to gain profit.[25]

Copyright also secures privacy. When Ian Hamilton quoted J. D. Salinger's unpublished letters in the draft of his biography of the author, Random House sued on Salinger's behalf in 1986. By 1987, Salinger successfully prevented the publication of the biography until the letters' content was expunged. He won because the quotations fell under copyright infringement, even though Hamilton accessed those letters legally in the libraries at Harvard, Princeton, and Texas. Hamilton's inability to quote or even paraphrase the letters ruined his manuscript, which was already out with reviewers. Forced to recall his book, Hamilton later revised it as a "literary adventure story," rather than a biography. The project got a new title—*In Search of J. D. Salinger: A Writing Life* (1988)—and a new promotional strategy when *People* published an account of Hamilton's struggles with his living subject.[26]

Authors and their estates may attempt to expand copyright to limit critical commentary. The James Joyce Estate, famous for preventing a generation of scholars and artists from citing or using Joyce's words, lost a settlement in 2007 and then again in 2009 to Carol Shloss, Stanford professor of English and author of *Lucia Joyce: To Dance in the Wake* (2003). The estate, headed by Joyce's grandson, Stephen James Joyce, who called academics "rats and lice," forced Shloss's publisher, Farrar, Straus and Giroux, to expunge quotations from fifty notebooks held at the University at Buffalo at the time of the book's publication. Without legal support from her publisher, Shloss capitulated. She was hardly alone. Many scholars before her faced similar pressure, among them Michael Groden, John Kidd, Eloise Knowlton, Brenda Maddox, and Danis Rose. One Joycean, Robert Spoo, was inspired by his experience battling the estate to start a new career—as a copyright lawyer. But Shloss was luckier than most. Hearing her complaints, the Stanford Law School Center for Internet and Society's Fair Use Project, aided by Doerner, Saunders, Daniel & Anderson of Tulsa and Howard Rice Nemerovski Canady Falk & Rabkin of San Francisco, eventually stepped in to help after the university declined to provide an indemnity. As a result, Shloss was able to make an effective appeal that the estate "attempt[ed] to interfere with Shloss' research, to stop publication of her book, to damage her relationship with her employer, and to misuse the copyrights they control" in 2007. Two years later, Shloss won legal fees of $240,000 from the estate.[27]

How copyright is interpreted is at stake in these battles. American copyright protections grew from the precedent of legal opinions. Samuel Warren and Louis Brandeis enumerated American privacy rights in 1890. Warren and Brandeis weighed examples from the United States, United Kingdom, and France to recognize that privacy extends to both person and property, but while personal privacy remained a stable category over time, conceptions of property rights shifted. Tangible and intangible property became equally weighed; Warren and Brandeis specifically named "the products and processes of the mind, as works of literature and art," as among one's intangible possessions.[28]

So-called yellow journalists, who entertained their readers with lurid tales and photographs at the turn of the century, provoked Warren and Brandeis to write their opinion. In it, Warren and Brandeis decried not only the use of cameras to peer into private domiciles but also the ways in which written content could be employed for salacious ends. For example, although a letter could be reprinted in full a newspaper to make a slanderous point, quotation was not necessary. A description of the letter alone could make a similar conclusion. As a result, they concluded that the right to protect one's privacy arose from an individual's innate right to be left alone. Additionally, they did not find a distinction between works created in response to professional or artistic interests and those created due to the course of life.[29]

Warren and Brandeis did not consider how privacy rights could be applied to literary archives. Their fourth provision, which summarizes that "the right to privacy ceases upon the publication of the facts by the individual, or with his consent," contains the language that is of most relevance to the Salinger case.[30] After all, placing papers in a repository open to the public would seem to support the concept that consent had been provided formally. But Warren and Brandeis's emphasis on protecting both the papers of work and life had residual effects on how the law would be imagined, articulated, and applied through intellectual property rights over the next hundred years, leading to Salinger's successful defense against Hamilton and Stephen James Joyce's effective intimidation of many scholars.

Intellectual property rights in the United States are quite strong. Historical accounts point out the twist in priorities that occurred when the United States transformed first from an agricultural to a manufacturing nation and then from a manufacturing hub to a country with an information economy. Each shift strengthened the enforcement of intellectual property rights. In the nineteenth century, the United States weakly applied intellectual property rights because the country had less innovation to protect. As the United States industrialized, enforcing these rights became more critical to support economic growth. Such rights remained just as valuable when the United States transitioned into an information and service-based economy aided in part by the digital revolution at the end of the twentieth century. Economic motives made intellectual property a value worth legally protecting over time.[31]

Salinger faced a conflict when he placed his papers in the literary archives market, thinking he could benefit from the trade while retaining his privacy. But what Salinger saw as private, scholars like Hamilton perceived as fair game. Disagreement was inevitable.[32] Furthermore, repositories need to satisfy their donors, but research institutions are predicated on the value of open information. Laws that sought to curtail unethical yellow journalists of the early twentieth century are being applied to today's researchers with unfortunate results.

Institutions need to protect both donor and researchers. Authors should carefully consider what it means to engage in the trade and imagine the drawbacks it entails as well as its possibilities. A sale or donation might be in a writer's financial self- interest, but authors who are not prepared to welcome researchers into their papers should limit their engagement with the literary archives market. Writers need to postpone placing their archival bodies until they feel comfortable opening their contents or opt to follow the example of James Baldwin's family from chapter 2. Baldwin's relatives closed the sections of his collection to which they were not comfortable providing access. While restriction is not ideal for repositories, when carefully negotiated it can be a middle ground that suits both parties.

THE PUBLIC

Authors' views of the public both parallel and diverge from their feelings toward scholars. Members of the public are just as driven by voyeurism, only they are more likely to seek an uncritical connection. As a result, authors may become uncomfortable with their readers' attention yet find themselves more willing to tolerate their interest.

Some repositories recognize fans' voyeurism by marketing to their interests directly. The Rosenbach, which holds an extensive set of papers related to the life and work of Marianne Moore, calls itself a "pilgrimage site for students and lovers of twentieth-century American art and literature." Granted, the Rosenbach does go above and beyond most repositories. Rather than providing visitors access to a literary collection in a workaday reading room, those who come to the repository can experience Moore's preserved living room complete with 2,500 personal items carefully moved from New York City to Philadelphia.[33]

The Ransom Center also is a pilgrimage site, albeit one that preserves only its authors' archival bodies, not their homes. One of the center's most significant recent additions, the David Foster Wallace collection, is the subject of intense popular interest. Wallace, a Generation X author not included in the seventh edition of the *NAAL*, is a rising star of late twentieth-century American literature.[34] Born in 1962, Wallace became a "high performance" product of the Program Era—which Mark McGurl defines as the postwar period in the United States during which the number of creative writing MFAs increased exponentially—before dying by suicide in 2008.[35] During his life, Wallace was most well-known for his book *Infinite Jest* (1996) and for winning the MacArthur "genius" award. His death was widely mourned. *GQ* even rhapsodized: "Here's a thing that's hard to imagine: being so inventive as a writer that when you die, the language is impoverished."[36]

Many readers focused their mourning on the papers associated with *The Pale King* (2011), Wallace's unfinished final novel. *The Pale King* documented the lives of Internal Revenue Service workers in Illinois. Bonnie Nadell, his agent, and Karen Green, his wife, found the novel's incomplete manuscript in his office. It was "a neat stack of manuscript, twelve chapters totaling nearly 250 pages" in addition to a disk with the chapters on it. As they continued to explore, they found "hundreds and hundreds of pages of his novel in progress . . . hard drives, file folders, three-ring binders, spiral-bound notebooks, and floppy disks."[37] Altogether, Nadell and Green found 150 potential chapters running to over a thousand pages.

Wallace's editor, Michael Pietsch, combed through *The Pale King*'s paper and digital manuscripts to piece together the novel. Pietsch acknowledged that his final product, which packaged Wallace's novel into 50 chapters and 548 pages, would look different if Wallace had been alive to finish it. But "given the choice between working to make this less-than-final text available as a book and placing it in a library where only scholars would read and comment on it, I didn't have a second's hesitation." Pietsch knew that the public wanted the final book. An incomplete book was better than no book at all. Plus, Pietsch believed Wallace wanted the work to be found due to how carefully the manuscript had been left; *The Pale King* was not "a classic case of Posthumous Great Novel, where scholars have gone into an estate and unearthed a manuscript the author probably would never want read," such as Harper Lee's *Go Set a Watchman*.[38]

In 2010, Nadell and Green, represented by Glenn Horowitz, first sent Wallace's earlier manuscripts and three hundred of his books to the Ransom Center. In April 2011, the papers related to *The Pale King* arrived after the novel was published. With the collection complete, Stephen Cooper immediately arranged the papers, and the Ransom Center digitized a few of the notes as a preview.[39]

Wallace's collection quickly found its academic and public audience, which became known collectively as the "Wallace Industry." Molly Schwartzburg reported the papers' extensive use by doctoral students in 2010, although she did not provide the number of researchers who came to use the collection. In 2011, the Awl, a popular news and culture website, dispatched a journalist to find "the paradox of Wallace's humor and good-natured candor, the qualities so many of his readers enjoyed most, set against the many secrets there have always been around his private life."[40] In 2012, the academic journal *Studies in the Novel* dedicated two issues to Wallace, one of which was entirely concerned with his final volume and other of which was a compilation of essays dedicated to Wallace's work. In 2014, *English Studies: A Journal of English Language and Literature* released a special issue dedicated only to *The Pale King*. Then, *The End of the Tour* (2015), a movie dedicated to the *Infinite Jest* book tour, was released. By 2017, Wallace's scholarly society had founded the peer-reviewed *Journal of David Foster Wallace Studies*. Few authors can boast of such quick and diverse interest in their papers.

Wallace's papers form the perfect archival body. He is a highly regarded contemporary author who incites public notice and academic credibility. To readers, Wallace is a genius—validated by the MacArthur grant, no less—who rejected academic life and wrote on topics like tennis and politics. To scholars, Wallace commands considerable intellectual authority for composing such novels as *Infinite Jest* and *The Pale King*.[41] Mark McGurl even described Wallace as "a leading candidate for contemporary canonization."[42]

Kathleen Fitzpatrick, former managing editor of the *Publications of the Modern Language Association*, responded in alarm to the widespread preoccupation with Wallace's literary collection. Fitzpatrick reminded her academic peers to be careful as they indulged their interest in Wallace's life and career. The collection at the Ransom Center might have rich research potential, but Fitzpatrick warned those visiting the manuscripts to avoid transference, the mistake of feeling a connection to an author is the same as having one. She chided scholars that affective connections felt in the archive do not translate into "a relationship, however imagined, with the man himself."[43] In other words, Fitzpatrick wanted her colleagues to avoid fetishizing Wallace's archival body.

Fitzpatrick saved her most important criticism for the public. She was especially wary of the phenomenon she observed when reading online articles about Wallace's death: "The public outpouring of grief in the wake of Wallace's death, for instance, was worryingly reminiscent of the spectacle surrounding Kurt Cobain's death—on the one hand, a clear indication of the deep connection that his fans felt, through his work, to Wallace himself; on the other, an unhealthy transformation of artist into celebrity fetish object, and of a private tragedy into a public performance."[44] Fitzpatrick recognized that Wallace was one of a few literary figures whose death could prompt such mourning. Wallace's achievements gained him a large academic and popular following, but Fitzpatrick realized that it was his suicide that transformed this acclaim into veneration.

Max Ross, a columnist for *Open Letters Monthly*, agreed with Fitzpatrick's observation even though he did precisely what Fitzpatrick warned against—he visited Wallace's literary collection due to the mode of his death. Ross wrote, "I'm positive that, even if the archives had nevertheless existed, we wouldn't have traveled to Texas if Wallace hadn't killed himself. This was the wholly known and fiercely unacknowledged component of the trip. Because acknowledging would force us to ask *why* we would travel 1700 miles to see the archives of a writer we admired to varying degrees, but only if he were dead."[45] Scholars know they should hide their inclination to turn their research materials into fetishized objects; likewise, members of the public are loathe to admit the reason behind their voyeuristic impulses.

Understanding the "exact brand of sadness" of an author such as Wallace reveals that the symbolic weight of a writer is based on his or her brand, one that current authors intentionally build to help create a legacy.[46] Yet successful brands, like J. D. Salinger's, invite academic and public interest. Public adulation is less critical of authors and therefore less threatening to their sense of their life and work, yet both scholars and general readers are prone to confuse an imagined connection with a real one. This phenomenon is how a literary collection becomes a fetishized archival body. Furthermore, as Wallace's career shows, an author's brand can be bolstered by suicide. Wallace's biography has a particularly apt title: *Every Love Story Is a Ghost Story*. The sentiment applies to any aspiring literary celebrity with a potential archival body.

CONCLUSION

In his documentation of voyeurism in contemporary American culture, Clay Calvert explained that "one of the major social forces driving voyeurism is our changing conception of what information should remain closed and private and, concomitantly, what information should be made open and available to the public."[47] Authors on the literary archives market are not immune to this greater cultural phenomenon.

Although writers try to retain their privacy in the face of scholarly and public interest, even if they achieve successful protections in the short term, in the long run their collections will be open. Future audiences will interpret content according to their own perception. The Salinger legal dispute shows that some authors have not fully grasped the repercussions of the decision to place papers on the literary archives market. Writers believe they are merely putting their works on display without recognizing that they have sold themselves on the market. Writers who use their intellectual property rights to protect themselves prove what University of Wisconsin–Madison Associate Professor Derek Johnson and his colleague Professor Jonathan Gray say: that authorship is "about control, power, and the management of meaning and of people as much as it is about creativity and innovation."[48]

Placing Papers analyzes the history of the twentieth-century American literary archives market through the perspective of each stakeholder in the trade: authors and families, literary agents and manuscript dealers, directors and curators, archivists, and scholars and the public. Fostering scholarship may be said to be the primary purpose of the literary collections market, but as soon as "the casket shuts," a more primal impulse takes over.[49] Access permits the voyeurism that powers the multimillion-dollar trade in writers' papers.

CONCLUSION

The Matthew Effect

> *What is archived is that which is worth studying and what academia deems worth studying is that which is in the archives.*
>
> —David M. Earle

William R. Reese, the rare book and manuscript dealer whose observation on the untold importance of the market introduced this book, also noted that "the rare book market seems two-tiered: the world of major trophy books, famous authors, and famous titles; and the remainder of the market."[1] Reese's reflection highlights that the market is divided between the most sought-after materials and everything else. Writers who already benefit from their standing by accruing more lucrative book contracts, speaking gigs, and other opportunities than do their peers continue to gain an advantage when they look for a home for their papers. Then, by landing a placement at a top repository, these select authors are more likely to enjoy an augmented posthumous legacy.

This phenomenon, the Matthew Effect, is neither limited to the rare book and manuscript trade nor is Reese the first to observe it. Daniel Rigney described the Matthew Effect as "one of the least known but most important principles in the social sciences."[2] To explain the effect, think of compound interest. Given enough time, invested money will grow exponentially from what was provided as the principal.

When sociologist Robert Merton first coined the term, he realized the theory had a long intellectual legacy. The idea takes its name from an ancient source: Bible verse 25 Matthew 29. In the King James Version from 1611, this verse reads: "For vnto euery one that hath shall be giuen, and he shall haue abundance but from him that hath not, shal be taken away, euen that which he hath." In the American 1946 edition, the verse is: "For to every one who has will more be given, and he will have abundance; but from him who has not, even what he has will be taken away."[3]

In other words, the best separate from the rest. Those who start ahead will accrue more advantage, while those behind become even more deficient. This truth may be unpleasant, but it is widely documented. For this reason, *Placing Papers* concludes by considering what the Matthew Effect's implications are for the future financial, scholarly, and public value of the trade in writers' papers.[4]

FINANCIAL VALUE

Not all authors will be able to sell their papers to institutions in the future, just as not all writers profited from their collections in the past. But what will likely occur is not only the perpetuation of the current state but also a widening divide between authors with and those without the highest level of cultural capital. After all, as this book observed for writers included in *The Norton Anthology of American Literature* (*NAAL*) and Kate Eichhorn's *The Archival Turn in Feminism* (2013) found for the authors of zines, "inaugurating private and semipublic collections as archives and donating them to established public and university archives and special collections" is a common strategy to obtain public legitimacy. Those with widespread name recognition and critical acclaim will be able to claim the right to demand high prices for their papers—after all, "the fact that higher status would be associated with higher prices is not surprising"—whereas the others will be lucky to sell theirs at all.[5]

It is predictable who these authors will be. Table 10 shows that twenty-three *NAAL* authors have yet to place their papers. Demographically, seven are white men, three are white women, four are minority men, and nine are minority women—a breakdown revealing the successful effort by *NAAL*'s

TABLE 10. *NAAL* unplaced authors by demographic and mortality

Unplaced demographics	Unplaced collections (n)
White men	7
Living	4
Dead	3
White women	3
Living	2
Dead	1
Minority men	4
Living	3
Dead	1
Minority women	9
Living	9
Dead	0
Total	23
Living	18
Dead	5

editors to diversify the contemporary literary canon. Due to the market's slow inclusion of minority women, all minority women who have not placed their papers are living, whereas three white men, one white woman, and one minority man died prior to placing their papers.

Jhumpa Lahiri is one of the living minority women whose papers remain unplaced and the youngest writer included in *NAAL*'s seventh edition. Born in 1967 into a Bengali family in London, England, Lahiri grew up in Rhode Island after her family moved to the United States. She attended Barnard College and Boston University before teaching at Princeton University. Her first collection of short stories, *Interpreter of Maladies* (1999), won the Pulitzer Prize.

Lahiri benefits from a variety of likely choices for her papers' eventual home. She may choose to lodge her collection at Princeton University like her colleague, Toni Morrison. Or she could prefer Boston University given her long history there, even if the school does not have any other *NAAL* writers currently in their holdings. And, as Lahiri's career continues to develop, other options may emerge. Since 2002, when *NAAL*'s seventh edition was published, Lahiri published three novels, *The Namesake* (2003), *The Lowland* (2013), *Dove mi trovo* (2018); a short story collection, *Only Goodness: Family Snapshots* (2013); and two nonfiction books, *In Other Words* (2016) and *The Clothing of Books* (2016).

Minority women like Lahiri will be the best situated to capture the future bounty of the trade in writers' papers. The early disadvantages this demographic faced, summarized earlier in chapter 2, now are advantages. As repositories attempt to diversify their holdings, the once-closed market has become both open and lucrative. That said, those most likely to profit are those with all the hallmarks of cultural capital already in place. Lahiri, who achieved early critical success and popular name recognition, is a prime example of who stands to succeed.

Lahiri may manage her papers herself or involve her agent. Eric Simonoff, with William Morris Endeavor (WME), currently administers Lahiri's copyright permissions. The 2009 merger of the William Morris Agency and Endeavor Talent Agency created WME. William Morris had a storied past. Established in 1898, it primarily concerned itself with representing vaudeville performers. It later signed such acts as Elvis Presley and Marilyn Monroe, who both joined the firm in 1955. Endeavor has a shorter legacy. Ariel Emanuel, David Greenblatt, Rick Rosen, and Tom Strickler began it in 1995. Together, they attracted clients like Matt Damon in 2001 before expanding into electronic music in 2008. With the merger, WME took a stake in brands such as Vice and IMG as well. The literary department is a small, but significant component of WME: it adds intellectual clout to the multimedia company. Simonoff, Lahiri's agent, is described as the department's alpha male and its prince. *Poets & Writers* explained to its audience that Simonoff is "known for representing some of the most impressive writers—and for making some of the most lucrative deals—in the business."[6]

Simonoff works in an office that resembles an investment bank, does not belong to the Association of Authors' Representatives, and attributes his success to being willing to "kill for the writer." One could imagine how Simonoff's desire to land his writers their advances could easily translate into an interest in gaining a high price for their papers.[7] Even if Simonoff does not take on the challenge for Lahiri, she is likely to become the client of an agent like Andrew Wylie or a dealer such as Glenn Horowitz. Due to her experience with Simonoff, she would be accustomed to their aggressive approach.

Lahiri could choose alternative representation, such as managing the transfer of her holdings herself or allowing her family members to represent her legacy. Nevertheless, the conflict between literary agents and repositories will not disappear. Wylie, Horowitz, and Ken Lopez successfully adapted their business structure to suit the needs of authors and the structure of the literary archives market. Although Stephen Enniss hopes to make the twenty-first-century trade resemble its early twentieth-century predecessor, top authors with star representation will be able to counterbalance Enniss and his colleagues. After all, the trade in writers' papers is a supplier's market.

Among professional executors, agents are more likely than dealers to be able to represent authors successfully because they better understand technology's challenges. Agents recognize that born-digital drafts are just as valuable as paper drafts and have begun to market them accordingly. After all, agents are used to managing intellectual content; format distinction is a lesser consideration. In contrast, dealers are more likely to falter when faced with the born-digital future. Their trade is predicated on print, the material qualities of paper or parchment. While translating the value of print into a digital realm is difficult, it is possible. Computers, phones, and other machines do carry traces of their owners through their unique patterns of wear. Savvy dealers will need to identify and exploit the physical properties of these machines to help their businesses prosper.

Born-digital content also will pose a challenge to institutions, archivists, and scholars, which must adapt their procedures and values. Institutions need to adjust what they consider meaningfully—as well as magically—valuable.[8] Archivists will have to reframe their value as preserving culture regardless of format and redirect their training and workflows accordingly. Likewise, researchers will want to become confident analyzing the effect of hardware and software on literature. Those places and people which best cope with these shifts are the most likely to be successful.

Fewer institutions will be able to pay high prices for literary collections given the divergence in endowment levels. As Charles T. Clotfelter explained in the *Chronicle of Higher Education*, "The richest colleges have become richer, gathering an increasing share of the most in-demand students and exposing them to the most sought-after faculty and the highest-quality facilities and campus resources."[9] As federal and state funding for higher education weakens, private universities, especially those with large endowments yielding greater rates of return, are better positioned to succeed in the trade. This fact can be seen historically, for only one of the top five collecting repositories is a public university.

The University of Texas at Austin may be exceptional, but it remains vulnerable. Texas's endowment suffered when oil prices began to drop over the summer of 2014. Commentators warned in 2015 that the shift could be "as disruptive as the quadrupling of oil prices that created the oil shock of 1974." A year later, their predictions seemed correct. The Texas endowment shrunk substantially once oil prices decreased by 30 percent.[10] While the Ransom Center sits in an enviable position, Enniss must contend with a tougher market as he continues to build the institution's legacy.

SCHOLARLY VALUE

The scholarly value of writers' papers is not immune to the Mathew Effect. Which authors' work gets preserved shapes which writers become subjects of study, setting in place the conditions for how the future canon will be determined.

Yet placing papers based on current perceptions of quality can be fallible. Yale University's curator of poetry Nancy Kuhl acknowledged this when she wrote that library collections are "at once fossil record and crystal ball," acting as both histories of the past and projections of the future. Curators must gamble limited resources—financial, human, and material—on their intuition as to what will be critical to scholars later. Doing so is an art, not a science, for determining what to keep is necessarily predicated on an individual's taste.[11] Subject gaps in holdings are a way to map a curator's interests alongside an institution's priorities, rather than an indicator of an author's long-term significance. Tracking curators' decisions about what they did not buy is difficult, if not impossible. Curators rarely keep formal records of what collections they were offered and turned down. And when they do, these records would be unlikely to be shared with researchers out of respect for donors' privacy.

Kuhl admitted that she worried about the impact of her own blind spots because her choices will help shape the future literary canon. Acclaim is a positively reinforcing feedback loop. Prominence leads to preservation which leads to future study. Authors who do not generate interest in their lifetime will lose out three times: first, when they do not receive interest in their work; second, when their work is not preserved; and third, when their contributions cannot be studied because their work was not saved. Anything not acquired risks being lost to history permanently, especially as born-digital content will make these types of authors more vulnerable to more immediate loss. Previously, papers remained accessible to future discovery unless they were thrown away. Now, electronic records are easily rendered unreachable due to bit rot and other complexities of digital preservation.

Curators' blind spots can be diagnosed only retrospectively. A way to map the problem is to consider the attrition rate between the number of people who seek to become authors and how many make it into the canon—determined in *Placing Papers* by inclusion in a teaching anthology like *NAAL*. Since the University of Iowa established the first creative writing master of fine arts (MFA) program in 1936, the field of American literature has grown tremendously. Now there are around 300 such programs in operation. Iowa alone chooses from among thirteen hundred applicants for fifty spots.[12] Yet few authors in any generation will make it into *NAAL*. Chapter 5 determined that the most *NAAL* representation that any one generation can hope for is fifty authors—the same number Iowa admits every year—and most generations receive substantially fewer anthology slots. As more people try to become writers by completing MFA programs, they face diminishing odds that they will gain the prominence they need to succeed. Those who achieve early acclaim will see their opportunities expand, whereas those who are passed over will face a lower likelihood to be discovered later given the more difficult odds.

But once a writer is included in *NAAL*, their collections are guaranteed to be sought. As table 10 depicts, only five *NAAL* authors are deceased and still without placed collections: Robert Duncan, Frank O'Hara, Hunter S. Thompson, Grace Paley, and Michael S. Harper. But all five of these writers do have collections in repositories, only these papers could not be included in this book's data set due to their size or owner. As this study sought to address only collections larger than 0.5 linear feet held by institutions such as private libraries or university repositories, papers that did not fit these criteria were not discussed. For example, Robert Duncan has four collections in his name at Kent State University; the University of California, Berkeley; University of California, Santa Cruz; and Washington University, St. Louis.[13] All four collections fall under the size limit, therefore none were recorded. Frank O'Hara, Grace Paley, and Michael S. Harper were excluded from discussion for the same reason.[14] Papers also can be in private rather than institutional hands. This situation occurred only once. Johnny Depp owns

Gonzo journalist Hunter S. Thompson's papers. The two were incredibly close; Depp described their relationship as "a pair of deviant bookends on the prowl." Depp wanted Thompson's papers when he was alive, but he "didn't want to be horrible actor-boy who says, 'OK, let's have everything now.' I wanted it to happen more naturally." So Depp waited. Three years after Thompson died by suicide, Depp bought Thompson's 800-box collection. Depp has indicated that he might share the papers in the future, but which institution is to benefit has yet to be determined.[15]

Even when a set of papers is sold or given to an institution, researchers do not immediately gain access. Sometimes authors' papers are processed quickly; other times they can linger in a backlog waiting to be arranged and described. Digitization adds another step to the workflow. More time and funding are required to bring a project to completion if digitization is an option. Additionally, if born-digital documents are present, migration and/or emulation often generates an even longer wait for scholars.

However, only writers who place their papers at the most moneyed repositories will benefit from the enhanced access provided by digitization and emulation.[16] Consider the case studies provided in this book: Gabriel García Márquez's collection at the Ransom Center illustrated digitization initiatives, while Salman Rushdie's papers at Emory demonstrated emulation. It is not an accident that both examples are from internationally acclaimed authors who sold their papers to the top five collecting institutions. In another example of the Matthew Effect, costly or experimental procedures will be tried first on the most valuable writers at the most moneyed repositories.

The scholarly value of literary collections will persist, but only top writers will be preserved. The possibility to discover overlooked authors will decline as technology diminishes the possibility of later access. Furthermore, writers of supposedly equal canonical standing will be sorted again into those who merit greater and lesser arrangement and description methods. Those authors given the opportunity to have their materials saved through digitization and emulation will benefit the most in future scholarship, which will further compound their advantages and cement their place in the canon.

PUBLIC VALUE

While most literary archives are currently found in academic settings, private cultural heritage institutions are the most likely candidates to support the market in the future. These organizations perceive literary archives as a way to bolster their cities' economy through tourism. Papers given their own repositories, complete with dedicated exhibition space, confer needed cultural capital to downtown revitalization projects. Yet this trend will only amplify the Matthew Effect. Very few authors will command enough public interest to justify the expense of stand-alone centers that function as concrete monuments to their subject's social status.[17]

At the start of the literary archives market in 1955, the three wealthiest philanthropic organizations in the United States were the Ford Foundation, the Rockefeller Foundation, and the Carnegie Corporation. These organizations invested in higher education to support the public good. For example, Ford decided faculty salaries needed to be increased to support the profession educating the emergent middle class—and then provided $210 million to achieve this objective nationally.[18] Such a goal would be unheard of today. While it is an oversimplification to say major contemporary private funders are uninterested in higher education, as many certainly are, when it comes to cultural heritage acquisitions, major purchases are more likely to be seen as better housed in independent centers that prioritize public attention over scholarly observation and tourist revenue over academic engagement.

Consider Woody Guthrie and Bob Dylan. Both placed their papers in Tulsa institutions dedicated exclusively to their works. Guthrie's papers are valuable to the public because he wrote one of the country's most popular songs and influenced a later generation of musicians. Known for "This Land Is Your Land," Guthrie was born in Okemah, a small town situated between Oklahoma City and Tulsa, in 1912. Once the Depression hit, he moved to California seeking work. There, he released his widely popular *Dust Bowl Ballads* (1940), one of the first American concept albums, and wrote what many consider the "alternative national anthem," "This Land Is Your Land."[19] Although Guthrie died in 1967, he was inducted into the Rock and Roll Hall of Fame in 1988 and the Oklahoma Music Hall of Fame in 1997. The Smithsonian celebrated his music by publishing a combination book and CD titled *Woody at 100: The Woody Guthrie Centennial Collection* (2012).

When the George Kaiser Family Foundation made a bid to purchase his papers in 2013 from the Woody Guthrie Foundation in Mount Kisco, New York, it wanted to open a center in his name in Tulsa, Oklahoma. Nora Guthrie, Woodie Guthrie's daughter, appreciated this vision. She agreed to the sale, and the museum and archive opened that same year. Now it sponsors near-weekly musical performances, serves as an events venue, and provides a store selling merchandise with Guthrie's quotations emblazoned on buttons, posters, shot glasses, and more. The center does retain facets of a traditional research facility: it has a dedicated archivist, Kate L. Blalack, and offers fellowships for scholars sponsored by the BMI Foundation.[20] Furthermore, it has started to attract similar collections. In 2014, the daughter of Phil Ochs, a singer-songwriter influenced by Guthrie, donated his papers to the center, expanding its profile from Woody Guthrie as an individual to his influence on folk musicians.

The Kaiser Foundation is funded by the Kaiser-Frances Oil Company and the BOK (Bank of Oklahoma) Financial Corporation. George B. Kaiser, the son of Herman Kaiser, took over the business his father created in 1969. George Kaiser not only is one of the wealthiest Americans but also is one of the wealthiest people in the world; as of May 12, 2018, he is worth $8.2 billion.[21] In addition to establishing the Woody Guthrie Center through his Tulsa Community Foundation, Kaiser purchased out the Bank of Oklahoma from the Federal Deposit Insurance Corporation (FDIC) in 1990 and invested in the Professional Basketball Club LLC, which controls the Oklahoma City Thunder and the Oklahoma City Blue, in 2014.[22]

Although Bob Dylan sung "there's not many men that done the things that you've done" on Guthrie's behalf, those who have achieved equal stature are more likely to obtain such centers for themselves in the future.[23] The establishment of Guthrie's center was shortly followed by one for Dylan himself. Unlike Guthrie, Dylan is not a native Oklahoman, nor are his works affiliated with the state. Rather, his connection to Oklahoma results from his ties to Guthrie's folk aesthetic.

Dylan is most recognized as a musician and became well-known for songs such as "Like a Rolling Stone" and albums like *Blood on the Tracks* (1975), but to the surprise of many, he won the Nobel Prize for Literature in 2016. Dylan then skipped the Nobel ceremony and gave his lecture—a requirement if he was to accept the prize—four months later during a private event. There, he answered his critics by revealing he never considered his songs literature. He admitted, "If someone had ever told me that I had the slightest chance of winning the Nobel Prize, I would have to think I'd have about the same odds as standing on the moon."[24]

Glenn Horowitz realized the opportunity presented by the Kaiser Foundation's interest in archives. He thought, "Dylan's material might be right at home down the street from the Guthrie collection, Bob back again near Woody, rather than buried in a university library stuffed with other important archives." Horowitz immediately acted on his intuition and successfully sold Dylan's collection to the Kaiser Foundation for about $20 million in 2016. The Kaiser Foundation did partner with the University of Tulsa for this purchase, but the acquisition could not have been managed by the university on its own accord. On October 25, 2017, Tulsa announced that it would create an Institute for Bob Dylan Studies with the goal to create "a broadly interdisciplinary" space that would welcome "pop culture historians to social scientists."[25]

The university and the foundation said that the goal of the acquisition was to make the papers and other materials related to Dylan's career available for public exhibitions as well as to increase access to them for future research. Dylan himself welcomed the purchase, saying: "I'm glad that my archives, which have been collected all these years, have finally found a home and are to be included with the works of Woody Guthrie . . . To me, it makes a lot of sense and it's a great honor." The foundation plans to open a center devoted to Dylan like the one it created for Guthrie; the two facilities will even be oriented opposite to one another in the Brady Arts District of Tulsa.[26]

Until the opening of the Bob Dylan Center in the future, access to his materials will be coordinated through the Helmerich Center for American Research, which prompted *Rolling Stone* to observe that those who want to visit the papers must peruse the finding aid and apply to the librarian with details on their project. However, Ken Levit, executive director of the Kaiser Foundation, hastened to inform the magazine's readers that the center itself would be devoted to public, not just scholarly interest: "I don't think we will be serving the mission of our foundation if that [public access] is not contemplated in a very broad way." *Rolling Stone* must have had substantial interest in the archive. Three months later the magazine reported on it again, this time noting high points in the collection, such as outtakes and song drafts, before focusing on the collection's security.[27]

Due to the rising interest in Dylan's papers, the center is asking for proposals from architectural firms to modify the building it plans to use to house the collection. Significantly, the center asks these firms to focus on the public, rather than the scholarly, side of the center. For example, proposals must include a museum, space for educational programs, and a store.[28] And these centers could expand even further—reports suggest that Johnny Cash's papers are likely to make the couple a triumvirate.[29]

The Kaiser Foundation's goals for the Guthrie and Dylan Centers in Tulsa, Oklahoma, are an echo of Harry Ransom's earlier ambitions for the University of Texas at Austin. Both George B. Kaiser and Harry Ransom wanted to use oil money to bring contemporary cultural artifacts to portions of the country previously devoid of national-level institutions. Texas may have chosen contemporary literature and Oklahoma contemporary music—with Dylan as an interloper in the former and a mainstay in the latter—but both sought to transmute business profits into arts patronage by using the allure of archives. Kaiser channels its money through private, philanthropic organizations, whereas Ransom acts as a steward on behalf of a public land-grant university.

The similarities in Kaiser's and Ransom's goals demonstrate the consistent interest in writers' papers since 1955. Yet the differences in how the goals are executed suggest how the market may develop in the future. Where before universities housed many authors' collections, increasingly corporate investments are building institutions devoted solely to the care, study, and exhibition of one blockbuster artist. The cultural capital universities tapped by acquiring literary archives is now sought by companies and cities, proving the accelerating financial power of the market.

GOING FORWARD

Additional predictions for the literary archives market require expanding the number of authors included in the data set. A wider data set could be accomplished by aggregating the writers included in several anthologies or across many editions of a single anthology. Yet what can be told from looking at the history and motivations of the market's stakeholders as defined here paints a stark picture. The trade in writers' papers follows the Matthew Effect. Those with the greatest standing acquire the most advantages, perpetuating and growing a hierarchy among the trade's stakeholders.

Only top authors, executors, institutions, archivists, and scholars will persist. Few writers will manage to build a brand in each generation. These authors' agents then will ensure that they command top dollar when placing their papers. If institutions want to control prices, they will need to do so en bloc and sacrifice a series of acquisitions to make good on the threat. However, this scenario is unlikely. Repositories would be required to concede their individual benefit—acquiring a desirable set of papers—to further a collective good, that of enforcing prices they see as more sustainable. Turning to archivists, these professionals will continue to be employed, but those with digital skills will earn more. Digital archivists will also be more likely to be recognized as contributing to scholarly research because of citation trends in digital humanities that emphasize naming all participants rather than only the faculty member associated with the project.[30] And although the trade's turn toward greater public engagement is a positive development, it comes with the specter of a lessened investment in university-based humanities research.

But research never was the primary motivator for the literary archives market. All stakeholders agree with the principle that the trade is designed to procure authors' papers on behalf of literary scholars. Yet the unsellable status of Paul Moran's collection of John Updike's trash demonstrates that repositories will keep materials away from researchers if necessary to preserve their cultural capital and financial interests. Access to cultural capital is the market's commodity, not the materials themselves. Acquiring authors' papers allows repositories to gain cultural capital; scholars gain research opportunities as a side benefit.

Only top writers with high cultural capital can be assured through the literary archives market that their corpus will outlive their corpse. When Norman Mailer was taken to tour the Ransom Center in 2005, he was shown his future neighbors: the boxes that held the archival bodies of his illustrious colleagues—Don DeLillo, Graham Greene, and Isaac Bashevis Singer. Mailer, leaning on his cane, imagined his future as an literary archive. After a moment, he accepted his fate. "We all wind up in boxes anyway," he said.[31] Perhaps so, but who we are determines how much those boxes cost, where they sit, what they look like, and who will peer into them.

Mailer died two years later. His physical body resided in one box; his archival body stretched to 957, each of which is carefully preserved for perpetuity owing to the contemporary American literary archives market.[32]

NOTES

INTRODUCTION: OUTSIDE THE LITERARY ARCHIVES MARKET

1. "Fiction," The Pulitzer Prizes, http://www.pulitzer.org/prize-winners-by-category/219.
2. Rebecca Rego Barry, "Updike's 'Trash' at Auction," *Fine Books & Collections*, February 17, 2016.
3. Paul Moran, "Finding John Updike: And Taking His Trash," *Texas Monthly*, November 19, 2014.
4. Moran, "Finding John Updike."
5. The Other John Updike Archive (johnupdikearchive.com) existed between 2009 and 2014; Paul Moran, "Finding John Updike."
6. Jennifer Lyons, Susan Pyzynski, Bonnie Salt, and Susan Sutherland, John Updike Papers, 1940–2009, MS AM 1793, Houghton Library, Harvard University; Adrienne LaFrance, "The Man Who Made Off with John Updike's Trash," *Atlantic*, August 28, 2014.
7. *California v. Greenwood* was a 1988 case that established the right to search and seize garbage left outside a home's curtilage (the land surrounding it). A curb is not included in a house's curtilage. California v. Greenwood, 486 U.S. 35 (1988).
8. Walter Benjamin, "Unpacking My Library: A Talk about Book Collecting," in *Illuminations*, ed. Hannah Arendt, trans. Harry Zohn (New York: Harcourt, Brace & World, 1968), 64.

9. Randal Johnson, "Pierre Bourdieu on Art, Literature, and Culture," in *The Field of Cultural Production: Essays on Art and Literature* (New York: Columbia University Press, 1993), 7, 9, 18.
10. Corydon Ireland, "Treasure Island: How Houghton Library Saves and Serves Famed Authors' Work," *Harvard Gazette*, November 9, 2011, http://news.harvard.edu/gazette/story/2011/11/treasure-island/.
11. Alison Flood, "Raiding John Updike's Rubbish—A Trashy Pursuit," *Guardian*, September 2, 2014.
12. Alex Beam, "John Updike's Trash Is Everyone's Treasure," *Boston Globe*, September 6, 2014.
13. LaFrance, "The Man Who Made Off."
14. Alan Burke, "Author John Updike's Trash Overrated," *CHNINews*, February 23, 2016.
15. Jan Goldstein, "Foucault among the Sociologists: The 'Disciplines' and the History of the Professions," *History and Theory* 23, no. 2 (May 1984): 175; Stephen Shapiro, "Intellectual Labor Power, Cultural Capital, and the Value of Prestige," *South Atlantic Quarterly* 108, no. 2 (2009): 250.
16. Paul Moran, The Other John Updike Archive, Wayback Machine, December 17, 2014, https://web.archive.org/web/20141217165105/http://johnupdikearchive.com/.
17. Paul Moran, "Culture Vulture," The Other John Updike Archive, Wayback Machine, December 17, 2014, https://web.archive.org/web/20150215195713/http://johnupdikearchive.com/culture-vulture/; Judith H. Dobrzynski, "Auctions Organized by Theme, with a Narrative Pull," *New York Times*, October 25, 2013.
18. Paul Moran, "Proust's Overcoat," The Other John Updike Archive, Wayback Machine, December 17, 2014, https://web.archive.org/web/20150215211650/http://johnupdikearchive.com/prousts-overcoat/; Stephanie Lacava, "In Search of Proust's Overcoat," *Paris Review*, August 30, 2010.
19. Paul Moran, "Talking Heads '77," The Other John Updike Archive, Wayback Machine, December 14, 2014, https://web.archive.org/web/20180826152047/http://johnupdikearchive.com/talking-heads-77/.
20. LaFrance, "The Man Who Made Off"; Matthew Kirschenbaum, *Track Changes: A Literary History of Word Processing* (Cambridge, MA: Harvard University Press, 2016), Image 21 and 224–25.
21. Johnson, "Pierre Bourdieu," 10; Pierre Bourdieu, "The Production of Belief: Contribution to an Economy of Symbolic Goods," in *The Field of Cultural Production: Essays on Art and Literature*, ed. Randal Johnson (New York: Columbia University Press, 1993), 75.
22. Michel Foucault, *Beyond Structuralism and Hermeneutics*, ed. Hubert L. Dreyfus and Paul Rabinow (Chicago: University of Chicago Press, 1983), 208–26.

23. Jamie A. Lee, "Be/longing in the Archival Body: Eros and the 'Endearing' Value of Material Lives," *Archival Science* 16, no. 1 (March 2016): 33–51.
24. Ann Cvetkovich, *An Archive of Feelings: Trauma, Sexuality, and Lesbian Public Cultures* (Durham, NC: Duke University Press, 2003), 9.
25. Max Horkheimer and Theodor W. Adorno, "The Culture Industry: Enlightenment as Mass Deception," in *Dialectic of Enlightenment*, trans. John Cumming (New York: Continuum, 1982), 158.
26. James F. English, *The Economy of Prestige: Prizes, Awards, and the Circulation of Cultural Value* (Cambridge, MA: Harvard University Press, 2005), 1–14.
27. The eighth edition came out in 2012 and the ninth in 2017. *The Norton Anthology of American Literature*, vol. E, *Literature since 1945*, WorldCat, https://www.worldcat.org/title/norton-anthology-of-american-literature-vol-e-literature-since-1945/oclc/980599291/editions?editionsView=true&referer=br.
28. *The Norton Anthology of American Literature* editors substantially altered which authors they included in each edition. Although the ninth edition includes three fewer authors than the seventh, nineteen new authors are featured, whereas twenty-three were dropped. Added writers include Edward Abbey, Frank Bidart, Edwidge Dandicat, Lydia Davis, Junot Diaz, Philip K. Dick, Don DiLillo, Richard Foreman, Patricia Highsmith, Edward P. Jones, Jamaica Kincaid, Barry Lopez, Charles Ludlam, Sharon Olds, George Saunders, Tracy K. Smith, Natasha Trethewey, August Wilson, and James Wright. Omitted authors are Julia Alvarez, Max Apple, Lorna Dee Cervantes, Robert Creeley, Robert Duncan, Brendan Galvin, Jorie Graham, Kimiko Hahn, Fanny Howe, Stanley Kunitz, Lorine Niedecker, Dennis Nurkse, Naomi Shihab Nye, George Oppen, Richard Powers, David Ray, Alberto Ríos, Pattiann Rogers, Cathy Song, Gerald Vizenor, William Vollman, C. D. Wright, and Charles Wright.
29. Repositories usually measure collections in linear feet. I asked repositories holding collections that did not conform to this standard measurement to convert their measurements. If they did not, I entered their measurements into the Beinecke Rare Book and Manuscript Library's Lineage Footage Calculator: https://beinecke.library.yale.edu/research-teaching/doing-research-beinecke/linear-footage-calculator.
30. A synthetic collection is an artificially created collection assembled over time through individual purchases from different people.
31. For example, Sylvia Plath's papers are held by both Indiana University and Smith College. As of April 2016, the guide to Sylvia Plath's papers at the Lilly Library includes eight separate collections that together equal 16 linear feet. In contrast, Plath's papers at Smith include two collections, one held in the Mortimer Rare Book Room and one held in the Smith College Archives, which together run to 33.5 linear feet. Plath's literary collection is marked as residing at Smith, rather than

Indiana, based on the size difference between the two sets of papers rather than a qualitative evaluation of these collections' content.

32. Christoph Schöch, "Big? Smart? Clean? Messy? Data in the Humanities," *Journal of Digital Humanities* 2, no. 3 (Summer 2013), http://journalofdigitalhumanities.org/2-3/big-smart-clean-messy-data-in-the-humanities/.

33. Charles Clay Doyle, Wolfgang Mieder, and Fred R. Shapiro, *Dictionary of Modern Proverbs* (New Haven, CT: Yale University Press, 2012), 168.

CHAPTER 1: INSIDE THE LITERARY ARCHIVES MARKET

1. Collins quoted in Jeanne Claire van Ryzin, "Stephen Enniss Puts Mark on Storied Ransom Center," *Austin American-Statesman*, August 27, 2016.

2. Jennifer Schuessler, "Poet's Archive Goes to University of Texas," *New York Times*, January 20, 2014; Nolan Feeney, "Toni Morrison's Papers to Be Housed at Princeton," *Time*, October 19, 2014; Courtney Crowder, "University of Illinois Acquires Gwendolyn Brooks Archive," *Chicago Tribune*, January 3, 2014; Richard Fausset, "University Receives Archive of Work by O'Connor," *New York Times*, October 7, 2014.

3. Rachel Donadio, "The Papers Chase," *New York Times*, March 25, 2007; Richard Cohen, "The Paper Chase," *Harry Ransom Center Magazine*, 2001.

4. Barry Newman, "As the Trash Goes, Authors' Clutter in the Right Hands Is Very Bankable," *Wall Street Journal*, January 2, 2013.

5. Helen Taylor, "What Will Survive of Us Are Manuscripts: Archives, Scholarship, and Human Stories," in *The Boundaries of the Literary Archive: Reclamation and Representation*, ed. Carrie Smith and Lisa Stead (Surrey, UK: Ashgate, 2013), 191.

6. Chris Arnot, "Stemming Flow of Literary Heritage across the Pond," *Guardian*, July 14, 2008; Kimberly Jones, "The Inevitability of Death and Texas," *Austin Chronicle*, July 18, 2008; Gary Martin, "The Meaning and Origin of the Expression: Nothing Is Certain but Death and Taxes," The Phrase Finder, 2019. https://www.phrases.org.uk/meanings/death-and-taxes.html.

7. Brian Friel, *Give Me Your Answer, Do!* (New York: Dramatists Play Service, 2000), 10, 14, 18.

8. Taylor, "What Will Survive," 191.

9. Arnot, "Stemming Flow."

10. Donadio, "The Papers Chase."

11. Newman, "As the Trash Goes."

12. Van Ryzin "Stephen Enniss."

13. Dan Piepenbring, "All Hail the Refrigerator, and Other News," *Paris Review*, August 23, 2016; Newman, "As the Trash Goes."

14. Phillip Lopate, "Selling My Papers: A Life's Work Out the Door," *American Scholar*, August 19, 2016.

15. Kevin Young, then the curator of literary manuscripts and the Raymond Danowski Collection at Emory University's Stuart A. Rose Manuscript, Archives, and Rare Book Library, informed me of this policy when I worked as his assistant between 2010 and 2013. With thanks to Joel Minor, curator of the Modern Literature Collection at Washington University in St. Louis, for sharing this fact.
16. Julie Thompson Klein, *Humanities, Culture, and Interdisciplinarity* (Albany: State University of New York Press, 2005), 34.
17. Lawrence W. Levine, *The Opening of the American Mind: Canons, Culture, and History* (Boston: Beacon Press, 1996), 85–88.
18. The Harry Ransom Center at the University of Texas at Austin acquired an excellent medieval and early modern manuscript collection after 1960.
19. Elizabeth Renker, "Resistance and Change: The Rise of American Literature Studies," *American Literature* 64, no. 2 (June 1992): 347–65.
20. Bernard Bergonzi, *Exploding English: Criticism, Theory, Culture* (Oxford: Clarendon Press, 1990), 80.
21. Thomas F. Staley, "Literary Canons, Literary Studies, and Library Collections: A Retrospective on Collecting Twentieth-Century Writers," *Rare Books and Manuscripts Librarianship* 5, no. 1 (1990): 13.
22. Henry Hart, "Richard Ellmann's Oxford Blues," *Sewanee Review* 117, no. 2 (Spring 2009): 268; Susan Dick, Declan Kiberd, Dougald McMillan, and Joseph Ronsley, "Richard Ellmann: The Critic as Artist," in *Essays for Richard Ellmann: Omnium Gatherem*, ed. Susan Dick, Declan Kiberd, Dougald McMillan, and Joseph Ronsley (Kingston: McGill-Queen's University Press, 1989), xiii.
23. William S. Brockman, "Learning to Be James Joyce's Contemporary? Richard Ellmann's Discovery and Transformation of Joyce's Letters and Manuscripts," *Journal of Modern Literature* 22, no. 2 (Winter 1998/1999): 253–63.
24. Brockman, "Learning to Be," 254–58.
25. Michael Basinski, "The James Joyce Collection: Its History and Future," James Joyce Collection, University at Buffalo University Libraries, November 2008, https://web.archive.org/web/20151003064145/http://library.buffalo.edu/pl/collections/jamesjoyce/collection/history-future.php.
26. Vassar College houses 29.8 cubic feet of Elizabeth Bishop's papers, Stanford University holds 1,000 linear feet of Allen Ginsberg's papers, the Rosenbach possesses 130.52 linear feet of Marianne Moore's papers, and Yale University stewards 40.37 linear feet of William Carlos Williams's papers. This range of collections led John Carter dismissively to portray the University at Buffalo as "writing round to every author they could think of." John Carter, *Taste and Technique in Book Collecting* (London: Private Libraries Association, 1970), 221, quoted in Staley, "Literary Canons," 13.
27. Aaron Welborn, "Mona and Jarvis: A Story in Manuscripts," *Off the Shelf: A Publication of Washington University Libraries* 3, no. 2 (Fall 2008): 8.

28. Joel Minor, "Modern Literature Collection and Manuscripts," University Libraries, Washington University in St. Louis, http://libguides.wustl.edu/c.php?g=47360&p=303469#s-lg-box-891530.
29. Robert Creeley's papers at Stanford are 443.5 linear feet. Washington University holds only 35 boxes.
30. James Merrill's collection at Washington University in St. Louis includes 175.5 linear feet, which grew from his repeated donations throughout his life as well as donations by his mother and other individuals. Yale University's 34.35 linear feet of Merrill material came from *Yale Review* editor J. D. McClatchy and Stephen Yenser, author of *The Consuming Myth: The Work of James Merrill* (1987). McClatchy and Yenser are coexecutors of Merrill's estate. With thanks to Joel Minor for clarifying this portion of Merrill's acquisition history. While Utah State University holds 5 linear feet of boxes related to May Swenson, Washington University in St. Louis possesses 223 linear feet.
31. Faye Phillips, "Developing Collecting Policies for Manuscript Collections," *American Archivist* 47, no. 1 (Winter 1984): 34.
32. The Poetry Collection at the University at Buffalo includes 137 collections pertaining to poetry. "The Poetry Collection," University at Buffalo, 2018, https://library.buffalo.edu/pl/; Collections Keyword Search, University at Buffalo, March 19, 2018, https://library.buffalo.edu/pl/collections/results.html?search=&submit=%EE%A4%A4; "Modern Literature Collection," University of Washington in St. Louis, https://library.wustl.edu/tag/modern-literature-collection/.
33. Jacques Derrida, *Archive Fever: A Freudian Impression*, trans. Eric Prenowitz (Chicago: University of Chicago Press, 1998), 2.
34. Megan Garber, "Harper Lee: The Sadness of a Sequel," *Atlantic*, February 3, 2015; William Giraldi, "The Suspicious Story behind Harper Lee's 'Go Set a Watchman,'" *New Republic*, July 13, 2015; Emily Langer, "Alice Lee, Sister of 'To Kill a Mockingbird' Author Harper Lee, dies at 103," *Washington Post*, November 18, 2014.
35. Boris Kachka, "The Decline of Harper Lee," *Vulture*, February 19, 2016, http://www.vulture.com/2014/07/decline-of-harper-lee.html.
36. Joe Nocera, "The Harper Lee 'Go Set a Watchman' Fraud," *New York Times*, July 24, 2015.
37. Agence-France Presse, "Harper Lee's *Go Set a Watchman* Tops US 2015 Bestseller List," *Guardian*, January 4, 2016; Jeffrey A. Trachtenberg, "Harper Lee Novel 'Go Set a Watchman' Sales Surpass 1.1 Million Copies," *Wall Street Journal*, July 20, 2015.
38. Nelle Harper Lee temporarily lost her copyright to her literary agent, Sam Pinkus, whom she later successfully sued to regain her rights. Kachka, "The Decline of Harper Lee."
39. Daniela Deane, "New Beatrix Potter Story Discovered and to Be Published This Year," *Washington Post*, January 26, 2016; Audrey Golden, "Copper Canyon's Release

of 'The Lost Poems of Pablo Neruda,'" www.BooksTellYouWhy.com, April 5, 2016, https://blog.bookstellyouwhy.com/copper-canyons-release-of-the-lost-poems-of-pablo-neruda.

40. Adrian Humphreys, "A Clockwork Original: McMaster University Bought Manuscript of Iconic Novel for $250," *National Post*, November 11, 2012; Anthony Burgess, *A Clockwork Orange* (New York: W. W. Norton, 2019).

CHAPTER 2: BRAND

1. "Types of Archives," Society of American Archivists, https://www2.archivists.org/usingarchives/typesofarchives; "Charles Bukowski's Literary Archive Comes to the Huntington," The Huntington, June 14, 2006, https://bukowskiforum.com/threads/a-public-event-celebrating-bukowski-at-7-30-p-m-on-september-20th.439/.
2. Charles Bukowski, "a 340 dollar horse and a hundred dollar whore," Poetry Foundation, https://www.poetryfoundation.org/poems/49569/a-340-dollar-horse-and-a-hundred-dollar-whore.
3. Joy Jacobsen, "Black Sparrow Folds Its Wings," *Poets & Writers*, September 1, 2012; "Black Sparrow: The Publisher Who Backed Bukowski," AbeBooks.com, https://www.abebooks.com/books/charles-bukowski-publisher-small-press/black-sparrow-press-books.shtml.
4. "Charles Bukowski, 1920–1994," Poetry Foundation, 2010, https://www.poetryfoundation.org/poets/charles-bukowski.
5. Common Language Marketing Dictionary, s.v. "brand," American Marketing Association, https://marketing-dictionary.org/b/brand/.
6. Naomi Klein, *No Space, No Choice, No Jobs, No Logo* (New York: Picador, 2002), 45.
7. *Placing Papers* does not study class, another important indicator of cultural capital. Future work on the literary archives market should address this topic, especially as "class is more threatening to capital than is ethnicity." Richard S. Pressman, "Is There a Future for the *Heath Anthology* in the Neo-Liberal State?," *symplokē* 8, no. 1/2 (2000): 64.
8. This book examines the acquisition histories of literary archives for authors appearing in the seventh edition of *The Norton Anthology of American Literature* to limit the scope of the study. Future research could expand my data set to track the literary archives of all authors included in the now nine editions of *NAAL*. For more discussion on this topic, see the conclusion.
9. Joel M. Podolny, *Status Signals: A Sociological Study of Market Competition* (Princeton, NJ: Princeton University Press, 2008), 24.
10. Glen M. Johnson, "The Teaching Anthology and the Canon of American Literature," in *The Hospitable Canon: Essays on Literary Play, Scholarly Choice, and Popular Presses*, ed. Virgil Nemoianu and Robert Royal (Philadelphia: John Benjamin's Publishing, 1991), 112.

11. Mark A. Eaton, "The Cultural Capital of Imaginary versus Pedagogical Canons," *Pedagogy* 1, no. 2 (2001): 306; emphasis in original.
12. John Guillory, preface to *Cultural Capital: The Problem of Literary Canon Formation* (Chicago: University of Chicago Press, 1993), ix.
13. This book identifies demographic representation of women and people of color in the seventh edition of *The Norton Anthology of American Literature* to create a data set to understand the history of the American literary archives market. Another assessment of the anthology could focus on genre, rather than sex and race, to investigate the market's history. *The Norton Anthology of American Literature*, vol. E, *1945 to the Present*, ed. Nina Baym, Jerome Klinkowitz, Arnold Krapat, and Patricia Wallace (New York: W. W. Norton & Company, 2007).
14. Sean Shesgreen, "Canonizing the Canonizer: A Short History of *The Norton Anthology of English Literature*," *Critical Inquiry* 35, no. 2 (Winter 2009): 296–97; Anthony Bradley, Edna Longley, and Colm Tóibín, "Review of the *Field Day Anthology of Irish Writing*," *Canadian Journal of Irish Studies* 18, no. 2 (December 1992): 117–18; Angela Bourke, ed., *The Field Day Anthology of Irish Writing*, vols. 4 and 5, *Irish Women's Writing and Tradition* (Cork: Cork University Press, 2002).
15. Judith Fetterley and Joan Schulz, "A *MELUS* Dialogue: The Status of Women Authors in American Literature Anthologies," *MELUS* 9, no. 3 (Autumn 1982): 5.
16. Joe Weixlmann, "Dealing with the Demands of an Expanding Literary Canon," *College English* 50, no. 3 (March 1988): 275–76, 281.
17. Nicole Tonkovich, "Of Compass Bearings and Reorientations in the Study of American Women Writers," *Legacy: A Journal of American Women Writers* 26, no. 2 (2009): 243.
18. Douglas Martin, "Selden Rodman, Writer and Folk Art Advocate, Dies at 93," *New York Times*, November 11, 2002.
19. Hoyt Fuller, "Racism in Literary Anthologies," *Black Scholar* 18, no. 1 (January/February 1987): 38.
20. Jennifer Jordan, "Arthur P. Davis: Forging the Way for the Formation of the Canon," *Callaloo* 20, no. 2 (Spring 1997): 452.
21. Cary Nelson, "Multiculturalism without Guarantees: From Anthologies to the Social Text," *Journal of the Midwest Modern Language Association* 26, no. 1 (Spring 1993): 48–52; Vincent B. Leitch, Barbara Johnson, John McGowan, Laurie Finke, and Jeffrey J. Williams, "Editing a Norton Anthology," *College English* 66, no. 2 (November 2003): 172–206.
22. Rachel Donadio, "Revising the Canon Wars," *New York Times*, September 16, 2007.
23. David Wyatt, "A Personal Note," in *Secret Histories: Reading Twentieth-Century American Literature* (Baltimore, MD: Johns Hopkins University Press, 2010), 331.
24. Pressman, "Is There a Future," 57.
25. Henry Louis Gates Jr., "On the Rhetoric of Racism in the Profession," *African Literature Association Bulletin* 15, no. 1 (Winter 1989): 12; Julie R. Enszer, "'She Who

Shouts Gets Heard!': Counting and Accounting for Women Writers in Literary Grants and Norton Anthologies," *Feminist Studies* 42, no. 3 (2016): 731.
26. Linda M. Morra, *Unarrested Archives: Case Studies in Twentieth-Century Canadian Women's Authorship* (Toronto: University of Toronto Press, 2014), 4.
27. Placement rates pictured in table 1 will be discussed in chapter 4. Writers without collections in institutions are discussed in the conclusion.
28. Corporate Author, "Administrative and Biographical History," Randall Jarrell Papers, 1915–1916, Martha Blakeney Hodges Special Collections and University Archives, University of North Carolina, Greensboro, http://libapps.uncg.edu/archon/index.php?p=collections/controlcard&id=24.
29. These components are all organized under a single guide linking to individual finding aids for each set of papers. Grouping sets of papers together creates a data set that allows the relative acquisition dates of *NAAL* authors to be compared at the cost of ignoring more precise details regarding a collection's provenance, hence the need for qualitative analysis to describe this variation. Cherry Williams, email correspondence with author, November 25, 2016; Corporate Author, "Guide to the Sylvia Plath Materials in the Lilly Library," http://www.indiana.edu/~liblilly/guides/plath/sylvia.shtml.
30. Chris Jackson, "Ishmael Reed, the Art of Poetry, No. 100," *Paris Review*, Fall 2016.
31. Jane Phillips, "Finding Aid to the Maxine Hong Kingston Papers, 1952–1999," Bancroft Library, University of California, Berkeley, http://oac.cdlib.org/findaid/ark:/13030/kt6w10293c/; Maxine Hong Kingston and Karen Horton, "Maxine Hong Kingston," *Conversations with Maxine Hong Kingston*, ed. Paul Skenazy and Tera Martin (Jackson: University Press of Mississippi, 1998), 7; University of California, Berkeley, English department, phone call with author, July 17, 2017.
32. Merrilee Lee, email correspondence with author, March 9, 2016.
33. Many collections are compiled over many years rather than in one single acquisition. This study requires a single date for computational purposes, so the year used is based on the best information found.
34. Lorine Niedecker, "5 Poems," *Poetry* (August 1965): 344; "Lorine Niedecker Wisconsin Poetry Festival Open Mic," Café Carpe Fort Atkinson, November 2, 2012, http://cafecarpe.com/event/lorine-niedecker-wisconsin-poetry-festival-open-mic/, and City of Fort Atkinson City Council Minutes, April 19, 2016, http://www.fortatkinsonwi.net/Minutes%2004-19-2016.pdf.
35. Charles McNair, "Grace Notes: Flannery O'Connor's Papers Add Richness to MARBL Special Collections," *Emory Magazine*, Winter 2015.
36. Richard Fausset, "Emory Receives Archive of Work by O'Connor: University Acquires Flannery O'Connor's Papers and Effects," *New York Times*, October 7, 2014.
37. Lauren Douglas-Brown, "'The Grace of Convergence': Emory Celebrates Acquiring the Archive of Flannery O'Connor," Emory News Center, October 9, 2014,

http://news.emory.edu/stories/2014/10/upress_flannery_oconnor_collection/campus.html.

38. Charles McNair, "Grace Notes"; Elaine Justice, "Flannery O'Connor Archive Comes to Emory University," Emory News, October 7, 2014, http://rose.library.emory.edu/about/news-events/news/archives/2014/flannery-oconnor-papers-emory.html.

39. Loretta Würtenberger and Karl von Trott, *The Artist's Estate* (Berlin: Hatje Cantz, 2016), 31, 68–69; Laura Millar, *The Story behind the Book: Preserving Authors' and Publishers' Archives* (Vancouver: Canadian Centre for Studies in Publishing Press, 2009), 118–19.

40. Toni Morrison, "James Baldwin: His Life Remembered; Life in His Language," *New York Times*, December 20, 1987.

41. Jordan Elgrably, "James Baldwin: The Art of Fiction, No. 78," *Paris Review*, Spring 1984.

42. David Lemming, *James Baldwin: A Biography* (New York: Arcade Publishing, 2015), 216–21; Debbie Elliott, "Integrating Ole Miss: A Transformative, Deadly Riot," NPR, October 1, 2012, https://www.npr.org/2012/10/01/161573289/integrating-ole-miss-a-transformative-deadly-riot.

43. Colm Tóibín, "The Last Witness," *London Review of Books* 23, no. 18 (September 20, 2001): 15–20; Gore Vidal, *Conversations with Gore Vidal*, ed. Richard Peabody and Lucinda Ebersole (Oxford: University Press of Mississippi, 2005), 109.

44. Corporate Author, "James Baldwin Early Manuscripts and Papers," Beinecke Rare Book and Manuscript Library, http://hdl.handle.net/10079/fa/beinecke.baldwin; Trudier Harris, introduction to *New Essays on "Go Tell It on the Mountain,"* ed. Trudier Harris (New York: Cambridge University Press, 1996), 1–28; Peter Travers, "'I Am Not Your Negro' Review: James Baldwin Meets #BlackLivesMatter in Bold New Doc," *Rolling Stone*, February 1, 2017.

45. Joan Sibley and Jamie Hawkins-Kirkham, "James Baldwin: An Inventory of His Papers at the Harry Ransom Center," Harry Ransom Center, University of Texas at Austin, 2011, http://norman.hrc.utexas.edu/fasearch/findingAid.cfm?eadid=00551; William J. Maxwell, *F. B. Eyes: How J. Edgar Hoover's Ghostreaders Framed African American Literature* (Princeton, NJ: Princeton University Press, 2015), 277.

46. "About the Schomburg Center for Research in Black Culture," New York Public Library, https://www.nypl.org/about/locations/schomburg; Herb Boyd, *Baldwin's Harlem: A Biography of James Baldwin* (New York: Atria Books, 2008); Lemming, *James Baldwin*, 13; Jennifer Schuessler, "James Baldwin's Archive, Long Hidden, Comes (Mostly) into View," *New York Times*, April 12, 2017; Candice Frederick, "The Schomburg Center Acquires Renowned Literary Icon James Baldwin's Papers," New York Public Library, April 13, 2017, https://www.nypl.org/blog/2017/04/13/james-baldwin-schomburg-center.

47. Audie Cornish and Kevin Young, "Schomburg Center for Research in Black Culture Receives James Baldwin Letters," *All Things Considered*, NPR, April 13, 2017,

http://www.npr.org/2017/04/13/523804448/schomburg-center-for-research-in-black-culture-receives-james-baldwin-letters.
48. Elgrably, "James Baldwin."
49. Ed Pavlić, "Come On Up, Sweetheart: James Baldwin's Letters to His Brother," *Boston Review*, October 14, 2015.
50. Hilton Als, "Family Secrets, PEN America, January 8, 2007, https://pen.org/family-secrets/.
51. Matt Theado, *Understanding Jack Kerouac* (Columbia: University of South Carolina Press, 2000), 24.
52. Mick Brown, "The Battle for Jack Kerouac's Estate," *Telegraph*, October 28, 2009; Sean O'Hagan, "America's First King of the Road," *Guardian*, August 5, 2007; Bruce Horovitz, "Raising the Dead: Past Legends Being Resurrected in New Gap Ads," *Los Angeles Times*, August 10, 1993; "Readers Guide: Questions and Topics for Discussion," in Jack Kerouac, *On the Road: The Original Scroll*, deluxe ed. (New York: Penguin Classics, 2008), n.p.
53. Jan Kerouac met her father only twice and died in 1996. Associated Press, "Jan Kerouac, 44, the Novelist and Daughter of a Beat Icon," *New York Times*, June 8, 1996.
54. Times Wire Service, "Stella Sampas Kerouac, 71; Widow of Beat Generation Novelist," *Los Angeles Times*, February 15, 1990; William R. Levesque, "The Fight over All Things Kerouac," *St. Petersburg Times*, November 24, 2002; "NYPL Acquires Kerouac Archive," *American Libraries*, August 27, 2001.
55. Dave Itzkoff, "Kerouac's Mother's Will Is a Fake, Judge Rules," *New York Times*, July 28, 2008.
56. Jack Boulware, "The Kerouac Obsession," *San Francisco Weekly*, July 19, 1998.

CHAPTER 3: PROFIT

1. Stephen Enniss, "Marketplace," Plenary Session II, Selected Presentations and Documents from the RBMS 2014 Preconference, Rare Book and Manuscripts Section, June 24–27, 2014, http://rbms.info/conferences/2014docs/.
2. Writers whose papers were placed with the support of manuscript dealers included William Gass (Washington University in St. Louis, 1968, House of Books); George Oppen (University of California, San Diego, 1985, an "antiquarian bookseller"); Raymond Carver (Ohio State, 1987, Charles Apfelbaum's Rare Books and Collections); Leslie Marmon Silko (Yale, 1992, Ken Lopez and Joseph the Provider); Robert Creeley (Washington University in St. Louis, 1964, Henry Wenning, and Stanford, 1993, George Minkoff); Philip Levine (NYPL, 1993, James S. Jaffe Rare Books); Kurt Vonnegut (Indiana, 1997, Glenn Horowitz); C. D. Wright (Yale, 2007, Lame Duck Books); Ishmael Reed (Delaware, 1980, Serendipity Books); Pattiann Rogers (Texas Tech, 2012, unnamed manuscript dealer); N. Scott Momaday (Yale, 2012, Ken Lopez); and Gerald Vizenor (Yale, 2000, Ken Lopez). Writers whose papers were placed with the support of agents were Yusef Komunyakaa (Yale, 2014,

Chris Calhoun Agency); James Dickey (Emory, 1993, Eugene H. Winick of McIntosh and Otis, Inc.); Tennessee Williams (Columbia, 1994, Glenn Horowitz); David Mamet (Texas, 2007, Howard Rosenstone); Amiri Baraka (Columbia, 2008, Glenn Horowitz); and Louise Glück (Yale, 2008, Andrew Wylie).

3. *Describing Archives: A Content Standard, Second Edition (DACS)*, Society of American Archivists, 2013, https://www2.archivists.org/standards/DACS/part_I/chapter_5/1_custodial_history, and https://www2.archivists.org/standards/DACS/part_I/chapter_5/2_immediate_source_of_acquisition; Tom Nesmith, "Seeing Archives: Postmodernism and the Changing Intellectual Place of Archives," *American Archivist* 65 (Spring/Summer 2002): 24–41.
4. Society of American Archivists, *A Glossary of Archives and Records Terminology*, s.v. "agent," http://www2.archivists.org/glossary/terms/a/agent.
5. Enniss, "Marketplace," minute 49–50.
6. Thomas F. Staley, "The Fleur Cowles *Flair* Symposium 2000: The Infinite Library, Old Worlds and New: Manuscripts, Archives, and Special Collections in the Twenty-First Century," *Libraries & Culture* 37, no. 1 (Winter 2002): 2–3.
7. Lisa Browar, "Pushing Paper: Dealers and Institutional Collectors," *Libraries & Culture* 37, no. 1 (Winter 2002): 55.
8. Debby Mayer, *Literary Agents: A Writer's Guide* (New York: Poets & Writers, 1998), 78.
9. James L. W. West III, *American Authors and the Literary Marketplace* (Philadelphia: University of Pennsylvania Press), 79.
10. Matthew Lavin, "It's Mr. Reynolds Who Wishes It: Profit and Prestige Shared by Cather and Her Literary Agent," *Cather Studies* 9 (2011): 173.
11. Mary Ann Gillies, *The Professional Literary Agent in Britain, 1880–1920* (Toronto: University of Toronto Press, 2007), 5.
12. Auden quoted in West, *American Authors*, 90.
13. Raymond Chandler, "Ten Per Cent of Your Life," *Atlantic Monthly*, February 1952, 48.
14. West, *American Authors*, 101.
15. Kenneth W. Rendell, "Tax Appraisals of Manuscript Collections," *American Archivist* 46, no. 3 (Summer 1983): 307.
16. Barbara J. Kaiser, "Problems with Donors of Contemporary Collections," *American Archivist* 32, no. 2 (April 1969): 106; William S. Reese, "The Rare Book Market Today," *Yale University Library Gazette* 73, no. 3/4 (April 2000): 153.
17. Rachel Donadio, "The Papers Chase," *New York Times*, March 25, 2007; Thompson, *Merchants of Culture*, 64–71.
18. Craig Lambert, "Fifteen Percent of Immortality," *Harvard Magazine*, July–August 2010, http://harvardmagazine.com/2010/07/fifteen-percent-of-immortality.
19. Laura Bennett, "The Andrew Wylie Rules," *New Republic*, October 7, 2013.

20. Lavin, "It's Mr. Reynolds," 164.
21. Andrew Wylie provided his client list, which included eleven *NAAL* authors. However, when institutions self-reported the use of literary agents—not just Wylie, but any agent—only six *NAAL* collections were earmarked as coming through this type of executor. The discrepancy between reported use and actual use is a problem of definition (what constitutes a literary agent, especially when a top one like Wylie does not belong to the professional organization); metadata (institutions elect to provide such information on a finding aid); and ethics (does reporting the use of agents and dealers violate the author's privacy). "Client List," Wylie Agency, http://www.wylieagency.com/clients.html.
22. Emma Brockes, "Agent Provocateur," *Guardian*, November 23, 2003; Robert McCrum, "Andrew Wylie," *Observer*, April 17, 2010.
23. McCrum, "Andrew Wylie"; Bennett, "The Andrew Wylie Rules."
24. "Lippincott Massie McQuilkin Acquires Russell & Volkening," *Publishers Weekly*, March 6, 2012.
25. Saul Bellow, *Letters*, ed. Benjamin Taylor (New York: Penguin Books, 2010), 327.
26. Harriet Wasserman, *Handsome Is: Adventures with Saul Bellow, a Memoir* (New York: Fromm, 1997), 186, 190.
27. Robert Worth, "Review of *Handsome Is: Adventures with Saul Bellow, a Memoir*," *New York Times*, June 29, 1997.
28. Claire Howorth, "Harriet Wasserman, Literary Agent Scandal, and Ted Mooney," *Daily Beast*, June 26, 2010, https://www.thedailybeast.com/harriet-wasserman-literary-agent-scandal-and-ted-mooney; Jonon Fisher, "Star Agent Scammed Us: Writers," *New York Post*, June 3, 2007; Chuck Sambuchino, "Harriet Wasserman Literary Agency Closes," *Writer's Digest*, November 19, 2007.
29. Ken Lopez, "Some Thoughts on the Maturing of the Rare Book Market at the Start of the 21st Century," Ken Lopez Bookseller, 2002, https://lopezbooks.com/articles/fabs/.
30. With thanks to W. Bartley Hildreth for making this observation. Barry Newman, "As Trash Goes, Authors' Clutter in the Right Hands Is Very Bankable," *Wall Street Journal*, January 3, 2013.
31. The *NAAL* data set records twelve collections managed by manuscript dealers but does not indicate which dealers were used. It is likely that the same self-reporting problem occurs in the dealer data that was highlighted in the agent data, namely, institutional self-reporting does not match agent/dealer self-reporting. Collections Handled, Ken Lopez Archives, http://archives.lopezbooks.com/.
32. Ken Lopez, Ken Lopez Archives, http://archives.lopezbooks.com/.
33. Michael Ryan, "Review of *Book Talk: Essays on Books, Booksellers, Collecting, and Special Collections* by Robert H. Jackson and Carol Z. Rothkopf," *Papers of the Bibliographical Society of America* 101, no. 2 (June 2007): 236.

34. Laura Barber, "10,000 Hours: Glenn Horowitz," *Port Magazine*, August 2013, http://www.port-magazine.com/literature/10000-hours-glenn-horowitz/; Brian Cassidy, "Chasing Tiger Woods and Rare Books: Hemingway Collection of Barry Levine," *Fine Books & Collections*, February 4, 2010.
35. Again, institutional self-reporting and dealer self-reporting do not generate the same picture of the market. The *NAAL* data record only 12 collections managed by manuscript dealers. As the data set does not record names, these dealers could be either Lopez or Horowitz—or another dealer not discussed in *Placing Papers*. As dealer self-reporting records that Horowitz managed nine and Lopez five collections, dealer self-reporting results in two more collections counted as moving through their possession than what institutions indicate. "Selected Archival Transactions," Glenn Horowitz, Bookseller, https://glennhorowitz.com/wp-content/uploads/2019/06/GHB_Project_List.pdf.
36. Michael Watts, "Lord of the Files," *Christie's*, September 22, 2016, https://www.christies.com/features/Glenn-Horowitz-literary-archives-broker-7686-1.aspx; Ben Sisario, "Bob Dylan's Secret Archive," *New York Times*, March 2, 2016; East Hampton Gallery, Glenn Horowitz Books, https://web.archive.org/web/20180808112009/glennhorowitz.com/easthampton (no longer available).
37. Donadio, "The Papers Chase."
38. Browar, "Pushing Paper," 53.
39. Browar, 53.
40. With thanks to W. Bartley Hildreth for supplying the terminology "asymmetric information."
41. Robert A. Wilson, *Modern Book Collecting: A Basic Guide to All Aspects of Book Collecting—What to Collect, Who to Buy from, Auctions, Bibliographies, Care, Fakes and Forgeries, Investments, Donations, Definitions, and More* (New York: Skyhorse, 2010), 65.
42. Michèle Kohler, "The British Trade and Institutional Libraries," in *Out of Print and into Profit: A History of the Rare and Secondhand Book Trade in Britain in the Twentieth Century*, ed. Giles Mandelbrote (London: British Library, 2006), 179.
43. Howard Rootenberg, "A Future Path of RBMS: A Bookseller's Point of View," *RBM: A Journal of Rare Books, Manuscripts, and Cultural Heritage* 14, no. 1 (2013): 33.

CHAPTER 4: COMPETITION

1. Fiona Mackay, Meryl Kenney, and Louise Chappell, "New Institutionalism through a Gender Lens: Towards a Feminist Institutionalism?," *International Political Science Review/Revue internationale de science politique* 31, no. 5 (November 2010): 579.
2. E. G. Austin, "Collecting with a Vengeance," *Economist*, June 28, 2011.
3. D. T. Max, "Final Destination," *New Yorker*, June 4, 2007.

4. Deanna B. Marcum, "Historical Context and Contemporary Challenges," *Academic Librarianship Today*, ed. Todd Gilman (Lanham: Rowman & Littlefield, 2017), 7.
5. Stephen Enniss, "Marketplace," Rare Book and Manuscript Section, June 2014, 57:00–1:00:00, http://rbms.info/conferences2/preconfdocs/2014/talks/2014_plenary2.mp3.
6. Library Investment Index Ranking, ARL Statistics, Association of Research Libraries, 2013–2014, http://www.arlstatistics.org/home.
7. Table 1 is provided in chapter 2.
8. The archival profession did not reflect on the economy in the 1980s in its journal of record, *American Archivist*. Instead, archivists preferred to focus on political, social, and professional concerns. To find this conclusion, I conducted a word search of issues of *American Archivist* 41–52 (1980–89). Rush Miller, "Damn the Recession, Full Speed Ahead," *Journal of Library Administration* 52, no. 3 (2012): 4.
9. Karen Grassmuck, "Slowdown Seen for Endowments," *Chronicle of Higher Education*, November 14, 1990.
10. This point is worth revising after 2020.
11. John L. Pulley and Anne Marie Borrego, "Wealthiest Colleges Lost Billions in Endowment Value in Last Year," *Chronicle of Higher Education*, October 19, 2001.
12. Charles B. Lowry, "Year Two of the 'Great Recession': Surviving the Present by Building the Future," *Journal of Library Administration* 51, no. 1 (2010): 39.
13. Don Troop, "Gifts to Colleges Hit $33.8 Billion, Topping Pre-Recession Levels," *Chronicle of Higher Education*, February 12, 2014; Chronicle Staff, "Early Data Show Double-Digit Growth in Endowment Returns," *Chronicle of Higher Education*, November 3, 2014.
14. Rush Miller, "Damn the Recession," 4.
15. Robert L. Houbeck Jr., "Leveraging our Assets: The Academic Library and Campus Leadership," *The Bottom Line: Managing Library Finances* 15, no. 2 (2002): 54.
16. Mark D. Winston and Lisa Dunkley, "Leadership Competencies for Academic Libraries: The Importance of Development and Fund-Raising," *College & Research Libraries* 63, no. 2 (March 2002): 171–82.
17. The Ransom Center operates separately from the rest of the libraries at the University of Texas–Austin. "UT Libraries' Org Structure," February 22, 2018, https://legacy.lib.utexas.edu/d7/sites/default/files/ut-libraries-org-structure.pdf. With thanks to Hannah Alpert-Abrams for this clarification.
18. Clifford Endres, "Paying the Price: Recipe for Trouble at UT-Austin: A Coveted Job, a Fat Budget, and an Expensive Taste for Rare Books," *Texas Monthly*, May 1988, 126; Max, "Final Destination."
19. Greg Barnhisel, *Cold War Modernists: Art, Literature, and American Cultural Diplomacy* (New York: Columbia University Press, 2015), 20, 2.

20. "Understanding PUF: What Is the Permanent University Fund?," University of Texas System, August 22, 2016, https://www.utsystem.edu/offices/chancellor/blog/what-is-the-permanent-university-fund; Mary G. Ramos, "Oil and Texas: A Cultural History," Texas Almanac, Texas State Historical Association, http://texasalmanac.com/topics/business/oil-and-texas-cultural-history; James Osborne, "Oil Boom Sends Gusher of Cash to Texas Universities," *Dallas News*, May 2014; John B. Thomas III, "Beginnings: The Rare Books Collection, 1897–1955," in *Collecting the Imagination: The First Fifty Years of the Ransom Center*, ed. Megan Barnard (Austin: University of Texas Press, 2007), 3.
21. Stephen C. Mielke, email correspondence with author, November 2, 2017.
22. "Harry Huntt Ransom," Office of the President, University of Texas at Austin, https://president.utexas.edu/past-presidents/harry-huntt-ransom.
23. Harry Huntt Ransom, "Harry Huntt Ransom," in *"The Conscience of the University" and Other Essays*, ed. Hazel H. Ransom (Austin: University of Texas Press, 1982), viii.
24. Margaret C. Berry, "Ransom, Harry Huntt," Handbook of Texas Online, Texas State Historical Association, accessed June 15, 2010, https://tshaonline.org/handbook/online/articles/fra59.
25. Alan Gribben, *Harry Huntt Ransom: Intellect in Motion* (Austin: University of Texas Press, 2008).
26. See the *Bibliography of D. H. Lawrence* (1963); *D. H. Lawrence and His World* (1966); and *Phoenix II: Uncollected, Unpublished, and Other Prose Work by D. H. Lawrence* (1968). Emily Grover, "Roberts, Francis Warren," Texas State Historical Association, https://tshaonline.org/handbook/online/articles/frogr.
27. "History," Harry Ransom Center, University of Texas at Austin, https://web.archive.org/web/20181110110304/http://www.hrc.utexas.edu/about/us/history/.
28. Adrian H. Goldstone also has his own manuscript collection, MS-1651, at the Ransom Center,.
29. James M. Dourgarian, "Interview with John R. Payne," James M. Dourgarian, Bookman, January 20, 2014, https://jimbooks.wordpress.com/2014/01/20/interview-with-john-r-payne/. In 2017, the William Reese Company listed Payne's personal copy on AbeBooks for $950. The other 22 copies on the market at the same time ranged between $90 and $683. "John Steinbeck: A Bibliographical Catalogue of the Adrian H. Goldstone Collection," AbeBooks.com, https://www.abebooks.com/book-search/title/steinbeck-bibliographical-catalogue/author/goldstone-adrian-john-payne/.
30. Megan Barnard, *Collecting the Imagination: The First Fifty Years of the Ransom Center* (Austin: Harry Ransom Research Center, 2007), 54; "US Business Cycle Expansions and Contractions," Public Information Office, National Bureau of Economic Research, September 20, 2010, http://www.nber.org/cycles.html; "US Business Cycle Expansions and Contractions," Public Information Office, National Bureau

of Economic Research, September 20, 2010, http://www.nber.org/cycles.html; "Oil Embargo, 1973–1974," Office of the Historian, https://history.state.gov/milestones/1969-1976/oil-embargo (no longer available); William S. Reese, "The Rare Book Market Today," *Yale University Library Gazette* 73, no. 3/4 (April 2000): 148; Dourgarian, "Interview with John R. Payne"; John R. Payne & Associates, "About," http://www.payne-associates.com/about.htm.

31. Monique Daviau, Richard Workman, and Catherine Stollar, "Carlton Lake: An Inventory of His Collection at the Harry Ransom Center," Harry Ransom Center, University of Texas at Austin, http://norman.hrc.utexas.edu/fasearch/findingAid.cfm?eadid=00291p1; "In Memoriam: Carlton Lake," Harry Ransom Center Newsletter, Summer 2006, http://www.hrc.utexas.edu/ransomedition/2006/summer/4.html (no longer available).

32. Lake coauthored *Life with Picasso* (1964) and wrote *A Dictionary of Modern Painting* (1956), *In Quest of Dali* (1969), and *Confessions of a Literary Archaeologist* (1990).

33. Mielke, email correspondence with author.

34. "Decherd H. Turner, Jr.," Bridwell Library, Perkins School of Theology, Southern Methodist University, https://www.smu.edu/Bridwell/SpecialCollectionsandArchives/Exhibitions/Archives/Bridwell/DecherdTurner; Philip R. Bishop, "Decherd Turner Dies," Mosher Press, July 18, 2002, http://www.thomasbirdmosher.net/publications-by-philip-r-bishop/other/decherd-turner-dies/.

35. US Inflation Calculator, accessed March 22, 2018, http://www.usinflationcalculator.com/; Gribben, *Harry Huntt Ransom*, 179.

36. Endres, "Paying the Price," 124, 128; "History," About the Harry Ransom Center, Harry Ransom Center, University of Texas at Austin, http://www.hrc.utexas.edu/about/us/history/ (no longer available).

37. Stuart Riley, "Thomas Staley, Director of the Harry Ransom Center, to Retire," *Daily Texan*, April 8, 2013; Max, "Final Destination."

38. E. G. Austin, "Collecting with a Vengeance," *Economist*, June 28, 2011; Max, "Final Destination."

39. Gloria Anzaldúa placed her papers at the Benson Latin American Collection at the University of Texas at Austin during Staley's tenure; however, Anzaldúa's papers would have been managed by a different director as the two libraries operate independently. Therefore, her collection is counted in the overall number of holdings attributed to Texas, although it is not included here in the description of Staley's career. "History," https://web.archive.org/web/20181110110304/http://www.hrc.utexas.edu/about/us/history/; Max, "Final Destination."

40. "Currents: Professionals on the Move," *American Libraries* 34, no. 10 (November 2003): 56–58; Jeanne Claire van Ryzin, "Stephen Enniss Puts Mark on Storied Ransom Center," *Austin American-Statesman*, August 27, 2016; Mielke, email correspondence with author.

41. Donald C. Gallup, "Aldis, Foley, and the Collection of American Literature at Yale," *Papers of the Bibliographical Society of America* 42, no. 1 (1948): 41–42; Donald Gallup, "The Collection of American Literature," *The Beinecke Rare Book and Manuscript Library: A Guide to Its Collections* (New Haven, CT: Yale University Library, 1974), 73–74.
42. Marjorie G. Wynne, "The Rare Book Collections at Yale Recollections, 1942–1987," in *Sol. M. Malkin Lectureship in Bibliography* (New York: Book Arts Press, 1987), 14.
43. Donald C. Gallup, *What Mad Pursuits! More Memories of a Yale Librarian* (New Haven, CT: Yale University Press, 1998), 50.
44. "Edith Wharton collection, 1868–1981 (inclusive)," Beinecke Rare Book & Manuscript Library, Yale University, https://orbis.library.yale.edu/vwebv/holdingsInfo?bibId=3435140.
45. "American Literature," Beinecke Rare Book & Manuscript Library, Yale University Library, https://web.archive.org/web/20160313081136/https://beinecke.library.yale.edu/collections/curatorial-areas/american-literature; Alvaro Ribeiro, SJ, "The Tinker Legacy: The Yale 'School' of Eighteenth-Century Studies," *Yale University Library Gazette* 80, no. 1/2 (October 2005): 23; Gallup, *What Mad Pursuits!*, 3–4; "Chauncey Brewster Tinker (1962)," Office of the Secretary and Vice President for Student Life, Yale University, http://secretary.yale.edu/department/chauncey-brewster-tinker-1962; "Chauncey Brewster Tinker letters and manuscripts," Beinecke Rare Book & Manuscript Library, Archives at Yale, http://hdl.handle.net/10079/fa/beinecke.tinklet.
46. Donald Gallup, *Pigeons on the Granite: Memories of a Yale Librarian* (New Haven, CT: Beinecke Rare Book & Manuscript Library, 1988), 3–4, 14, 77, 215.
47. Frank M. Turner, "Meditations on the Beinecke Rare Book and Manuscript Library," *Yale University Library Gazette* 82, no. 3/4 (April 2008): 143; Donald Gallup, "The Ezra Pound Archive at Yale," *Yale University Library Gazette* 60, no. 3/4 (April 1986): 161–63; Eric Homberger, "Donald Gallup," *Guardian*, September 13, 2000; Donald Gallup, "The William Carlos Williams Collection at Yale," *Yale University Library Gazette* 56, no. 1/2 (October 1981): 50–59; William H. Honan, "Donald Gallup Dies at 87; Bibliographer of T. S. Eliot," *New York Times*, September 10, 2000.
48. Gallup, *Pigeons on the Granite*, 191–210; Gallup, "Ezra Pound Archive at Yale," 161–77.
49. Donald Gallup, "The Gertrude Stein Collection," *Yale University Library Gazette* 22, no. 2 (October 1947): 22.
50. Joseph Reed, "Remarks on the Occasion of the Thirtieth Birthday of the Beinecke Rare Book and Manuscript Library," *Yale University Library Gazette* 68, no. 3/4 (April 1994): 105.
51. Aaron D. Purcell, *Academic Archives: Managing the Next Generation of College and University Archives, Records, and Special Collections* (Chicago: Neal-Schuman, 2012),

55; Marjorie G. Wynne, "Donald C. Gallup, 1913–2000," *Yale Library Gazette* 76, no. 1/2 (October 2001): 18; Gallup, *Pigeons on the Granite*, 328.

52. Patricia C. Willis, "The Collection of American Literature," *The Beinecke Library of Yale University*, ed. Stephen Parks (New Haven, CT: Beinecke Rare Book & Manuscript Library, 2003), 126.

53. Patricia C. Willis, "Petals on a Wet Black Bough: American Modernism and the Orient," *Yale University Library Gazette* 71, no. 1/2 (October 1996): 61–71.

54. Adrienne Raphel, "The Marianne Moore Revival," *New Yorker*, April 13, 2016.

55. Raphel, "The Marianne Moore Revival"; Jeredith Merrin, "Hummingbird—for Patricia C. Willis," Marianne Moore Society, June 13, 2015, https://mooresociety.org/2015/06/13/hummingbird-a-poem-for-patricia-c-willis-by-jeredith-merrin/.

56. Nancy Kuhl, email correspondence with author, April 2, 2018; Nancy Kuhl, Melissa Barton, and Anna Franz, email correspondence with author, November 7, 2017.

57. "David F. Swensen, B.A., B.S., '80, Ph.D., '14 L.H.D.," Leadership and Organization, Yale University, https://www.yale.edu/about-yale/leadership-organization/david-swensen; Seth Zweifler, "At Yale, an Investment Guru Grooms a New Generation," *Chronicle of Higher Education*, August 12, 2013.

58. Brenda Cronin, "Yale Set to Reopen Its Renovated Beinecke Rare Book and Manuscript Library," *Wall Street Journal*, July 21, 2016.

59. Mattie Taomina, Twitter Direct Message with author, April 17, 2017; Larry Scott, email correspondence with author, October 30, 2017.

60. Terrence McCarthy, "The College Died, but the Students Really Lived," *New York Times*, March 14, 1992.

61. Corporate Author, "The Charles Olson Research Collection," University of Connecticut Library, http://lib.uconn.edu/libraries/asc/collections/the-charles-olson-research-collection/.

62. Stephen J. Potchatek, Steven Mandeville-Gamble, and Diana Kohnke, "Guide to the Robert Creeley Papers, 1950–2011 M0662," Stanford University, Department of Special Collections and University Archives, http://pdf.oac.cdlib.org/pdf/stanford/mss/m0662.pdf; Stephen Burt, "What Life Says to Us," *London Review of Books* 30, no. 4 (February 21, 2008): 20–22.

63. Washington University in St. Louis sought the papers of both Denise Levertov and Robert Creeley in 1964. Levertov was not yet ready to part with her papers in 1964. Creeley, however, chose to accept Washington's offer. As a result, Washington holds Creeley's collection from the 1950s through early 1970s. Creeley decided to sell the remainder of his papers to Stanford in 1993 using the assistance of manuscript dealer George Minkoff. As a result, Creeley's collection is split between the two institutions, with Washington holding papers from the earlier years, while Stanford owns a larger set mainly from the later years. With thanks to Joel Minor

for this information; also see Potchatek, Mandeville-Gamble, and Kohnke, "Guide to the Robert Creeley Papers, 1950–2011, M0662."

64. Allen Ginsberg, "Howl," Poetry Foundation, https://www.poetryfoundation.org/poems/49303/howl.
65. Corrie Goldman, "Through Photos and Memorabilia, Stanford's Allen Ginsberg Collection Captures a Generation," *Stanford Report*, July 19, 2013.
66. Steven Mandeville-Gamble, "Guide to the Allen Ginsberg Papers M0733," Stanford University, Department of Special Collections and University Archives, http://pdf.oac.cdlib.org/pdf/stanford/mss/m0733.pdf.
67. Jennifer B. Lee, email correspondence with author, January 8, 2016.
68. David Margolick, "An Unlikely Home for Ginsberg's Archive," *New York Times Books*, September 20, 1994.
69. Mark Ford, "The Dreams of Allen Ginsberg," *New York Review of Books*, September 27, 2007; Margolick, "An Unlikely Home."
70. "Stanford Unveils Plan to Address Budget Shortfalls," News Release, Stanford University News Service, May 2, 1991, https://news.stanford.edu/pr/91/910502Arc1406.html; "Stanford Management Company," Stanford Management Company, Investment Office, Stanford University, http://www.smc.stanford.edu/; "Stanford Names Van Etten New Chief Financial Officer," News Release, Stanford University News Service, June 14, 1991, https://news.stanford.edu/pr/91/910614Arc1307.html.
71. "Centennial Campaign Surpasses Goal of Raising $1.1 Billion," News Release, Stanford University News Service, June 13, 1991, https://news.stanford.edu/pr/91/910613Arc1309.html; "Libraries and Information Resources Cuts to Focus on Computing Areas," News Release, Stanford University News Service, April 13, 1994, https://news.stanford.edu/pr/94/940413Arc4333.html; "Stanford Acquires Archive of Beat Poet Allen Ginsberg," News Release, Stanford University News Service, September 7, 1994, https://news.stanford.edu/pr/94/940907Arc4140.html.

CHAPTER 5: PROVENANCE

1. Molly Schwartzburg, "Conclusion: Observations on the Archive at the Harry Ransom Center," in *The Legacy of David Foster Wallace*, ed. Samuel Cohen and Lee Konstantinou (Iowa City: University of Iowa Press, 2012), 251–52.
2. Jeff Rice, "Occupying the Digital Humanities," *College English* 75, no. 4 (March 2013): 360.
3. Trevor Muñoz, "Recovering a Humanist Librarianship through Digital Humanities," in *Laying the Foundation: Digital Humanities in Academic Libraries*, ed. John W. White and Heather Gilbert (West Lafayette, IN: Purdue University Press, 2016), 11.
4. Howard D. White, "Citation Analysis and Discourse Analysis Revisited," *Applied Linguistics* 25, no. 1 (2004): 89–116.

5. Malcolm Tight, "Working in Separate Silos? What Citation Patterns Reveal about Higher Education Research Internationally," *Higher Education* 68, no. 3 (September 2014): 380–81; Richard Delgado, "The Imperial Scholar: Reflections on a Review of Civil Rights Literature," *University of Pennsylvania Law Review* 132, no. 3 (March 1984): 561–78; Paula Chakravartty, Rachel Kuo, Victoria Grubbs, and Charlton McIlwain, "#CommunicationSoWhite," *Journal of Communication* 68, no. 4 (April 2018): 254–66; Carrie Mott and Daniel Cockayne, "Citation Matters: Mobilizing the Politics of Citation toward a Practice of 'Conscientious Engagement,'" *Gender, Place & Culture* 24, no. 7 (2017): 954–73; Moya Bailey and Trudy, "On Misogynoir: Citation, Erasure, and Plagiarism," *Feminist Media Studies* 18, no. 4 (March 2018): 762–68.
6. Deborah Jones Merritt, "Scholarly Influence in a Diverse Legal Academy: Race, Sex, and Citation Counts," *Journal of Legal Studies* 29, no. S1 (January 2000): 345–68; Molly M. King, Carl T. Bergstrom, Shelley J. Correll, Jennifer Jacquet, and Jevin D. West, "Men Set Their Own Cites High: Gender and Self-Citation across Fields and over Time," *Socius: Sociological Research for a Dynamic World* 3 (2017): 1–22.
7. Heather Sarson, "Recognition for Group Work: Gender Differences in Academia," *American Economic Review: Papers and Proceedings* 107, no. 5 (2017): 141–45. With thanks to Judith Pascoe for this citation, which was given in the context of her talk, "It's Alive! *Frankenstein*, Collaboration, and the Iowa Salary Data," Workshop for the Digital Scholarship & Publishing Studio, Iowa City, IA, February 2016.
8. Maha Bali, "Inclusive Citation: How Diverse Are Your References?," ProfHacker, February 22, 2018, https://www.chronicle.com/blogs/profhacker/inclusive-citation-how-diverse-are-your-references/65070; Christen A. Smith, Cite Black Women, CiteBlackWomencollective.org, with thanks to Jodi Reeves Eyre for pointing me to this resource.
9. Anne J. Gilliland, "Standardizing and Automating American Archival Description and Access," in *Conceptualizing 21st-Century Archives* (Chicago: Society of American Archivists, 2014), 83–109.
10. Kathleen Fenney, email correspondence with author, August 30, 2017.
11. Hilary Dorsch Wong, email correspondence with author, August 28, 2017.
12. Jackie Dooley, "Feeding Our Young," *American Archivist* 77, no. 1 (April 2014): 11.
13. Elizabeth Snowden Johnson, "Our Archives, Our Selves: Documentation Strategy and the Re-Appraisal of Professional Identity," *American Archivist* 71, no. 1 (Spring/Summer 2008): 191–93.
14. Jacqueline Goggin, "That We Shall Truly Deserve the Title of 'Profession': The Training and Education of Archivists, 1930–1960," *American Archivist* 47, no. 3 (Summer 1984): 243; Sara Powell, "LIS 438: Literature Review, on the Necessity of Historical Studies in Archival Education," Simmons College, November 12, 2014, 2.
15. "Master of Archival Studies (MAS)," University of British Columbia, https://www.grad.ubc.ca/prospective-students/graduate-degree-programs/master-of-archival

-studies. With thanks to Sara Powell, Kathleen Roe, John Russell, and Eric Willey for responding to my Twitter query on March 28, 2018.
16. Goggin, "That We Shall Truly Deserve," 250; "GPAS Curriculum," Society of American Archivists, https://www2.archivists.org/prof-education/graduate/gpas/curriculum.
17. Stacie Williams, "Implications of Archival Labor," *On Archivy*, April 11, 2016, https://medium.com/on-archivy/implications-of-archival-labor-b606d8d02014.
18. Kate Eichhorn, *The Archival Turn in Feminism: Outrage in Order* (Philadelphia: Temple University Press, 2013), 1–2.
19. James F. English, *The Economy of Prestige: Prizes, Awards, and the Circulation of Cultural Value* (Cambridge, MA: Harvard University Press, 2005), vii–viii.
20. Maarja Krusten, Twitter conversation with author, December 26, 2017.
21. Mark A. Greene, "MPLP: It's Not Just for Processing Anymore," *American Archivist* 73, no. 1 (Spring/Summer 2010): 177–78.
22. Mark A. Greene and Dennis Meissner, "More Product, Less Process: Revamping Traditional Archival Processing," *American Archivist* 68, no. 2 (Fall/Winter 2005): 208–63; Emily R. Novak Gustainis, "Processing Workflow Analysis for Special Collections: The Center for the History of Medicine, Francis A. Countway Library of Medicine, as a Case Study," *RBM: A Journal of Rare Books, Manuscripts, and Cultural Heritage* 13, no. 2 (2012): 115–19; Stephanie Bennett and Tanya Zanish-Belcher, Twitter conversation with author, July 19, 2017; Carl Van Ness, "Much Ado about Paper Clips: 'More Product, Less Process' and the Modern Manuscript Repository, or Reply to Mark A. Greene and Dennis Meissner," *American Archivist* 73, no. 1 (Spring/Summer 2010): 129–45; Daniel A. Santamaria, *Extensible Processing for Archives and Special Collections: Reducing Processing Backlog* (Chicago: American Library Association, 2015), 2.
23. Santamaria, *Extensible Processing for Archives*, 139–40.
24. Erin Lawrimore, Twitter conversation with author, July 19, 2017; Marika Cifor and Jamie A. Lee, "Towards an Archival Critique: Opening Possibilities for Addressing Neoliberalism in the Archival Field," *Journal of Critical Library and Information Studies* 1, no. 1 (2017): 12–13.
25. Only Brendan Galvin's papers remain unprocessed as of April 2018. However, the papers of Gwendolyn Brooks and Ursula Le Guin are undergoing processing, and the literary archives of John Ashbery, Toni Cade Bambara, John Cheever, Robert Hayden, Audre Lorde, and Lorine Niedecker do not have online finding aids.
26. Larisa K. Miller, "All Text Considered: A Perspective on Mass Digitizing and Archival Processing," *American Archivist* 76, no. 2 (Fall/Winter 2013): 521–41; Geneva Henry, *Core Infrastructure Considerations for Large Digital Libraries* (Washington, D.C.: Council on Library and Information Resources, July 2012), https://www.clir.org/pubs/reports/pub153/; Ricky Erway and Jennifer Schaffner, *Shifting*

Gears: Gearing Up to Get into the Flow (Dublin, OH: OCLC, 2007), https://www.oclc.org/content/dam/research/publications/library/2007/2007-02.pdf.
27. Bradley J. Daigle, "The Digital Transformation of Special Collections," *Journal of Library Administration* 52, nos. 3–4 (April–June 2012): 244–64.
28. Stephen Enniss, "The Role of the Artifact in a Facsimile Age," *RBM: A Journal of Rare Books, Manuscripts, and Cultural Heritage* 1, no. 1 (2000): 46–47.
29. Leslie Perrin Wilson, "Presentation of Archival Materials on the Web: A Curator's Model Based on Selectivity and Interpretation," in *American Literature Scholar in the Digital Age*, ed. Amy E. Earhart and Andrew Jewell (Ann Arbor: University of Michigan Press and University of Michigan Library, 2011), 85.
30. Miller, "All Text Considered"; Alexandra Mills, "User Impact on Selection, Digitization, and the Development of Digital Special Collections," *New Review of Academic Librarianship* 21, no. 2 (May–August 2015): 160–69.
31. Katherine Fisher, "Barriers to Digital Preservation in Special Collections Departments," *Preservation, Digital Technology & Culture* 45, no. 4 (February 2017): 180–85.
32. Anne R. Kenney, "Mainstreaming Digitization into the Mission of Cultural Repositories," in *Collections, Content, and the Web* (Washington, D.C.: Council on Library and Information Resources, 2000), 11, https://clir.wordpress.clir.org/wp-content/uploads/sites/6/pub88.pdf.
33. Governmental agencies include the National Endowment for the Humanities (NEH), the National Endowment for the Arts (NEA), the Institute of Museum and Library Services (IMLS), and the National Historical Publications and Records Commission (NHPRC); private foundations include the Luce, Knight, Mellon, Sloan, Gates, and Whiting Foundations; and organizations include the American Library Association (ALA), the Digital Public Library of American (DPLA), and the Council on Library and Information Resources (CLIR).
34. Copyright Act, 17 U.S.C. §108 (2016), 19.
35. Social Security Administration, "Benefits Planner/Life Expectancy: Life Expectancy Calculator," https://www.ssa.gov/planners/lifeexpectancy.html.
36. Jeff Cavallin, "University of Texas Paid $2.2 Million for Garcia Márquez Archive," *Dallas News*, February 25, 2015; Gabriel García Márquez, WorldCat, accessed May 18, 2017.
37. "Contact Us," Harry Ransom Center, http://www.hrc.utexas.edu/contact/.
38. Jennifer Tisdale, "Award Supports Digitization of More Than 24,000 Images from the Gabriel García Márquez Archive," *Ransom Center Magazine*, Harry Ransom Center, University of Texas at Austin, January 4, 2016, https://blog.hrc.utexas.edu/2016/01/04/clir-grant/; "Sharing 'Gabo' with the World: Building the Gabriel García Márquez Online Archive from His Papers at the Harry Ransom Center," CLIR Digitizing Hidden Special Collections and Archives Funded Projects 2015, http://registry.clir.org/projects/18602827.

39. Shaheen quoted in Jullianne Ballou, "Scrapbooking Gabo," *Ransom Center Magazine*, Harry Ransom Center, May 15, 2017, https://blog.hrc.utexas.edu/2017/05/15/scrapbooking-the-gabo-way/.
40. Anna R. Craft, David Gwynn, and Kathelene McCarty Smith, "Uncovering Social History: An Interdepartmental Approach to Scrapbook Digitization," *American Archivist* 79, no. 1 (Spring/Summer 2016): 186–200.
41. Jullianne Ballou, "Thousands of Images from Gabriel García Márquez Archive Now Online," Press Release, Harry Ransom Center, University of Texas at Austin, December 12, 2017, https://web.archive.org/web/20181205074956/http://www.hrc.utexas.edu/press/releases/2017/ggm.html.
42. "Timeline: American Generations since 20th Century," Southern California Public Radio, https://web.archive.org/web/20190411155532/http://projects.scpr.org/timelines/american-generations-timeline/.
43. Michael Forstrom, "Managing Electronic Records in Manuscript Collections: A Case Study from the Beinecke Rare Book and Manuscript Library," *American Archivist* 72, no. 2 (Fall/Winter 2009): 460–77.
44. Adrian Cunningham, "The Archival Management of Personal Records in Electronic Form: Some Suggestions," *Archives and Manuscripts* 22 (May 1994): 94–105; Paul Conway, *Preservation in the Digital World* (Washington, D.C.: Council on Library and Information Resources, March 1996), https://www.clir.org/pubs/reports/conway2/index/.
45. Susan E. Davis, "Electronic Records Planning in 'Collecting' Repositories," *American Archivist* 71, no. 1 (Spring/Summer 2008): 168, 177; Gabriela Redwine, Megan Barnard, Kate Donovan, Erika Farr, Michael Forstrom, Will Hansen, Jeremy Leighton John, Nancy Kuhl, Seth Shaw, and Susan Thomas, *Born Digital: Guidance for Donors, Dealers, and Repositories* (Washington, D.C.: Council on Library and Information Resources, October 2013), https://www.clir.org/pubs/reports/pub159/; Ricky Erway, *Swatting the Long Tail of Digital Media: A Call for Collaboration* (Dublin, OH: OCLC Research, 2012), https://www.oclc.org/content/dam/research/publications/library/2012/2012-08.pdf.
46. Ricky Erway and Julianna Barrera-Gomez, *Walk This Way: Detailed Steps for Transferring Born-Digital Content from Media You Can Read In-House* (Dublin, OH: OCLC, 2013), http://www.oclc.org/content/dam/research/publications/library/2013/2013-02.pdf; "AIMS—Born Digital Collections: An Inter-Institutional Model for Stewardship," July 16, 2010, http://files.archivists.org/conference/dc2010/researchforum/MatienzoHandout.pdf; Redwine et al., *Born Digital*, 9; Laura Carroll, Erika Farr, Peter Hornsby, and Ben Ranker, "A Comprehensive Approach to Born-Digital Archives," *Archivaria: The Journal of the Association of Canadian Archivists* 72 (Fall 2011): 61–92.

47. "About the Digital Preservation Coalition," Digital Preservation Coalition, 2019, http://www.dpconline.org/about; Society of American Archivists, "List of SAA Sections," https://www2.archivists.org/governance/handbook/section9/list-of-saa-sections; "Welcome to bloggERS!," January 21, 2015, https://saaers.wordpress.com/2015/01/.
48. Society of American Archivists, "DAS Curriculum Structure," 2017, https://www2.archivists.org/prof-education/das-curriculum-structure; Society of American Archivists, "DAS Courses," April 5, 2017, https://www2.archivists.org/prof-education/das/course-list.
49. These numbers are not mutually exclusive as programs can offer multiple types of degrees and usually provide a variety of specialization options. American Library Association Committee on Accreditation, *Directory of Institutions Offering ALA-Accredited Master's Programs in Library and Information Studies*, 2017, http://www.ala.org/CFApps/lisdir/directory_pdf.cfm.
50. Stephanie L. Maata, "Placements and Salaries 2013: The Emerging Databrarian," *Library Journal*, October 17, 2013.
51. Mary Kendig, Linkedin.com profile, March 27, 2018, https://www.linkedin.com/in/kendigmary/; Mary Kendig, "Identity Crisis: The Reality of Preparing MLS Students for a Competitive and Increasingly Digital World," *Signal*, Library of Congress, April 14, 2017, https://blogs.loc.gov/thesignal/2017/04/identity-crisis-the-reality-of-preparing-mls-students-for-a-competitive-and-increasingly-digital-world/.
52. Richard Pearce-Moses, "The Archival Lexicon," Glossary of Archival and Records Terminology, Society of American Archivists, 2005, http://www2.archivists.org/glossary/archival-lexicon.
53. Tanya Clement, Wendy Hagenmaier, and Jennie Levine Knies, "Toward a Notion of the Archive of the Future: Impressions of Practice by Librarians, Archivists, and Digital Humanities Scholars," *Library Quarterly: Information, Community, Policy* 83, no. 2 (April 2013): 121; Edward Nawotka, "Long at Helm, U.T. Collector Leaves Legacy with His Exit," *New York Times*, August 31, 2013.
54. Matthew G. Kirschenbaum, Erika Farr, Kari M. Kraus, Naomi L. Nelson, Catherine Stollar Peters, Gabriela Redwine, and Doug Reside, *Approaches to Managing and Collecting Born-Digital Literary Materials for Scholarly Use* (Washington, D.C.: NEH Office of Digital Humanities, May 2009), 7, https://drum.lib.umd.edu/bitstream/handle/1903/9787/Born-Digital%20White%20Paper.pdf.
55. Bradley J. Daigle, "The Digital Transformation of Special Collections," *Journal of Library Administration* 52 (2012): 250.
56. Although some institutional projects like the UCSB Cylinder Audio Archive exist to provide access to the music locked in wax cylinders, more repositories hold wax

cylinders than participate in these projects. "UCSB Cylinder Audio Archive," University of California–Santa Barbara Library, http://cylinders.library.ucsb.edu/.

57. Ricky Erway, Ben Goldman, and Matthew McKinley, *Agreement Elements for Outsourcing Transfer of Born Digital Content* (Dublin, OH: OCLC Research, 2014), http://www.oclc.org/content/dam/research/publications/library/2014/oclcresearch-born-digital-content-transfer-2014.pdf.

58. Erway, *Swatting the Long Tail*, 3–7.

59. Adam Kirsch and Anna Holmes, "How Has Twitter Changed the Role of the Literary Critic?," *New York Times*, November 3, 2013.

60. Lorraine York, *Margaret Atwood and the Labour of Literary Celebrity* (Toronto: University of Toronto Press, 2013), 125, 130.

61. Alison Flood, "Jonathan Franzen: 'Twitter Is the Ultimate Irresponsible Medium,'" *Guardian*, March 7, 2012.

62. "Social Media Crawling and Scraping Services for Brand Monitoring," Prompt Cloud, https://www.promptcloud.com/social-media-networking-sites-crawling-service/.

63. Sarah Kim, Lorraine A. Dong, and Megan Durden, "Automated Batch Archival Processing: Preserving Arnold Wesker's Digital Manuscripts," *Archival Issues* 30, no. 2 (2006): 92–93, 95.

64. Lise Jaillant, "Reading Ian McEwan's Correspondence," *Times Literary Supplement*, November 21, 2017.

65. Society of American Archivists, *Glossary of Archival and Records Terminology*, s.v. "migration," https://www2.archivists.org/glossary/terms/m/migration.

66. Margaret L. Hedstrom, Christopher A. Lee, Judith S. Olson, and Clifford A. Lampe, "'The Old Version Flickers More': Digital Preservation from the User's Perspective," *American Archivist* 69, no. 1 (Spring–Summer 2006): 160.

67. Jeff Rothenberg, *Avoiding Technological Quicksand: Finding a Viable Technical Foundation for Digital Preservation* (Washington, D.C.: Council on Library and Information Resources, 1998), https://clir.wordpress.clir.org/wp-content/uploads/sites/6/pub77.pdf.

68. Anne Gilliland-Swetland, "From Education to Application and Back: Archival Literature and an Electronic Records Curriculum," *American Archivist* 56, no. 3 (Summer 1993): 535.

69. Erika Farr, phone interview with author, September 6, 2012; Jennifer L. Brady, Laura Carroll, Liz Chase, Pat Clark, and Amy Hildreth [Chen], Salman Rushdie Papers, Stuart A. Rose Manuscript, Archives, and Rare Book Library, Emory University, https://findingaids.library.emory.edu/documents/rushdie1000/.

70. Dan Rockmore, "The Digital Life of Salman Rushdie," *New Yorker*, July 29, 2014; Patricia Cohen, "Fending Off Digital Decay, Bit by Bit," *New York Times*, March 15,

2010; Devyani Saltzman, "Snooping through Salman Rushdie's Computer," *Atlantic*, April 21, 2010.
71. Hedstrom et al., "'The Old Version Flickers More,'" 160.
72. Kathryn C. Montgomery, *Generation Digital: Politics, Commerce, and Childhood in the Age of the Internet* (Cambridge, MA: MIT Press, 2007), 33.

CHAPTER 6: ACCESS

1. John Cawelti, "The Writer as Celebrity: Some Aspects of American Literature as Popular Culture," *Studies in American Fiction* 5, no. 1 (Spring 1977): 164, quoted in Joe Moran, *Star Authors: Literary Celebrity in America* (London: Pluto Press, 2000), 3.
2. Daniel H. Borus, *Writing Realism: Howells, James, and Norris in the Mass Market* (Chapel Hill: University of North Carolina Press, 1989), 126.
3. Ronna C. Johnson, "'You're Putting Me On': Jack Kerouac and the Postmodern Emergence," *College Literature* 27, no. 1 (Winter 2000): 22.
4. Paul David Grainge, "Advertising the Archive: Nostalgia and the (Post) National Imaginary," *American Studies* 41, no. 2/3 (Summer/Fall 2000): 140.
5. Susan Orlean and Manjula Martin, "Running the Widget Factory," *Scratch: Writers, Money, and the Art of Making a Living* (New York: Simon & Schuster, 2017), 54.
6. Clay Calvert, *Voyeur Nation: Media, Privacy, and Peering in Modern Culture* (Boulder, CO: Westview Press, 2000), 74.
7. Dana Gioia, "The Hand of the Poet: The Magical Value of Manuscripts," *Hudson Review* 49, no. 1 (Spring 1996): 11–12.
8. Gioia, "The Hand of the Poet," 21.
9. Karl Marx, *Capital*, vol. 1, trans. Ben Fowkes (Harmondsworth, UK: Penguin, 1976), 163–65, quoted in Francis Mulhern, "Critical Considerations on the Fetishism of Commodities," *ELH* 74, no. 2 (Summer 2007): 483–84.
10. Maynard Mack, "The Tinker Legacy: The Yale 'School' of Eighteenth-Century Studies," *Yale University Library Gazette* 80, no. 1/2 (October 2005): 25.
11. Pierre-Marc de Biasi, "Toward a Science of Literature: Manuscript Analysis and the Genesis of the Work," *Genetic Criticism: Texts and Avant-textes*, ed. Jed Deppman, Daniel Ferrer, and Michael Groden (Philadelphia: University of Pennsylvania Press, 2004), 39; Daniel Morris, *Not Born Digital: Poetics, Print Literacy, New Media* (New York: Bloomsbury, 2016), 153.
12. Anita Helle, "Archival Matters," in *The Unraveling Archive: Essays on Sylvia Plath*, ed. Anita Helle (Ann Arbor: University of Michigan Press, 2007), 6; Michael Basinski, Marie Elia, Nancy Kuhl, James Maynard, and Edric Mesmer, "Acts of Curation: The Curating of Poetry and the Poetics of Curating: A Roundtable Discussion," *Reading Room: A Journal of Special Collections* 1, no. 1 (2016): 49; Rose Eveleth, "Victorians Made Jewelry Out of Human Hair," SmartNews, Smithsonian.com,

December 24, 2013, https://www.smithsonianmag.com/smart-news/victorians-made-jewelry-out-of-human-hair-180948192/; Harry Huntt Ransom, "Prelude: 'The Collection of Knowledge in Texas,'" in *Collecting the Imagination: The First Fifty Years of the Ransom Center*, ed. Megan Barnard (Austin, TX: Harry Ransom Humanities Research Center, 2007), xvii; Barry Newman, "As Trash Goes, Authors' Clutter in the Right Hands Is Very Bankable," *Wall Street Journal*, January 3, 2013, A1.

13. Kristen Schutjer, John Hawk, and Alison E. Bridger, "Finding Aid to the Richard Brautigan Papers, 1942–2003," University of California, Berkeley, Online Archive of California, http://www.oac.cdlib.org/findaid/ark:/13030/tf096n97xn/; Andrei Codrescu, *Bibliodeath: My Archives with Life in Footnotes* (Williamsburg, NY: Antibookclub, 2012), 117.

14. Matthew Kirschenbaum, *Track Changes: A Literary History of Word Processing* (Cambridge, MA: Belknap Press of Harvard University Press, 2016), 7.

15. Margrit Shildrick, "Some Speculations on Matters of Touch," *Journal of Medicine and Philosophy* 26, no. 4 (2001): 402.

16. Catherine Bates, "'In the Hope of Making a Connection': Rereading Archival Bodies, Responses, and Love in Marian Engle's *Bear* and Alice Munro's 'Meneseteung,'" in *Basements and Attics, Closets and Cyberspace: Explorations in Canadian Women's Archives*, ed. Linda M. Morra and Jessica Schagerl (Waterloo, Canada: Wilfrid Laurier University Press, 2012), 103.

17. Valerie de Craene, "Fucking Geographers! Or the Epistemological Consequences of Neglecting the Lusty Researcher's Body," *Gender, Place & Culture: A Journal of Feminist Geography* 24, no. 3 (April 2017): 450.

18. Jamie A. Lee, "Be/longing in the Archival Body: Eros and the 'Endearing' Value of Material Lives," *Archival Science* 16, no. 1 (March 2016): 47, 35.

19. "The Hand of the Poet—Part Two: E. E. Cummings to Julia Alvarez," New York Public Library, August 16, 1996 to February 22, 2017, https://www.nypl.org/events/exhibitions/hand-poet-part-two-e-e-cummings-julia-alvarez.

20. Fiona Candlin, *Art, Museums, and Touch* (Manchester, UK: Manchester University Press, 2010), 91, 2.

21. Michelle Moravec, "How Digitized* Changed Historical Research," On Archivy, Medium.com, August 23, 2016, https://medium.com/on-archivy/how-digitized-changed-historical-research-d77c78540878; April Hathcock, "Creative Commons Requires Consent," At the Intersection, March 20, 2016, https://aprilhathcock.wordpress.com/2016/03/20/creative-commons-requires-consent/.

22. Society of American Archivists, Code of Ethics for Archivists (Chicago: Society of American Archivists, 1992), not paginated, quoted in Sara S. Hodson, "In Secret Kept, in Silence Sealed: Privacy in the Papers of Authors and Celebrities," *American Archivist* 67, no. 2 (Fall–Winter 2004): 196.

23. Hodson, "In Secret Kept," 197.
24. "What Does Copyright Protect?," FAQ, U.S. Copyright Office, https://www.copyright.gov/help/faq/faq-protect.html. With thanks to Joel Minor for reminding me of Donald Barthelme's novel.
25. "Trademark, Patent, or Copyright?," United States Patent and Trademark Office, https://www.uspto.gov/trademarks-getting-started/trademark-basics/trademark-patent-or-copyright; "Snow White," United States Patent and Trademark Office, November 19, 2008, http://tsdr.uspto.gov/#caseNumber=77618057&caseType=SERIAL_NO&searchType=statusSearch; John Hartley, "Authorship and the Narrative of the Self," *A Companion to Media Authorship*, ed. Jonathan Gray and Derek Johnson (Chichester, UK: Wiley-Blackwell, 2013), 29.
26. William M. Landes and Richard A. Posner, "Copyright in Unpublished Works," in *The Economic Structure of Intellectual Property Law* (Cambridge, MA: Harvard University Press, 2009), 125; Patrick J. Leahy and Paul Simon, "The Salinger Papers," *New York Times Opinion*, July 19, 1991; Douglas Martin, "Ian Hamilton, 63, Whose Salinger Book Caused a Stir, Dies," *New York Times*, January 7, 2002; Andrea Chambers and Jonathan Cooper, "In Search of J. D. Salinger, Biographer Ian Hamilton Discovers a Subject Who Didn't Want to be Found," *People*, June 6, 1988.
27. Cynthia Haven, "Stanford Researcher Gets Six-Figure Settlement from James Joyce Estate," *Stanford News*, September 28, 2009; D. T. Max, "The Injustice Collector," *New Yorker*, June 19, 2006.
28. Loren Glass, *Authors Inc.: Literary Celebrity in the Modern United States, 1880–1980* (New York: New York University Press, 2004), 9–11; Samuel D. Warren and Louis D. Brandeis, "The Right to Privacy," *Harvard Law Review* 4, no. 5 (December 1890): 194–95.
29. Warren and Brandeis, "The Right to Privacy," 193–220.
30. Warren and Brandeis, 218.
31. Frederick S. Lane, *American Privacy: The 400-Year History of Our Most Contested Right* (Boston: Beacon Press, 2009); "Copyright Timeline: A History of Copyright in the United States," Association of Research Libraries, http://www.arl.org/focus-areas/copyright-ip/2486-copyright-timeline#.WjFCqFWnGUk; William W. Fisher III, "The Growth of Intellectual Property: A History of the Ownership of Ideas in the United States," in *Eigentumskulturen im Vergleich* (Göttingen, Germany: Vandenhoeck & Ruprecht, 1999), http://cyber.harvard.edu/property99/history.html.
32. Gordon F. Proudfoot, *Privacy Law and the Media in Canada* (Ottawa: Canadian Bar Foundation, 1986), 3.
33. Corporate Author, "Marianne Moore Collection," Rosenbach, https://rosenbach.org/collection/marianne-moore-collection/.

34. 100 hits, "David Foster Wallace," MLA International Bibliography, November 17, 2017.
35. Mark McGurl, "The Institution of Nothing: David Foster Wallace in the Program," *boundary 2: an international journal of literature and culture* 41, no. 3 (2014): 27–54.
36. John Jeremiah Sullivan, "Too Much Information," *GQ*, March 31, 2011.
37. Michael Pietsch, "Editor's Note," in *The Pale King: An Unfinished Novel*, by David Foster Wallace (New York: Little, Brown, 2011), vi.
38. Pietsch, "Editor's Note," ix; Sullivan, "Too Much Information."
39. Patricia Cohen, "David Foster Wallace Papers Are Bought," *New York Times*, March 8, 2010; "David Foster Wallace Materials Related to 'The Pale King' Now Open for Research," UT News, September 27, 2012, https://news.utexas.edu/2012/09/27/david-foster-wallace-materials-related-to-the-pale-king-now-open-for-research; "David Foster Wallace Archive Acquired by the Harry Ransom Center," March 9, 2010, http://www.hrc.utexas.edu/press/releases/2010/dfw/acquisition.html (no longer available); "About This Collection," David Foster Wallace's *The Pale King*, Harry Ransom Center Digital Collections, University of Texas at Austin, http://hrc.contentdm.oclc.org/cdm/landingpage/collection/p15878coll20#nav_top (no longer available).
40. Molly Schwartzburg, "Observations on the Archive at the Harry Ransom Center," in *The Legacy of David Foster Wallace*, ed. Samuel Cohen and Lee Konstantinou (Iowa City: University of Iowa Press, 2012), 243; Maria Bustillos, "Inside David Foster Wallace's Private Self-Help Library," Awl, April 5, 2011, https://www.theawl.com/2011/04/inside-david-foster-wallaces-private-self-help-library/.
41. 54 citations, "*Infinite Jest*," MLA International Bibliography, December 12, 2017.
42. McGurl, "The Institution of Nothing," 33.
43. Kathleen Fitzpatrick, "Infinite Summer: Reading, Empathy, and the Social Network," in *The Legacy of David Foster Wallace*, ed. Samuel Cohen and Lee Konstantinou (Iowa City: University of Iowa Press, 2012), 185.
44. Fitzpatrick, "Infinite Summer," 185.
45. Max Ross, "From the Archives: A Voyeur in the Archives," *Open Letters Monthly: An Arts and Literature Review*, September 1, 2012, https://www.openlettersmonthly.com/voyeurs-in-the-archives/.
46. Ross, "From the Archives."
47. Calvert, *Voyeur Nation*, 78.
48. Derek Johnson and Jonathan Gray, introduction to *A Companion to Media Authorship*, ed. Jonathan Gray and Derek Johnson (Chichester, UK: Wiley-Blackwell, 2013), 4.
49. D. T. Max, "D. F. W.: Tracing the Ghostly Origins of Phrase," *New Yorker*, December 11, 2012.

CONCLUSION: THE MATTHEW EFFECT

1. William S. Reese, "The Rare Book Market Today," *Yale University Library Gazette* 73, no. 3/4 (April 2000): 157.
2. Daniel Rigney, preface to *The Matthew Effect: How Advantage Begets Further Advantage* (New York: Columbia University Press, 2010), not paginated.
3. Matt. 25:29 (King James Version); Matt. 25:29 (Revised Standard Version).
4. Michael Boydon, *Predicting the Past: The Paradoxes of American Literary History* (Leuven, Belgium: Leuven University Press, 2009), 146–52.
5. Kate Eichhorn, introduction to *The Archival Turn in Feminism: Outrage in Order* (Philadelphia: Temple University Press, 2013), 15; Joel M. Podolny, *Status Signals: A Sociological Study of Market Competition* (Princeton, NJ: Princeton University Press, 2005), 23.
6. "Jhumpa Lahiri," WATCH: Writers Artists and their Copyright Holders, Harry Ransom Center at the University of Texas at Austin and the University of Reading, http://norman.hrc.utexas.edu/watch/record_detail.cfm?contactid=1432&IndivID=3918&ArtistID=15998; "Our Story," WME, http://wmeentertainment.com/story/; Leon Neyfakh, "Why Did Janklow Prince Eric Simonoff Defect to William Morris," *Observer*, March 16, 2009; Michael Szczerban, "Agents & Editors: Eric Simonoff," *Poets & Writers* (July/August 2013): 1.
7. Szczerban, "Agents & Editors," 2.
8. Dana Gioia, "The Hand of the Poet: The Magical Value of Manuscripts," *Hudson Review* 49, no. 1 (Spring 1996): 9–29.
9. Charles T. Clotfelter, "How Rich Universities Get Richer . . . and Leave Everyone Else Behind," *Chronicle of Higher Education*, October 27, 2017.
10. Moisés Naím, "The Hidden Effects of Cheap Oil," *Atlantic*, March 31, 2015; Todd Davis, "University of Texas' Energy-Driven Endowment Shrinks; Why Is It Investing More in Oil, Gas?," *Dallas News*, February 2016.
11. Michael Basinski, Marie Elia, Nancy Kuhl, James Maynard, and Edric Mesmer, "Acts of Curation: The Curating of Poetry and the Poetics of Curating: A Roundtable Discussion," *Reading Room: A Journal of Special Collections* 1, no. 1 (2016): 40.
12. Edward J. Delaney, "Where Great Writers Are Made," *Atlantic*, August 2007.
13. Robert Duncan's collections at Kent State University and the University of California, Berkeley, are 1 box; the University of California, Santa Cruz, holds only 11 folders; and Washington University in St. Louis has 2 boxes.
14. Louise Erdrich's collection at the University of North Dakota is 0.25 linear feet. Frank O'Hara's collection at the Museum of Modern Art is 2 linear feet, but it cannot be counted as it does not relate to his literary career, only his professional work as a curator. His other collections are too small to be counted: he has 1 box at Columbia University, 1 folder at the University of Chicago, and 1 centimeter of files

at the University of Victoria. Eudora Welty's collection at LSU is too small to be counted at 53 items. Grace Paley's collection at the Ransom Center is too small to be counted at 0.42 linear feet. Michael S. Harper appears only in other poets' collections or in institutional holdings as a conference presenter, guest author reading from his works, or honoree.

15. Johnny Depp, introduction to *Gonzo: The Life of Hunter S. Thompson, An Oral Biography*, by Jann S. Wenner and Corey Seymour (New York: Little, Brown, 2007), xxiii; Chris Heath, "Johnny Depp's Savage Journey into 'Fear and Loathing in Las Vegas,'" *Rolling Stone*, June 11, 1998.
16. B. J. Daigle, "The Digital Transformation of Special Collections," *Journal of Library Administration* 52, nos. 3–4 (July 2, 2012): 253.
17. For more on monuments, see Barbara Godard, "Canadian Women Writers in and out of the Archive," *Trans/Acting Culture, Writing, and Memory: Essays in Honour of Barbara Godard*, ed. Eva C. Karpinski, Jennifer Henderson, Ian Sowton, and Ray Ellenwood (Waterloo, UK: Wilfrid Laurier University Press, 2013), 308–12.
18. Greg Barnhisel, *Cold War Modernists: Art, Literature, and American Cultural Diplomacy* (New York: Columbia University Press, 2015), 184.
19. Nick Spitzer, "The Story of Woody Guthrie's 'This Land Is Your Land,'" The NPR 100, February 15, 2012, https://www.npr.org/2000/07/03/1076186/this-land-is-your-land.
20. "About the WGC Archives," Woody Guthrie Center, http://woodyguthriecenter.org/archives/history-of-archives/; "Archives," Woody Guthrie Center, http://woodyguthriecenter.org/archives/; "BMI Foundation Woody Guthrie Fellowship," Woody Guthrie Center, http://woodyguthriecenter.org/archives/bmi-fellowship/.
21. "George Kaiser," profile, *Forbes*, May 12, 2018, https://www.forbes.com/profile/george-kaiser/.
22. Alan Gallindoss, "George Kaiser Buys into Oklahoma City Basketball Team," *Jewish Business News*, April 19, 2014.
23. Bob Dylan, "Song to Woody," Bob Dylan, https://bobdylan.com/songs/song-woody/.
24. Agence France-Presse, "Bob Dylan Finally Accepts Nobel Prize in Literature at Private Ceremony in Stockholm," *Guardian*, April 2, 2017.
25. Karen Heller, "A Billionaire's Quirky Quest to Create a Mecca for Bob Dylan Fans—in Tulsa, Oklahoma," *Chicago Tribune*, October 13, 2017; Ben Sisario, "Bob Dylan's Secret Archive," *New York Times*, March 2, 2016; "TU Institute for Bob Dylan Studies Announced," University of Tulsa, October 25, 2017, https://utulsa.edu/news/tu-institute-bob-dylan-studies-announced/.
26. Reuters Staff, "Bob Dylan Sells Treasure Trove of Archive Material," Reuters, March 2, 2016, https://www.reuters.com/article/us-people-bobdylan/bob-dylan-sells-treasure-trove-of-archive-material-idUSKCN0W42FU; "Coming Home: The Woody Guthrie Center Opens in Tulsa," NPR, May 28, 2013, https://www.npr

.org/2013/05/28/186893611/coming-home-the-woody-guthrie-center-opens-in-tulsa.
27. Jon Blistein, "Massive Bob Dylan Archive Opens in Oklahoma," *Rolling Stone*, March 28, 2017; Andy Greene, "Exclusive: A Look Inside Bob Dylan's Secret Archives, *Rolling Stone*, June 27, 2017; Heller, "A Billionaire's Quirky Quest."
28. "The Bob Dylan Archive," George Kaiser Family Foundation, http://www.gkff.org/bobdylancenter/ (no longer available).
29. Michael Overall, "Johnny Cash Archives Could Follow Bob Dylan's to Tulsa," *Tulsa World*, October 12, 2017.
30. Adam Crymble and Julia Flanders, "FairCite," *DHQ: Digital Humanities Quarterly* 7, no. 2 (2013), http://www.digitalhumanities.org/dhq/vol/7/2/000164/000164.html.
31. D. T. Max, "Final Destination," *New Yorker*, June 11, 2007.
32. Monique Daviau, Jennifer Hecker, Katy Hill, Stephen Mielke, Gabriela Redwine, Joan Sibley, and Apryl Sullivan, "Norman Mailer: An Inventory of His Papers at the Harry Ransom Center," Harry Ransom Center, University of Texas at Austin, 2005–2007, http://norman.hrc.utexas.edu/fasearch/findingAid.cfm?eadid=00480p1.

INDEX

Abbey, Edward, 137n28
Abbott, Charles D., 18
Abrams, M. H., 27
access. *See* scholars and the public
acknowledgments of archivists, 86–87
Adaptation (film), 107
African American Review, 37
age disparities at time of deposit, 32–33, 35, 42
agents and dealers, 1–2, 9, 43–54; agents, 46–50, 145–46n2, 147n21; agents vs. dealers, 43–45, 48, 126; dealers, 50–53, 145n2, 147n31, 148n35; profit, 44–48, 50, 53–54
Albers, Josef, 74
Aldis, Owen Franklin, 68, 73
Alexander, Elizabeth, 29
Allen, Donald, 75
Alvarez, Julia, 67, 82, 137n28
American Archivist, 84, 97, 149m8
American Library Association (ALA), 98, 157n33
American Marketing Association, 25

Anderson, James and Morag, 38
Angiletta, Anthony, 77
anthologies, 24, 26–29, 42, 75. *See* also *Norton Anthology of American Literature, The*
Anthology of American Negro Literature, 28
Anzaldúa, Gloria, 151n39
Apple, Max, 137n28
appraisal process, 15–16
archival education, 84–85, 98, 159n49
Archival Outlook, 97
archival repositories. *See* repositories
Archival Turn in Feminism, The (Eichhorn), 123
Archive Fever (Derrida), 20
archivists and digital archivists, 2, 9–10, 80–105; archivists, 88–94, 134; arrangement and description by, 79, 81–83, 87–89, 104, 129; author privacy issues and, 113; born-digital content as challenge to, 126, 129; British, 13; costs of acquisitions and, 14; digital archivists, 94–104, 134; focus in the

169

archivists and digital archivists (*continued*)
1980s, 149n8; professional identity of, 84–86, 105; provenance and, 81–88. *See also* finding aids
Arcus Foundation, 38
Ashbery, John, 75, 156n25
Asian American Authors (anthology), 29
Associated Press, 14–15
Association of College and Research Libraries (ACRL), 44
Association of Research Libraries (ARL), 57–61, 78, 98
Association to Protect the Rights of Authors, 46
asymmetric information, 52–53
Atlantic, 103
Atwood, Margaret, 101
Auden, W. H., 47
Austin American-Statesman, 14–15
authors and families, 1–2, 10, 24–42; access and privacy issues, 106, 108, 112–16, 120–21; authors, 29–35, 42, 54, 145–46n2; brand, 24–29, 38, 107, 120; commodification of personal papers of, 8–9, 16; cultural capital and, 12, 23–24, 26, 47–48, 123–25, 134; fame and celebrity, 107; families, 36–42; financial value and, 16, 123–26; scholarly value and, 127–29
Authors' Syndicate, 46
autonomy and professions, 6
Awl (website), 118

baby boomers (1946–60), 94
Baldwin, James, 36–39, 41–42, 71, 82, 116
Ballou, Jullianne, 93–94
Bambara, Toni Cade, 29, 58, 83, 89, 94, 156n25
Bancroft Library, University of California, Berkeley, 32, 41, 128, 165n13
B & L Rootenberg Rare Books & Manuscripts, 53
Bank of Oklahoma (BOK) Financial Corporation, 131

Baraka, Amiri, 52, 145–46n2
Barnett, Ross, 36–37
Barrios and Borderland: Cultures of Latinos and Latinas in the United States (anthology), 29
Barthelme, Donald, 49, 113–14
Barton, Melissa, 72–73
batch archival processing, 101–2
Bates, Catherine, 110–11
Beat movement, 40, 75–76
Begley, Adam, 5–6
Beinecke, Edwin, 70
Beinecke, Frederick, 70
Beinecke, Walter, 70
Beinecke Library, Yale University: acquisition of collections by, 61–62, 68–73; archivists rarely named in finding aids at, 82; Baldwin collection at, 37–39, 41; competition and, 78–79; digital media in collections at, 96; director of, 61; Lopate collection at, 15; Merrill collection at, 140n30; Momaday collection at, 12; Pound's papers and, 45; W. C. Williams collection at, 18, 139n26
Belfast Group, 14
Bellow, Saul, 44, 49
Benjamin, Walter, 4
Benson Latin American Collection, University of Texas at Austin, 151n39
Beuys, Joseph, 7
Biasi, Pierre-Marc de, 106, 109
Bible and the Matthew Effect, 123
Bibliodeath (Codrescu), 110
Bidart, Frank, 137n28
Bishop, Elizabeth, 18, 30, 139n26
Biswell, Andrew, 22
Black Fire: An Anthology of Afro-American Writing (anthology), 29
Black Mountain College, 74–75
Black Mountain Review, The, 74–75
Black Sparrow Press, 25
Blake, Paul, Jr., 40

INDEX 171

Blalack, Kate L., 131
Bliss, Anthony, 41
Blood on the Tracks (album), 131
Blue Crush (film), 107
BMI Foundation, 131
Bob Dylan Center, 132–33
Book Talk (2006), 51
born-digital content, 94–103, 126–29
Boston University, 56, 124
Boulware, Jack, 41
boundary condition, 26
Bourdieu, Pierre, 5, 8
Bradley, Anthony, 27
brand. *See under* authors and families
Brandeis, Louis, 115–16
Brautigan, Richard, 110
Brewster, Kingman, 70
Bridwell Library, Southern Methodist University, 66
British Library, 99
Brooks, Gwendolyn, 11–12, 20, 23, 51, 156n25
Browar, Lisa, 45–46
Brown, Curtis, 47
Bukowski, Charles, 25–26
Bunshaft, Gordon, 70
Burgess, Anthony, 22
Burghes, A. M., 47
Burroughs, William S., 40, 75
Byatt, A. S., 67

Cage, John, 74
California v. Greenwood, 135n7
Calvert, Clay, 120
Calverton, V. F., 28
Canada, 22, 98
canon wars, 28
Carnegie Corporation, 130
Carter, John, 139n26
Carter, Tonja, 21
Carver, Raymond, 49, 145n2
case studies, 10
Cash, Johnny, 132

celebrity authors, 107–8
Cervantes, Lorna Dee, 137n28
Chandler, Raymond, 47–48
Cheever, John, 52, 156n25
Chicago Tribune, 121
Chronicle of Higher Education, 126
citation analysis, 81–82
City Lights Books, 41
civil rights movement, 36–37, 59
class and cultural capital, 141n7
Clifton, Lucille, 35
Clockwork Orange, A (Burgess), 22
Clotfelter, Charles T., 126
Clothing of Books, The (Lahiri), 124–25
Codrescu, Andrei, 110
Cohen, Patricia, 103
Cold War, 63
collecting instinct, 4
collections: backlogs in processing of, 88–89; gradual acquisition of, 33–34, 143n33; grouping of papers in, 31, 143n29; measurement of, 9–10, 137–38nn29–31. *See also under Norton Anthology of American Literature, The*
collective good vs. private good, 56
College Library, Yale University, 68
Collins, Billy, 11–12, 15, 20, 44, 68, 82, 89
Columbia University, 77–78, 86, 165n14
competition. *See under* directors and curators
Conway, Paul, 96–97
Cooper, Stephen, 118
Copper Canyon Press, 22
Copyright Act of 1976, 92
copyrights, 47–48, 92, 113–15. *See also* intellectual property rights
Corman, Cid, 74
Cornell, Joseph, 7
Cornell University, 18
corporate authorship on finding aids, 83, 87, 105
Corso, Gregory, 40
Costello, Bonnie, 71

Council on Library and Information Resources (CLIR), 91, 93, 157n33
Crace, Jim, 13
Creeley, Robert, 19, 73–75, 137n28, 145n2, 153n63
Cuba, 76
Cullen, Countee, 27–28
cultural capital: archivists and, 84, 86, 89; authors and, 12, 23–24, 26, 47–48, 123–25, 134; brand and, 24–26; changing rules of the game and, 55; class and, 141n7; Cold War and, 63; competition and, 56–57, 79; defined, 5; Moran's lack of, 5–6, 8; private cultural heritage institutions and, 129–30, 133; race and, 36; repositories and, 8, 55–57, 79, 89, 134; social media and, 101; widening divide between authors and, 123–25
Cunningham, Adrian, 96–97
Cunningham, Merce, 74
curators. *See* directors and curators
Czechoslovakia, 76

Damon, Matt, 125
Dandicat, Edwidge, 137n28
Davis, Lydia, 137n28
Davis, Susan E., 96–97
Dawson's Creek (TV show), 104
deconstruction, 19
Delaney, Beauford, 36
DeLillo, Don, 134, 137n28
demand side vs. supply side, 45, 54–56
demographic deposit rate of *NAAL* authors, 29–30, 32
Department of Rare Books and Special Collections, Princeton University, 11–12, 124
Depp, Johnny, 128–29
Derrida, Jacques, 20
Dewey, John, 74
Diaz, Junot, 137n28
Dick, Philip K., 137n28
Dickens, Charles, 101

Dickey, James, 35, 145–46n2
digital archives specialist (DAS), 98
digital archivists. *See* archivists and digital archivists
digital content: born-digital content, 94–103, 126–29; emulation of, 102–4, 129; migration of, 102–3, 129
digital humanities, 81
digital preservation, 96–104, 128
Digital Preservation Coalition (DPC), 97
Digital Public Library of America (DPLA), 157n44
digitization, 89–94, 112, 129, 157n33. *See also* born-digital content
Dillard, Annie, 71
di Prima, Diane, 40
directors and curators, 1–2, 9–10, 55–79; appraisal process and, 16; archives of contemporary writers and, 18–20; author privacy issues and, 113; competition, 56–61; curators, 50, 60–62, 66, 68–78, 127; directors, 60–68, 78; negotiations with sellers and, 53
diversification of the market, 26–32, 42, 59–60, 78, 84, 125
Doerner, Saunders, Daniel & Anderson, 115
Dooley, Jackie, 84
Dove mi trovo (Lahiri), 124–25
Doyle, Arthur Conan, 47
Drexel University, 96
Duchamp, Marcel, 7
Duncan, Robert, 74, 128, 137n28, 165n13
Dust Bowl Ballads (album), 130
Dylan, Bob, 52, 130–33

Earle, David M., 122
Eastlake, William, 73–74
Economist, 67
Economy of Prestige, The (English), 86
Eggers, Dave, 67
Eichhorn, Kate, 86, 123

INDEX

Eisgruber, Christopher L., 11–12
Electronic Records Section, 97
Eliot, T. S., 69, 109
Ellison, Ralph, 49
Ellmann, Richard, 17–18
Emanuel, Ariel, 125
embodiment of authors in collections, 109–11
emulation of digital content, 102–4, 129
End of the Tour, The (film), 118
endowments, 59–60, 67, 72–73, 78, 126–27
energy crisis (1970s), 62, 65
England, 46–47, 97
English, James F., 86–87
English Studies, 118
enhanced curation, 99–100
Enniss, Stephen: appointed director of Ransom Center, 68, 99; career of, 68; complaint about expense of literary archives, 55; dealers vs. agents and, 44–46, 50, 54; enhanced curation and, 99; García Márquez collection price and, 14–16; ideal market of the past portrayed by, 45, 52, 126; Ransom Center as top collecting repository and, 61, 63, 68; Ransom Center's financial vulnerability and, 127; suggestion to limit competition, 56–57, 78
ephemera, 8, 12
Erdrich, Louise, 154n14
Erwin, Micah, 82
Evers, Medgar, 37
Every Love Story Is a Ghost Story (Wallace biography), 120
executors, 1, 8, 10, 15, 22, 31, 33–35. *See also* agents and dealers

Facebook, 100–101
Fales Library, New York University, 52
fame and scholarly value, 107
families. *See* authors and families
Farr, Erika, 103

Farrar, Straus and Giroux, 114
"Faulkner and Desegregation" (Baldwin), 37
FBI archives, 38, 40–41
Felt Suit (Beuys), 7
feminists and feminism, 27, 111, 123
Ferlinghetti, Lawrence, 40–41, 76
fetishism, 108–11, 119–20
Fetterley, Judith, 27
Field, Douglas A., 37
Field Day Anthology of Irish Writing, The, 27
financial crisis (2008), 60, 78
financial value, 12–16, 123–27
finding aids: archivists unnamed in, 80–84, 87, 105; authors' executors and, 44–45; corporate authorship on, 83, 87, 105; cultural capital and production of, 89; for digitized collections, 91; for Ginsberg's materials, 76; literary archives lacking, 156n25. *See also* archivists and digital archivists
"Finding John Updike" (Moran), 3
Fitzgerald, Sally, 35
Fitzpatrick, Kathleen, 119
Fleur Cowles *Flair* Symposium, 45
Flood, Alison, 101
Folger Shakespeare Library, 68
Ford Foundation, 38, 130
Foreman, Richard, 137n28
Forstrom, Michael, 96
Fort Atkinson Historical Society/Hoard Historical Museum, 33–34
Foschini, Lorenza, 7
Fountain (Duchamp), 7
Fourth Amendment, 4
France, 36–37, 41, 115
Franzen, Jonathan, 101
"Freaks and the American Ideal of Manhood" (Baldwin), 37
Freedman, Jenna, 86
Freedom of Information Act, 14–15
Friel, Brian, 13

friendship between dealers and institutions, 53
Fundación Pablo Neruda, 22

Gallup, Donald, 69–73
Galvin, Brendan, 137n28, 156n25
Gap, 40, 107
García Márquez, Gabriel, 14–16, 92–94, 129
Gass, William, 145n2
Gates Foundation, 157n33
Generation X (1961–80), 94–95
Generation Y "millennials" (1981–2000), 94–95
George Kaiser Family Foundation, 130–33
Georgia College, 34–35
Gewirtz, Isaac, 14
GI Bill, 17
Gilliland-Swetland, Anne, 102
Ginsberg, Allen: Beat movement and, 40, 75–76; Gap ads and, 107; price paid for collection of, 12, 76–77; provenance of collection, 76; Stanford's possession of collection of, 18, 73, 75–77, 139n26; University at Buffalo and papers of, 18; as Wylie's client, 49, 76
Gioia, Dana, 108–9
Give Me Your Answer, Do! (Friel), 13
Glossary (SAA), 45
Glück, Louise, 49, 71, 145–46n2
Goldstone, Adrian H., 65, 150nn28–29
Goodman, Mitchell, 74
Google Books, 91
Go Set a Watchman (N. H. Lee), 21–22, 118
GQ, 117
Graham, Jorie, 137n28
Gray, Jonathan, 120–21
Greatest Generation (1901–24), 94–95
Green, Karen, 117–18
Greenblatt, David, 125
Greene, Graham, 134
Greene, Mark A., 88
Groden, Michael, 114

Group for Literary Archives and Manuscripts (GLAM), 13–14
Guardian, 13, 101
Guérin, Jacque, 7
Guild of Literature and Art, 46
Guthrie, Nora, 130
Guthrie, Woody, 130–33

habitus, violation of norms of, 47, 51
Hahn, Kimiko, 137n28
hair, collection of, 109–10
Hall, Donald, 75
Hamilton, Ian, 114, 116
"Hand of the Poet, The" (Gioia), 108
Handsome Is (Wasserman), 49
Hanks, Jo, 22
Hansen, Grace, 82
haptic access to materials, 111–12
Hardy, Thomas, 47
Harlem Renaissance, 36
Harper, Michael S., 128, 166n14
HarperCollins, 21
Harry Ransom Center, University of Texas at Austin: acquisition of collections by, 18, 52, 61–62, 65–68, 78; archivists named in finding aids at, 82; Baldwin collection at, 38; Collins collection and, 11; competition and, 56–57, 70, 78–79; directors of, 63–64; energy crisis and, 62; Enniss's appointment to the directorship of, 68, 99; financial vulnerability of, 127; García Márquez collection and, 14–16, 92–94, 129; Mailer collection and, 134; Mamet collection and, 52; organizational structure of libraries at University of Texas at Austin and, 149n17; Paley collection at, 166n14; Pound's papers and, 45; prices paid for collections by, 13–16; Updike collection and, 3–4; Wallace collection and, 117–20; Wesker collection and, 101; Yale contrasted with, 73
Hathcock, April, 112

INDEX 175

Hayden, Erma, 31
Hayden, Robert, 31–32, 156n25
Heaney, Seamus, 14
Heath Anthology, 29
Helmerich Center for American
 Research, 132
Henry W. and Albert A. Berg Collection
 of English and American Literature,
 14, 40–42
Hester, Betty, 35
Highsmith, Patricia, 137n28
Hodson, Sara S., 112
Holmes, Anna, 101
Holt, Henry, 47
homophobia, 36–37, 41, 77
Hoover Institute, Stanford University, 77
Horowitz, Glenn, 12, 50–53, 118, 125–26,
 131–32, 148n35
Houbeck, Robert, Jr., 60
Houghton Library, Harvard University,
 3–6, 61–62
Howard Rice Nemerovski Canady Falk
 & Rabkin, 115
Howe, Fanny, 44, 73, 137n28
Howe, Susan, 109
"Howl" and Other Poems (Ginsberg), 75–76
Hughes, Langston, 27–28
Hughes, Ted, 14, 31
Humanities Research Center (HRC). *See*
 Harry Ransom Center, University of
 Texas at Austin
"Hummingbird—for Patricia C. Willis"
 (Merrin), 71
Huntington, the, 25–26
Hyry, Thomas, 61

I Am Not Your Negro (documentary), 37–38
IMG, 125
inclusive citation practices, 82, 87
Infinite Jest (Wallace), 117–19
In Other Words (Lahiri), 124–25
In Search of J. D. Salinger (Hamilton), 114
Instagram, 100–101

Institute for Bob Dylan Studies, 132
Institute of Museum and Library
 Services (IMLS), 157n33
intellectual property rights, 115–16, 120–21.
 See also copyrights; trademarks
Interpreter of Maladies (Lahiri), 124
Ireland, 14
Irish literary holdings, 68
Irsay, Jim, 40
Italy, 65
item-level review, 88–93

Jackson, Samuel L., 37
James, Henry, 107
James Baldwin Now (McBride), 37
James Baldwin Review, 37
James Joyce Estate, 114–15
James Joyce Quarterly, 67
Jarrell, Randall, 30
Joans, Ted, 41
John Rylands Library, University of
 Manchester, 13–14
John S. and James L. Knight Foundation,
 38
Johnson, Derek, 120–21
Johnson, Ronna C., 107
John Steinbeck (Goldstone), 65
Jones, Chelsea S., 82
Jones, Edward P., 137n28
Josef and Anni Albers Foundation, 74
Journal of David Foster Wallace Studies,
 118–19
Joyce, James, 17–18, 67, 114–15
Joyce, Justin A., 37
Joyce, Nelly, 18
Joyce, Stephen James, 114–16

Kaiser, George B., 131, 133
Kaiser, Herman, 131
Kaiser Foundation. *See* George Kaiser
 Family Foundation
Kaiser-Frances Oil Company, 131
Kaplan, Bart, 37

Karefa-Smart, Gloria, 39
Keller, Michael, 73
Kendig, Mary, 98
Kennedy, John F., 37
Kennedy, Robert F., 36–37
Kenney, Anne R., 91
Kent State University, 128, 165n13
Kerouac, Gabrielle, 40
Kerouac, Jack, 36, 40–42, 49, 75, 107
Kerouac, Janet "Jan," 40, 145n53
Kerouac, Stella Sampas, 40
Kidd, John, 114
Kill Your Darlings (film), 75
Kincaid, Jamaica, 137n28
King, Martin Luther, Jr., 37
Kingston, Maxine Hong, 32
Kipling, Rudyard, 47
Kirsch, Adam, 101
Kirschenbaum, Matthew G., 8, 110
Knight Foundation, 157n33
knowledge and professions, 6
Knowlton, Eloise, 114
Knox, Jane Shaw, 34
Koch, Kenneth, 75
Kohler, Michèle, 53
Komunyakaa, Yusef, 72, 145–46n2
Krusten, Maarja, 87
Kuhl, Nancy, 72–73, 127
Kunitz, Stanley, 137n28
Kyrle, Ifan, 31

Lahiri, Jhumpa, 92, 94, 124–26
Lake, Carlton, 63, 65–66
Lamantia, Philip, 41
Lameyer, Gordon Ames, 31
Lapsley, Gaillard, 69
La Trahison des images (Magritte), 7
Lawrence, D. H., 64–65
Leavell, Linda, 71
Lee, Alice "Miss Alice," 21
Lee, Jamie A., 111
Lee, Nelle Harper, 21–22, 118, 140n38
Le Guin, Ursula, 156n25

Levertov, Denise, 73–75, 153n63
Levine, Philip, 52, 145n2
Levit, Ken, 132
Lewis, C. S., 17
librarians, 14, 66, 68, 86–87, 98
Libraries & Culture, 45
library directors. *See* directors and curators
library funding levels, 57–60, 62–63, 66
Library Investment Index, 57–58
"Life's Swell" (Orlean), 107
"Like a Rolling Stone" (song), 131
Lilly Library, Indiana University, 31, 137–38n31, 143n29
linotype machines, 46
literary agents. *See* agents and dealers
literary archives market: agents and dealers (profit), 43–54; archivists and digital archivists (provenance), 80–105; authors and families (brand), 24–42; directors and curators (competition), 55–79; inside, 11–23; Matthew Effect, 122–34; outside (introduction), 1–10; scholars and the public (access), 106–21
literary history, 3–4, 27–29
Longley, Edna, 27
Lopate, Phillip, 15
Lopez, Barry, 137n28
Lopez, Ken, 50–51, 53, 126, 148n35
Lorde, Audre, 156n25
Lorine Niedecker: An Original Biography (Knox), 34
Lorine Niedecker: A Poet's Life (Peters), 34
Louisiana State University, 165–66n14
Lowell, Robert, 30, 66, 82
Lowland, The (Lahiri), 124–25
Lowry, Charles B., 60
Lozano, Daniela, 82, 93
Luce Foundation, 157n33
Lucia Joyce (Shloss), 114
Ludlam, Charles, 137n28

Mack, Maynard, 109
Macmillan, Frederick, 47

INDEX

Maddox, Brenda, 114
Magee, Rosemary, 34, 61
magical value of manuscripts, 108–9, 112, 126
Magritte, René, 7
Mailer, Norman, 12, 134
Malamud, Bernard, 52
Malcolm X, 37
Mamet, David, 52, 67, 145–46n2
Mandeville-Gamble, Steven, 76
Manning, Olivia, 56
Manual of Marvels (Cornell), 7
manuscript dealers. *See* agents and dealers
manuscripts, magical and meaningful values of, 108–9, 112, 126
Margaret Atwood and the Labour of Literary Celebrity (York), 101
Martin, John, 25
Martin, Manjula, 107
Marx, Karl, 109
master's programs and archival education, 84–85, 98, 159n49
Matheson, William, 19
Matthew Effect, the, 2, 122–34; defined, 122–23; financial value, 123–27; public value, 129–33; scholarly value, 127–29
McBride, Dwight A., 37
McClatchy, J. D., 140n30
McEwan, Ian, 67
McGurl, Mark, 117, 119
McKay, Claude, 27–28
McMaster University, 22
McPheron, William, 73–75, 77
meaningful value of manuscripts, 108–9, 112, 126
Meissner, Dennis, 88
Mellon, Paul, 69
Mellon Foundation, 157n33
Meredith, James, 36–37
Merrill, James, 19, 49, 52, 140n30
Merrin, Jeredith, 71–72
Merton, Robert, 123
Merwin, W. S., 12, 51–52

Mielke, Stephen, 82
migration of digital content, 102–3, 129
millennials, 94–95
Miller, Arthur, 49, 65, 82
Minkoff, George, 153n63
modernists and modernism, 17–19, 30, 63, 69–71, 73, 78
Momaday, N. Scott, 12, 51, 72, 145n2
monopolies and professions, 6
Monroe, Marilyn, 125
Montgomery, John, 41
Moore, Marianne, 18, 71, 117, 139n26
Moran, Paul, 3–9, 134
Moravec, Michelle, 112
more product, less process (MPLP) method, 88–89, 91–92
Morgan, Bill, 76
Morra, Linda M., 29–30
Morris, Leslie A., 5–6, 8
Morrison, Toni, 11–12, 15, 20, 36, 44
Mosley, Katharine, 82
Murray, Liz, 82
Museum of Modern Art, 165n14
music on wax cylinders, 100, 159n56

Nabokov, Vladimir, 12, 52
Nadell, Bonnie, 117–18
Namesake, The (Lahiri), 124–25
National Archives' Electronic Access Project, 91
National Association of College and University Business Officers, 59
National Bahá'í Archives, 31
National Endowment for the Arts (NEA), 157n33
National Endowment for the Humanities (NEH), 99–100, 157n33
National Historical Publications and Records Commission (NHPRC), 157n33
National Library of Ireland, 18
National Public Radio, 11
Neruda, Pablo, 22

New American Poetry, 1945–1960, The, 75
New Anthology of Modern Poetry, 27
New Criticism, 17–19
newspaper penny tax, abolition of, 46
New Yorker, 67, 71, 101, 103, 107
New York Life, 38
New York Public Library (NYPL), 14, 38–42, 52, 74, 111
New York Times, 12, 21, 101, 103
New York University Press, 37
Niedecker, Lorine, 33–35, 94, 137n28, 156n25
Nixon, Richard, 65
nonfungible assets, 52
nonliquid assets, 52
North American Man/Boy Love Association, 77
Northwestern University, 74
Norton Anthology of American Literature, The (*NAAL*), 9–10; agent data and, 147n21; archivists and finding aids of collections, 82–83, 87, 89; authors' cultural capital and, 24, 26, 123; authors' executors, 44; authors included and omitted from, 137n28; authors' top 5 collecting repositories, 61–62; authors with placed collections, 29–35; authors with unplaced collections, 29–30, 123–24, 128–29; collection sizes, 88–89; competition to be included in, 128; competitor to, 29; copyright protections and, 92; dealer data and, 147n31, 148n35; demographic deposit rate by decade, 29–30, 32; deposit rates with born-digital content by decade of deposit, 95–96; deposit rates with born-digital content by generation, 94–95; diversification of contemporary literary canon, 123–24; funding levels of institutions acquiring authors' collections, 57–60, 62; Horowitz's clients in, 52; paper-based literary collections of authors, 88; racism and, 28, 42; Ransom Center's acquisitions of collections, 65, 67; sexism and, 27, 42; Stanford's acquisitions of collections, 75–78; Wylie's clients in, 49, 147n21; Yale's acquisitions of collections, 68, 71
Norton Anthology of English Literature, The (*NAEL*), 27
Nurkse, Dennis, 137n28
Nye, Naomi Shihab, 137n28

occupational privilege, 6
Ochs, Phil, 131
O'Connor, Flannery, 11–12, 20, 33–35
off-site access of collections, 90–94
O'Hara, Frank, 75, 128, 165–66n14
Oklahoma City Blue, 131
Oklahoma City Thunder, 131
Olds, Sharon, 137n28
Olson, Charles, 74–75
One Hundred Years of Solitude (García Márquez), 92
Online Computer Library Center (OCLC), 97, 100
Only Goodness (Lahiri), 124–25
On the Road (Kerouac), 40
Open Letters Monthly, 119–20
Oppen, George, 137n28, 145n2
optic access to materials, 111–12
optical character recognition (OCR) systems, 90–91
Orchid Thief, The (Orlean), 107
Organization of Petroleum Exporting Countries (OPEC), 65
Origin (magazine), 74
Original Manuscripts by 100 Masters from John Donne to Julia Alvarez (exhibition), 111
Orlean, Susan, 107
Other John Updike Archive, The (website), 3, 6–7
Outside, 107

Pale King, The (Wallace), 117–19
Paley, Grace, 128, 166n14

INDEX

paper duty, elimination of, 46
papers, writers', inside the literary archives market, 11–23; financial value of, 12–16; public value of, 20–22; scholarly value of, 16–20
papers, writers', outside the literary archives market, 1–10
paraprofessionals, 83–84
Paris Review, 15
Patterson, Jennifer, 82
Pavlić, Ed, 39
Payne, John, 63, 65–66, 150n29
Pearce-Moses, Richard, 80, 99
Peck, Raoul, 37
Penguin Books, 40
People, 114
Permanent University Fund (PUF), 63
Peters, Margot, 34
Piepenbring, Dan, 15
Pietsch, Michael, 118
Pinkus, Sam, 140n38
Pinsky, Robert, 73
Plath, Sylvia, 31, 51, 137–38n31, 143n29
Poetry Collection, University at Buffalo Libraries, 19, 140n32
Poets & Writers, 125
Possession (Byatt), 67
postmodern assemblages, 6–8
postmodernists, 73
poststructuralism, 19
Potter, Beatrix, 22
Pound, Ezra, 45, 69–71, 75
Powers, Richard, 137n28
Presley, Elvis, 125
privacy and access, 106, 108, 112–16, 120–21
privacy rights, 115–16
private cultural heritage institutions, 129–33
private good vs. collective good, 56
Professional Basketball Club LLC, 131
professional identity and archivists, 84–85
profit. *See under* agents and dealers
Program Era, 117

"Project Independence," 65
property rights, 115–16
Proust, Marcel, 7
Proust's Overcoat (Foschini), 7
provenance. *See* archivists and digital archivists
public value, 20–22, 129–33
Puglia, Steve, 91
Pynchon, Thomas, 52, 65, 82

quantitative data, 9–10

racial essentialism, 28
racism, 27–28, 36–37, 41–42, 59, 81–82
Random House, 22, 114
Ransom, Harry, 62–66, 110, 133
Ransom, Hazel, 64
Ransom Center. *See* Harry Ransom Center, University of Texas at Austin
Raphel, Adrienne, 71
rare books: curators' shift away from, 50; two-tiered market, 122; value of relationships and, 51
Rare Books and Manuscripts Section (RBMS), 44–45, 55
Ray, David, 44, 137n28
Rayner, Katharine J., 38
RBM (journal), 53
Readings from Negro Authors for Schools and Colleges (1931), 28
Ready, William, 22
Reed, Ishmael, 31–32, 145n2
Reese, William R., 1, 122
relationships, value of, 43–44, 50–51, 53
Remember This House (Baldwin), 37
repositories: agents vs. dealers and, 43–45; author age disparities at time of deposit in, 32–33; cultural capital and, 8, 55–57, 79, 89, 134; defined, 29–30; demographic deposit rate of *NAAL* authors, 29–30, 32; digital, ingesting files into, 101–2; digital content appearance in, 95–96, 126; diversification of holdings, 125;

repositories (*continued*)
  emulations of literary collections and, 103; funding levels and acquisitions by, 57–60, 62–63, 66; funding levels and digitization by, 89–94, 129, 157n33; measurement of collections in, 9–10, 137–38nn29–31; price control and, 133–34; private cultural heritage institutions, 129–33; SWAT and, 100; top 5 in literary archives market, 61–62, 126–27, 129; voyeurism of fans and, 117
Reynolds, Paul Revere, 48–49
Rigney, Daniel, 122–23
Ríos, Alberto, 137n28
RLG DigiNews, 91
Roberts, F. Warren, 63–66
Rockefeller Foundation, 130
Rockmore, Dan, 103
Rodman, Selden, 27–28
Roethke, Theodore, 92
Rogers, Pattiann, 137n28, 145n2
Rolling Stone, 37–38, 132
Roosevelt, Franklin D., 52
Rootenberg, Howard, 53
Rose, Danis, 114
Rose, Jacqueline, 109
Rose Library, Emory University: acquisition of collections by, 61–62; British literary archives and, 14; curators and directors, 61, 68; emulation of Rushdie's digital content at, 103–4, 129; O'Connor collection and, 11, 34–35; third-party appraisers and, 16; Walker collection and, 52
Rosen, Rick, 125
Rosenbach, the, 18, 71, 117, 139n26
Ross, Max, 119–20
Roth, Philip, 49
Rothenberg, Jeff, 102
Roub, Bonnie and Gail, 34
Rushdie, Salman, 14, 68, 103–4, 129
Russell & Volkening, 49
Ryan, Michael, 51

Salinger, J. D., 114–16, 120
Saltzman, Devyani, 103
Sampas, John, 40–41
San Francisco Renaissance, 75–76
San Francisco Weekly, 41
Saroyan, William, 110
Saunders, George, 137n28
Schiff, Robyn, 71
scholarly value, 16–20, 127–29
scholars and the public, 1–4, 8, 10, 106–21; access, 107–10, 129, 132; authors' privacy and, 106, 108, 112–16, 120–21; born-digital content and, 126, 129; ephemera and, 12; the public, 117–20; scholars, 108–16, 118–20; value of literary archives and, 16–22
Schomburg Center for Research in Black Culture, 38–39, 41–42
Schroeder, E. C., 61
Schulz, Joan, 27
Schwartzburg, Molly, 81, 118
scraping social media feeds, 101
"Secrecy, Archives, and the Public Interest" (Zinn), 84
self-branding, 107
service and professions, 6
Servicemen's Readjustment Act, 17
sexism, 27–28, 42, 59, 81–82
Sexton, Anne, 66, 82, 113–14
Shaheen, Celia, 93
"Sharing 'Gabo' with the World" (digitization project), 93
Shepard, Sam, 67, 82
Shildrick, Margrit, 110–11
Shloss, Carol, 114–15
Sibley, Joan, 82
Silent Generation (1925–45), 94–95
Silko, Leslie Marmon, 49, 51, 71, 145n2
Simonoff, Eric, 125
Sinclair, Upton, 48
Singer, Isaac Bashevis, 134
Sloan Foundation, 157n33
Smith, Tracy K., 137n28

INDEX   181

Smith, Zadie, 99
Smith College, 31, 137–38n31
Smithsonian, 130
Snow White (Barthelme), 113–14
Snow White and the Huntsman (film), 113
Snow White and the Seven Dwarfs (film), 114
"Snow White and the Seven Dwarfs" (Sexton), 113–14
Snyder, Gary, 40
social capital, 47–48, 54
social media platforms, 100–101
Society of American Archivists (SAA), 44–45, 84–85, 97–98, 112
Society of Authors, 46
software and workstations for antiquated technology (SWAT), 100
Song, Cathy, 137n28
Southwestern Historical Quarterly, 64
Soviet Union, 63
Spoo, Robert, 114–15
stakeholders, 1–2, 4, 8–10, 55, 64, 79, 134
Staley, Thomas F., 11, 17, 63, 66–68, 151n39
Stanford Law School Center for Internet and Society's Fair Use Project, 115
Stanford University, 18, 19, 61–62, 73–78, 110, 139n26, 153n63
steam printing, 46
Stein, Gertrude, 48, 69–70
Steinbeck, John, 65, 73–74
Sterling Library, Yale University, 68–70
Stevenson, Robert Louis, 70
Streep, Meryl, 107
Street, Robert, 73
Strickler, Tom, 125
structuralism, 19
Stuart A. Rose Manuscript, Archives, and Rare Book Library, 14
Studies in the Novel, 118
Sukenick, Ronald, 67, 82
supply side vs. demand side, 45, 54–56
Swann Auction, 6–7
Swensen, David F., 72–73

Swenson, May, 19, 140n30
synthetic collections, 10, 137n30

Tax Reform Act, 48
Taylor, Marvin, 52
Texas, 63, 67. *See also* Harry Ransom Center, University of Texas at Austin; University of Texas
Texas A&M, 63
Texas Folklore Publications, 64
Texas Quarterly, 64
theory, 19
"This Land Is Your Land" (song), 130
Thompson, Hunter S., 49, 52, 128–29
Time, 11–12, 37
Tinker, Chauncey Brewster, 68–70, 109
Tinker Library, The (Tinker), 69
Tóibín, Colm, 27, 37
To Kill a Mockingbird (N. H. Lee), 21
touching archival materials, 110–12
tourism, 130
Track Changes (Kirschenbaum), 8
trademarks, 114. *See also* intellectual property rights
Transformations (Sexton), 113
Trethewey, Natasha, 137n28
Trujillo, Robert G., 61
Turner, Decherd, 63, 66–67
Twitter, 100–101

UCSB Cylinder Audio Archive, 159n56
United Kingdom, 13–14, 115
United Kingdom Literary Heritage Working Group, 14
United States: automatic copyright in, 113–14; Cold War and, 63; digital preservation in, 97; generations in, 94–95; global collections coming to, 67; Lawrence's papers and, 65; literary market prices in, 12–13; market for collections of contemporary authors in, 2; master's programs in library and information studies, 98; privacy rights

United States (*continued*)
and property rights in, 115–16; publication of new editions in, 22; tax benefit for donating collections and, 48
United States Securities and Exchange Commission, 52
Universal Studios, 114
University at Buffalo, 18–19, 75, 114, 139n26, 140n32
University of California, Santa Cruz, 128, 165n13
University of Chicago Library, 83, 165n14
University of Connecticut, 74
University of Delaware, 31
University of Illinois, 11, 23, 51
University of Iowa, creative writing MFA program, 128
University of Kansas, 18
University of Maryland's College of Information Studies, 98
University of Michigan, 96
University of Michigan-Flint, 60
University of Mississippi, 36–37
University of North Carolina at Greensboro, 30
University of North Dakota, 165n14
University of Texas, 63–64
University of Texas at Austin, 127, 133, 151n39. *See also* Harry Ransom Center, University of Texas at Austin
University of Tulsa, 52, 132
University of Victoria, 165–66n14
Updike, John: as Horowitz's client, 52; literary collection of, 2–9, 134; as Wylie's client, 49
Utah State University, 140n30

Van Duyn, Mona, 19
Vassar College, 18, 139n26
Vice, 125
Victoria and Albert Museum, 22
Vietnam War, 74–76

Vizenor, Gerald, 51, 71, 137n28, 145n2
Vollman, William, 137n28
Vonnegut, Kurt, 89, 145n2
voyeurism, 103, 105, 108, 110–12, 117, 119–21

Wales, 97
Walker, Alice, 14, 35, 52
Wallace, David Foster, 67, 117–20
Wallace Industry, 118–19
Wall Street Journal, 12, 15, 50–51
Walt Disney (company), 114
Walther, Bob, 86
Warren, Robert Penn, 71
Warren, Samuel, 115–16
Washington University, St. Louis, 16, 18–19, 128, 140n30, 153n63, 165n13
Wasserman, Harriet, 49–50
Waste Land, The (Eliot), 69
Watt, A. P., 47
Waugh, Alec, 56
Waugh, Evelyn, 56
wax cylinders, music on, 100, 159–60n56
WB (television network), 104
Weber, David C., 73
Weinberg, Jeffrey, 40
Welty, Eudora, 166n14
Wesker, Arnold, 101
Wesleyan University, 74
West, Cornel, 24
Whalen, Philip, 41
Wharton, Edith, 69
White, Heather, 71
Whiting Foundation, 157n33
Whitman, Walt, 109
Whitney, John Hay, 69
Wilde, Oscar, 18, 101
William Morris Endeavor (WME), 125
William Reese Company, 150n29
Williams, Stacie, 85
Williams, Tennessee, 145–46n2
Williams, William Carlos, 18, 30, 69, 75–76, 139n26

Willis, Patricia C., 71–73
Wilson, August, 137n28
Wilson, Leslie Perrin, 90–91
Wilson, Robert A., 53
Winged Serpent: American Indian Prose and Poetry, The (anthology), 29
Woodruff, Robert W., 62
Woody at 100 (book and CD), 130
Woody Guthrie Center, 130–33
Woody Guthrie Foundation, 130
Wright, C. D., 71, 137n28, 145n2
Wright, Charles, 137n28
Wright, James, 137n28
Wright, Richard, 36
W. W. Norton & Company, 22

Wylie, Andrew, 5–6, 43, 48–50, 54, 125–26, 147n21
Wylie Agency, 48

Yale University, 68–70, 78. *See also* Beinecke Library, Yale University
Yeats, William Butler, 18
yellow journalists, 115–16
Yenser, Stephen, 140n30
York, Lorraine, 101
Young, Kevin, 38
Young, Timothy G., 82

zines, 123
Zinn, Howard, 84

www.ingramcontent.com/pod-product-compliance
Lightning Source LLC
Chambersburg PA
CBHW032214230426
43672CB00011B/2559